Musician
For
A While

A Biography of
Walter Bergmann

by Anne Martin

Re published by Peacock Press, 2018
Scout Bottom Farm
Mytholmroyd
Hebden Bridge
HX7 5JS (UK)

ISBN 978-1-912271-29-0

Designed by Gustav

Printed by Lightning Source, UK

© Anne Martin 2002

Contents

Acknowledgements

Family and Childhood	Page 1
Lawyer and Musician	9
Walter Bergmann in 1939	29
The first few months in England	33
The War Years	39
Post-war years up to the end of 1959	61
The Sixties	85
The Seventies	119
The last years	157

Appendices

Catalogue of Walter Bergmann's compositions and summary of his edited works (composers)	173
Biographical notes	177
Bibliography	189
Index	191

'Possibly the most far-reaching influence on post-war music came from a group of musicians who were centred at Morley College, London and included Michael Tippett, Walter Goehr, Walter Bergmann and Matyas Seiber.'

Lewis Foreman
(From Parry to Britten, Batsford 1987)

Acknowledgements

There are many people whom I need to thank for the help and support they have given me in writing this book, several who sadly did not live to see it completed. First and foremost I must thank Walter Bergmann's daughter Erica Bendix for trusting me with her father's diaries and a great deal more in the way of documents and papers and answering questions, without which the book could not have been written; Herbert Hersom and Edgar Hunt, who gave me the encouragement to start the project; Margret Biss, who spent time writing out WB's tiny pre-war handwritten Gothic script in Roman script for me, and Brian and Mary Bonser who were kind enough to read my partially finished manuscript, note corrections and make helpful comments.

I must thank the numerous people who took time to write to me or answer questions, in particular John Amis, Frans Brüggen, Douglas Craig, Dietrich Gerhardt, Antony Hopkins, Ken Kenworthy, Joan Lambe, Margaret Murray, Evelyn Nallen, Janivere Rowell, Erika Seelig, Hugh Strecker, John Mansfield Thomson, Philip Thorby, David Walters, Theo Wyatt and Charlotte Zimmermann.

The following have kindly given me permission to quote from letters, documents, books and articles; John Amis, Erica Bendix, Meirion Bowen [Michael Tippett Estate], Monica Coles, Catherine Marwood, Michael Muskett, Janivere Rowell, Hugh Strecker; Britsh Broadcasting Corporation, Chrysalis Books [Batsford], Express & Echo (Exeter), Faber & Faber, *Financial Times, Ham & High, Music Teacher, Musical Times,* Orpheus Publications [*The Stradj*] Oxford University Press (*Early Music*), Peacock Press, Random House Group (Hutchinson), The Society of Recorder Players (*Recorder News*], *Sussex Express, Times Ed, Worcester Evening News, Yorkshire Post;* and to reproduce photographs, Erica Bendix, Cambridge Newspapers and Simon Cuerden.

I have made every effort to trace and clear copyright, but in a small number of cases this had proved impossible; I apologise to any surviving copyright holders I failed to reach.

Finally I must thank my family and friends who believed I could complete the book and my husband, Alan, without whom it would not have been completed.

Anne Martin
March 2002

Hans, Walter; Fritz
The Three Bergmann Boys
c. 1905

I. Family and Childhood

Walter Bergmann was born in Altona, part of Hamburg, on September 24th 1902. He was the youngest of three sons born to Oskar and Alice Bergmann. Hans, the elder, was born in 1896 and Fritz in 1899. Oskar Bergmann was a building engineer involved in railway construction. Walter Bergmann grew up in a comfortable professional home in a close-knit family.

The Bergmann family's origins appear to have been in southern Germany. Their earliest known ancestor was a coppersmith, Johann Georg Bergmann (1745? - 1809), who travelled from Speyer, near Karlsruhe, to the Thüringer Wald, and settled in Walterhausen, which lies close to Erfurt and Weimar, southwest of Leipzig. Johann Georg's grandson, Johann Daniel Bergmannn (1823 - 1907), grew up in Walterhausen and then moved to Berlin to work as a skilled craftsman making plaster mouldings to decorate ceilings. He was Walter Bergmann's grandfather. Walter Bergmann just remembered him. He was very skilled with his hands, and made charming model plaster animals for his grandchildren. Walter Bergmann was only four when his Grandfather died in Weimar. His Grandmother, Wilhelmine Bergmann (née Erdmann, 1825 - 1868), died young from cancer. Although Walter Bergmann only had a few, vague memories of his Grandfather, he was very familiar with the Thüringer Wald as he explored it as a child with his favourite aunt, Anna. Tante Anna used to tell him stories of his Grandparents' courtship, and how his Grandfather would walk for an hour and a half after a long arduous day just to catch a glimpse of his future wife.

Johann Daniel and Wilhelmine Bergmann had eight children. Oskar Gustav Bergmann, Walter Bergmann's father, was born in Berlin in 1859. He was the sixth child and only boy in the family and had to contend with the love of seven sisters all his life.[1] Oskar was almost nine when his mother died; his youngest sister was four and the eldest twenty-two. His father did not remarry, and Oskar Bergmann was brought up largely by his sisters. The Bergmanns came from a Protestant background, but they were not religious.

As a young man Oskar Bergmann served as a First Lieutenant in the Third Guards Regiment, and then studied civil engineering. He entered into the service of the Preussischen Eisenbahn Verwaltung (Prussian Railway Administration), which became the Reichsbahn after the First World War. During the war he served as a Captain. Oskar Bergmann's main involvement in the railways was in the design and construction of several main line stations, including those at Altona, Bremen and Halle. He eventually became engineering adviser to the Railway Board. Walter Bergmann remembered visiting his father in his office and described it as being a room full of authority.[2]

Oskar Bergmann first saw his future wife, Alice König, through an open window, while he was studying in Berlin. Alice and her sister Vera were still both young girls, aged about twelve and eight. The two girls looked out of the window at the handsome young man and apparently discussed which of them should marry Herr Bergmann. They decided that he should marry the eldest, Alice, first, and then the younger, Vera, when Alice died. This is what actually happened. Alice König married Oskar Bergmann in 1893 at the age of nineteen. In 1926, at the age of forty-eight, Vera married Oskar, a year and a half after her sister's death.

The König family was of Jewish ancestry, but were not practising Jews. Originally the family name was Königsberger. Both of Alice Bergmann's parents, Hermann and Clothilde König, were born in Germany, but they spent a significant part of their lives in Russia, where Alice was born in Moscow in 1874. The family left Russia during the pogroms. (Alexander II was assassinated in March 1881. His death was followed by anti-Jewish riots and massacres. In 1882, laws were enacted that expelled many Jewish communities.) The family returned to Germany, changed their name from Königsberger to König and made sure all the documents dealing with their immediate past were destroyed. There were eventually four children in the family, Oswald, Alice, Vera and Georg.

After their marriage, Oskar and Alice Bergmann moved with Oskar's work. Walter Bergmann was born in Altona-Othmarschen in a house in the Lindenallee, where the Bergmanns lived until he was about four. He had several memories from this time, and was amazed that when he revisited Altona in 1932[3] he recognised the house and garden, although they seemed smaller. The Lindenallee was a quiet side road adjoining the main road that ran alongside the River Elbe. In winter there was tobogganing and skating nearby, and Walter Bergmann remembered his cousin, Grete Hoffmann, coming to the house after a skating accident. He also recalled his mother looking for a piece of jewellery. The Bergmann boys used to visit an elderly lady nearby, who made Pfannkuchen (pancakes) for them. In 1905, while still living in Altona, the family holidayed in the Thüringer Wald. The visit to Luisenthal made a strong impression on Walter Bergmann. He remembered the presence of his father's colleague, Karl Marcus, the small railway, the trout stream, the still and quietness of the woods and the smell of wood. He noted that smell played an important role in his memories[4].

In 1906 the Bergmann family moved to Bremen. Their new home was situated on a piece of ground close to the railway embankment. It was a paradise for children, with stables, a flower garden, a kitchen garden and a vine. Walter Bergmann remembered the beauty of the garden and the roar of the trains. While living in Bremen, the family made their first visit to the cinema. The silent movie they saw was accompanied by a gramophone. From this time on, cowboys and indians began to feature in the boys' games. The boys also had their first sight of an airship and it was then the family began to realise that Walter Bergmann was short-sighted, as it took him a long time to see it and recognise what it was. In Bremen the Bergmanns acquired a dog. She was called Molly and was given to them by a cousin, who brought her from Teneriffe. She was small, white and woolly and had an enchanting appearance, which was deceptive, as she bit without warning. She attached herself to Alice Bergmann and Tante Anna. She had two obsessions, cigarette ends and sailors. However the latter interest diminished during the war, when there were large numbers of sailors on the streets.

Other general memories from childhood concerned clothing and food. Walter Bergmann remembered uncomfortable sailor suits, which were complicated to put on and had starched collars that made a noise. All three boys were fussy eaters and considered much food 'disgusting', such as chicken, fish, game and mushrooms. At one point, Hans Bergmann ate little more than bread and milk. The other two boys liked simple food, such as bread and butter, eggs, potatoes and lean meat either minced or roasted. Meals were apparently often a miserable experience. Their attitude to food changed during the war.

Most of Walter Bergmann's childhood memories came from Halle, to where the family moved in March 1909 when he was aged eight and a half and Oskar Bergmann became a Railway Board Adviser. Walter Bergmann spent the rest of his childhood and most of his adult life until he left Germany in Halle. Although the family were not active Protestants, all three boys were confirmed in the Protestant Stephanskirche in Halle. (The family's Jewish ancestry through Alice Bergmann would have remained forgotten had Walter Bergmann's first wife not raised it in acrimonious divorce proceedings.)

From 1909 to 1914 the Bergmann family lived in a rented house in the Handelstrasse (no. 21). Walter Bergmann described it as a hateful house with no garden[5]. The children had to play in the street. To compensate for the lack of a garden and a not particularly pleasant environment, Oskar Bergmann purchased a piece of land in Weimar, on which he built a house. The family went there regularly at weekends and in the holidays. Walter Bergmann's aunts were frequent visitors to the Bergmann homes. It must have been daunting for Alice Bergmann to marry a man with seven sisters, all older than her, who had looked after their brother since he was nine. Walter Bergmann's earliest musical memories were of his aunts singing.

Walter Bergmann started school in April 1909. For all of his school years he attended the Halle Stadtgymnasium. The school consisted of three years Vorschule (preparatory/ elementary school *) and nine years Gymnasium (grammar school) offering a classical education. He enjoyed his first year at school, but found it difficult to grasp the Greek alphabet and he did not excel academically, particularly during the war years. At one point he just avoided having to repeat a school year. He made a small circle of friends within his class, which he retained during his school years, but did not continue on leaving school. Both his brothers were outstanding pupils, which must have been daunting for a younger brother. Hans shone at everything, and Fritz was good at Maths and Physics. Walter Bergmann had problems with Maths and German, and in retrospect saw himself as lazy[6]. Music played a very minor role in school life. It was well after he had started school that it was established that Walter Bergmann needed glasses. His parents finally realised he needed them when he could not read the small print on a visit to the cinema.

Both of Walter Bergmann's parents were musical. His father played the piano and the cello. He had a pleasant singing voice and a good ear for music. Alice Bergmann played the violin, viola and piano. Oskar Bergmann possessed a collection of musical instruments, 2 cellos, 2 violins, a viola, trumpet, guitar, zither, harmonium, flute and 2 pianos. Walter Bergmann observed[7] that his father approached music theoretically and would practise over a considerable period of time to master the notes of a particular piece. However his musical ear helped him appreciate that musicality did not stem from technical mastery. All of the Bergmann boys were musical. Hans played the piano and the cello and had singing lessons for a while. He did not pursue his musical interests as an adult. Fritz played violin, viola and piano. Walter Bergmann was the most musically gifted of the three.

His aunts remembered him singing a great deal as a small boy, and accurately beating time to music. The first piece of serious music Walter Bergmann consciously remembered listening to was Beethoven's first *Piano Trio*, when he was around nine. He began having piano lessons at the age of eight. Initially his Mother taught him, but then he had a series of five teachers, each with completely different personalities, capabilities and ideas. It was an erratic progression, which perhaps contributed to the lack of technical skill Walter Bergmann lamented in later life. Probably, like many excellent sight-readers, he was able to 'get by' without a great deal of practice.

* until 1918

His first teacher was Herr Uschmann, a gifted cellist from the theatre orchestra, who also gave theory lessons to both Walter and Fritz Bergmann. Walter Bergmann remembered him as a nice man, but a bad teacher[8]. He played operatic extracts with Herr Uschmann. His second piano teacher was a daughter of a colleague of Oskar Bergmann, called Fräulein Hedwig Nottebahn. She was considered to be an 'enfant terrible' because she gave gymnastic lessons and danced in public - somewhat risqué activities around 1911. She taught in a Greek toga. Walter Bergmann described her teaching as very theoretical, but she phrased well[8]. He studied Bach's simple *Preludes* with her. Fräulein Nottebahn was succeeded by Fräulein Scheringer, a robust, forceful and sentimental older single lady, who loved the piano pedals. She adored the music of Schumann, as did Walter Bergmann. However he found it painful to play the music as she expected it to be played[8].

Walter Bergmann's next teacher was Herr Univerzitätsmusikdirektor Professor Dr. Rahlwes, the most distinguished teacher in Halle. The lessons were not successful as Walter Bergmann described himself as having being paralysed with respect[9]. He played a variety of music with Dr Rahlwes including Haydn sonatas, the simpler sonatas of Beethoven, and music by Handel, Couperin and Scarlatti. Walter Bergmann's relations with Rahlwes became strained when he did not admire his teacher's *Piano Quintet*. Rahlwes eventually gave up piano teaching to concentrate on other aspects of his career.

By then in his teens, Walter Bergmann was finally taught by Felix Wolfes, whom he considered to be the first real musician and good teacher he had encountered. Felix Wolfes was an excellent accompanist and arranger, and Walter Bergmann commented that he could make even the worst piano sound like an orchestra[9]. Wolfes had studied with Hans Pfitzner and made piano arrangements for him. He respected his pupil's love of Schumann, but refrained from criticising how Walter Bergmann approached the music, although the latter admitted later there was much to criticise. Walter Bergmann learnt a great deal from Wolfes, who was an excellent conductor, especially of opera and in particular of the operatic works of R. Strauss and Wagner, and a charming and witty man. He later became Director of the Dortmund Opera (in 1931).

Walter Bergmann began to play the flute around the time he was confirmed, but he did not feel comfortable playing it and only began to enjoy playing and appreciating it much later as an adult. He very much regretted that he was unable to sing as an adult, although he was able to do so as a child.

The Bergmanns played a great deal of music as a family. Initially this consisted of quite simple arrangements, but later they played chamber music. The family put a great deal of effort into their music- making, but the end result apparently suffered from a lack of ability in all the players. Walter Bergmann observed[10] that all the piano trios, quartets and quintets they attempted to play were too difficult both technically and musically. Possibly Fritz and himself had sufficient musical understanding, but the end result was not satisfactory. Other music they tried to play included music for light orchestra and Brahms string quartets. Walter Bergmann played piano duets with his father, which were more successful, and later they played works for two pianos. This was how he became acquainted with symphonies by Haydn and Schumann.

Walter Bergmann received little music teaching at school, and what he did receive was very limited and unrewarding. A Herr Henckel was the music teacher during his twelve years at school, and in 1938 Walter Bergmann described him as the worst musician he had ever met[11]. When his pupils made a mistake in a singing lesson, Herr Henckel hit them over the head with a wooden stick. Walter Bergmann commented that he wondered how the music teacher believed he would awaken a love of music through such methods[12]. He also noted that Henckel did not have a good sense of pitch. The school choir bellowed and the orchestra played arrangements for light orchestra very slowly. Henckel held no professional musical qualification, neither had he received any musical training, and was a poor performer. As well as his teaching post, he held a senior post in musical administration in connection with the organ. Walter Bergmann described him as a 'dangerous, incompetent man'[13]. From a musical point of view, the most rewarding experience at school for Walter Bergmann was meeting Arnold Matz, a violinist who became a life-long musical friend.

Arnold Matz was the brother of one of Walter Bergmann's classmates, Karl Alfred. When they first met, Arnold Matz had only been playing the violin for a few years, but already he had an astonishing technique and a vital, beautiful tone. Walter Bergmann described him as a born musician[14]. The two boys became close friends and saw each other daily. They had the same 'unfathomable passion' for music which gave them a mutual outlook on life. Whenever the two friends spent time apart, they were always at ease with each other when they were reunited[15]. Together they played the violin and keyboard sonatas of Bach, Handel, Mozart, Beethoven, Brahms and Dvorak, and any other music they could find. Their favourites included the Beethoven *A Minor Sonata* and Dvorak's *Sonatine*. Walter Bergmann and Arnold Matz became the mainstay of school music, and they managed to remain on amiable terms with Herr Henckel, in spite of the lack of respect they had for him.

In 1914 the Bergmanns moved within Halle to 24 Magdeburgerstrasse into a large, attractive apartment spread over two floors, which also had a garden. (The street had become Hindenburgstrasse by 1938.) Oskar Bergmann had problems with the lease. The property was sold just after the family had moved there, and the new landlord wanted to live in it himself. The matter was finally resolved several years after the First War, during the time of inflation, when the Bergmanns relinquished part of the apartment. It was situated directly opposite the University Hospital, which in wartime was filled with wounded soldiers. Hans Bergmann studied there, and Walter Bergmann spent six weeks in the hospital in February 1918, following appendicitis. The family remained in Magdeburgstrasse for ten years through the First World War and the difficult post-war years, when Germany experienced an unsuccessful revolution. Both Alice and Hans Bergmann were seriously ill during the post-war years.

The war disrupted school life and caused enormous changes. In the autumn of 1918 the pupils were put to work in fields near Magdeburg. There were no teachers or headmaster, and the Stadtgymnasium was closed for weeks at a time because there was no heating. Whenever possible lessons were given in other buildings that had heating. Cocoa and food were distributed to the neediest children by the Quakers. By the end of the war there were severe shortages of food and fuel. Matters improved little after the war ended, with days and nights without water and light. The years between 1914 and 1918 had been very difficult, with long periods with little to eat and virtually no fuel or heating, but everyone had suffered together and held to a hope of victory and a successful conclusion to the war. After it ended, the war was argued about and politicised. The deprivations continued and life was extremely depressing without the common motivation that helped to keep people together during the war years. Oskar, Hans and Fritz Bergmann all had to serve in the war. Hans Bergmann reached the age of 18 in 1914, and Fritz in 1917. All three survived without serious injury, but Fritz Bergmann was injured outside the house in Magdeburgerstrasse in the disturbances of 1919, when Germany struggled to attain stability in the vacuum left at the end of the war. Civil unrest spread to most German cities. In Berlin alone, 1000 people were killed in March 1919.

By 1919 life had changed irrevocably from pre-war days. The Bergmanns' life style changed in common with all their contemporaries. Their social circle shrank and large scale entertaining disappeared. Walter Bergmann remembered[15] playing the piano at pre-war dinners given for the Railway Management. (He later learnt that Grete Haase, his second wife, first saw him at one of these occasions.) Throughout their married life Oskar and Alice Bergmann strove to provide a happy atmosphere at home. Friends were always welcome, and they held open house on Saturday evenings. Such social gatherings were curtailed during the war, but they resumed again after the war on a more limited scale, with music, cards, roulette, cocoa and sandwiches. The lack of food and heat limited all social activities, but dancing and dancing classes were popular, as they could function with little cost. Walter Bergmann started to attend dancing classes in 1918. It was the first time he had had any real contact with the opposite sex. He did not succeed in learning to dance, and was not popular with the girls, who were all younger than him. He became aware of what he saw as his physical deficiencies. Earlier gym lessons had also been a disaster. He became very depressed and, like any sixteen year old, miserable when teased about it by his Father and brothers. Walter Bergmann was asked to several dances at private houses. Guests were expected to bring their own sandwiches to eat. He remembered meeting Grete Haase on such an occasion held at the home of a colleague of Oskar Bergmann, Oberbaurat Meyer. His musical activities were still of prime importance to him, and he continued to make music with the Matz and Wolfes families.

School life was apparently back to normal by 1920, the year of the 150th Anniversary of Beethoven's birth. The Gymnasium joined in the Beethoven Fest. Herr Henckel put together a programme that included the slow movement of Beethoven's *First Symphony*, played very slowly by the school orchestra, and the Adagio from the *Appassionata Sonata* sung by the choir. Each item commenced with Henckel calling out 'dr-rei, heraus damit' - a phrase that passed in to the pupils' vocabulary. He audibly counted 'eins, zwei, drei' throughout the performance[16]. Walter Bergmann and Arnold Matz were the most senior musicians in the school, and were expected to play one movement from a Beethoven Trio with a third student who played the cello. Walter Bergmann suggested that they play a complete Beethoven trio. Herr Henckel dismissed this idea, saying that such a work would be too difficult for the younger schoolchildren to listen to. He gave the three boys a performance limit of six minutes. The three students then decided they would play all of Beethoven's *Geister Trio*. Henckel insisted that they play to him before the concert. With true schoolboy cunning, they agreed on a plan of action. At the rehearsal attended by Herr Henckel, they played straight through all the movements, increasing the tempo markings, omitting the repeats and shortening the slow movements. They thus managed to keep to the six-minute deadline. Of course in the actual concert performance, they played the work as intended. Walter Bergmann did not record the reaction of Herr Henckel!

Walter Bergmann took his Abitur (school leaving certificate) at Easter in 1921. In German and mathematics he achieved a grade 2 (grade 1 being the highest). His essay, which he had to present as a paper, was praised by his teachers and was also awarded a grade 2 in spite of the fact he had not finished it and had improvised the conclusion just before he delivered the paper. Its title was *Weimar oder Potsdam?* (In 1938 he reflected that this was typical of his character; he always left finishing things until the last possible moment and ended up improvising.) He had not enjoyed school, but had got through it as best he could[17]. He later observed that some of his schooling had been rewarding and had provided a good basis for thinking, though not for life. He had not been unpopular at school - at one point Walter Bergmann was elected to be the class representative. However he surmised that this happened because he was the most apolitical member of the class and would follow the lead of others, which made him popular with the teachers. His lack of sporting ability still depressed Walter Bergmann and he developed an inferiority complex due to the fact he was not good at any kind of physical activity. It took him ten years to overcome this feeling of inferiority, and during this time he began to escape from reality by half living in a dream world. He fantasised about being a champion or a soldier[18]. He finally began to live completely in the real world when he began his career as a lawyer.

By the time he was nineteen and had left school, nearly all of Walter Bergmann's musical experience had been acquired outside of school life. He had made music at home with his family and friends. His musical experience had been broadened through his friendship with Arnold Matz and contact with the Matz family. All of the Matz family, with the exception of Karl Alfred, were gifted musicians. Frau Matz had studied the violin with Joachim, her daughter Issi had an excellent singing voice and Gottfried and Rudi Matz played the piano and violin. By 1921, Walter Bergmann was well acquainted with the keyboard and chamber music of Bach, Handel, Haydn, Mozart, Beethoven and Dvorak. He had developed a passion for the music of Schumann, both for his songs and piano music. Walter Bergmann believed that it was through Schumann's music that he first came to understand the true nature of music[19]. With Professor Dr. Rahlwes he had studied the music of Couperin and Scarlatti. He had sung in large choral works such as Beethoven's *Missa Solemnis* and the *Ninth Symphony*, Handel's *Susanna* and Haydn's *The Seasons*. Felix Wolfes had introduced him to opera, an interest he was to develop further during the 1920s. He also had a growing interest in and knowledge of contemporary music, but Walter Bergmann's greatest love at this time was Schumann and Lieder.

[1] 'Er hatte zeit sieben Lebens sich der Liebe von 7 Schwestern zu erwehren.' WB's notes made on the Isle of Man in 1940.

[2] 'der Raum so autoritätsgeladen'; WB's notes 1940

[3] WB's handwritten autobiographical notes written in prison in 1938

[4] WB's hand written notes 1938, p. 7

[5] WB's hand written notes 1938, p. 21

[6] WB's hand written notes 1938, p. 14

[7] Autobiographical notes handwritten by WB in prison in 1938 and typed later, p. 13

[8] WB's typed notes 1938, p. 3

[9] WB's typed notes, 1938, p. 4

[10] WB's typed notes, 1938, p. 13

[11] WB's hand written notes, 1938, p.15

[12] WB's typed notes, 1938, p.15

[13] 'Ein gefährlicher Nichtskönner',

WB's typed notes, 1938, p.15
[14] WB's typed notes, 1938, p.16
[15] WB's hand written notes, 1938, p.25
[16] WB's typed notes, 1938, p. 15
[17] WB's hand written notes, 1938, p.20
[18] WB's hand written notes, 1938, p.29
[19] WB's typed notes, 1938, p.5

The Bergmann Family c. 1918

2. Lawyer and Musician

On his last day at school, Walter Bergmann considered whether he should study law or music.[1] His inclination was towards music but he really did not know what career he wished to follow, and felt that he did not have any particular gifts other than his musical abilities. His father was willing for him to have the opportunity to study music, and he auditioned for the Leipzig Conservatoire. Walter Bergmann described his audition performance as appalling[2], but in 1921 he was accepted as a student. He studied the piano with Beresel, who worked hard at improving Walter Bergmann's technique. In particular he studied music by Mozart, Beethoven and Chopin, and enjoyed playing a Mozart piano concerto in E flat. Walter Bergmann also studied the flute with Maximilian Schwedler (editor of Handel sonatas for Peters). Schwedler did not think much of his pupil's abilities as a flautist, but soon discovered that he had an excellent accompanist. He made good use of Walter Bergmann as accompanist for his other flute pupils. Walter Bergmann also studied harmony at Leipzig, with Ludwig, which he did not enjoy, and in Halle he studied musicology with Schering and Klose.

During the winter of 1921/22, Walter Bergmann initially lived at home and travelled daily to Leipzig by train. The journey lasted an hour in unheated carriages. It was an extremely cold winter, and he had no opportunity to get warm or to practise in Leipzig during the day. He then found a room to rent in the Thomasinstrasse in Leipzig. There was a piano in the house, but it was difficult for him to get access to it and the house was very cold, making practising difficult. Walter Bergmann led an uncomfortable, lonely and miserable existence. It was a stark contrast to home; he made no new friends and ate all his meals alone in the Conservatoire canteen. In 1938 he reflected that he was surprised that his mother had not intervened and sorted out his problems. He concluded that she may have already been seriously ill, or perhaps she had felt that he was old enough to sort out his own problems, and ought to do so without parental assistance. The misery of Walter Bergmann's living conditions were exacerbated by the escalating inflation in Germany. He began to doubt the wisdom of studying music. He knew he did not have the talent to become a concert pianist, although he was aware of his gift as an accompanist. He saw little future for himself in music, and could see no way of using accompanying as the basis of a career. He took the decision to study law instead of music. He felt that such a course had to have a better prospect of a successful career. Studying music involved the prospect of hardship and struggle without any likelihood of a livelihood at the end of it. He later attributed his choice to pursue a legal career to the fact he had 'a strong feeling for injustice and saw red if violence or injustice was done'.[3] His decision was supported by his father, who probably felt a great deal of relief at what he saw as his unrealistic son becoming realistic about life. He advocated 'Musik als Hobby und niemals als Brotfach'[4]. (Music as a hobby and never as a livelihood.)

Walter Bergmann returned home and for a year from Easter 1922 he studied law in Halle. Economically life was bleak, but he was much happier. As well as being back living comfortably at home, he had fallen in love with Issi Matz. Since leaving school he had continued to make music with the Matz family, particularly with Arnold and Issi. Walter Bergmann meticulously kept copies of the concerts he performed in throughout his life, and the earliest he preserved dates from March 17th 1921, at the time he left school, when he gave a concert with Arnold Matz and a singer named Ursula Meyer. The programme included Beethoven's *Sonata in A minor, op. 23* and Schumann's *Sonatine in A minor*, both for violin and piano, and songs by Schumann and Brahms. Walter Bergmann's love of Schumann continued, but from 1922 he began to explore contemporary music with Arnold and Issi. They experienced 'the opening of the ears at that time, which unfortunately became named atonal'[5]. Writing in 1938, Walter Bergmann stated his belief that it was important to compare the new music from the first decades of the twentieth century with Expressionism in painting. Such music should not be considered to be a style of music, but a breakthrough in musical thought. He felt it should have been a time of exultation, and in retrospect it could be seen as the breaking of new ground[6]. From the perspective of 1938, Walter Bergmann believed that from this period of musical thought emerged the 'great works' of Bartok, Hindemith and Stravinsky. He felt a particular affinity with Hindemith's music, whom he met briefly in 1922. German music and art could be seen to reflect the turbulence of Germany itself, and dissatisfaction with old ideas and beliefs.[7] Hindemith was one of those exploring new and radical means of expression. (In his four-movement suite *Kammermusik no.I*, for example, premiered at the 1922 Donaueschingen Festival, he wrote for a small band, which included an accordion, a siren and a canister of sand.)

The contemporary music was difficult to play and understand, and had many critics. Arnold Matz and Walter Bergmann found few musicians willing to play it with them. Walter Bergmann also began to compose himself, as well as regularly accompanying Issi Matz as she sang a variety of music. They began to spend a great deal of time making music together. He described her as having a good singing voice, but poorly developed technique[8]. In 1938 he wrote that there were songs that he had not heard anyone sing as well as she did, for example Schumann's *Mondnacht*. They sight-read music together, particularly Schumann songs, but also songs by contemporary composers such as Hindemith and Pfitzner. Issi Matz became a frequent welcome visitor to the Bergmann home in Magdeburgerstrasse[9]. The house was often filled with visitors, as well as members of the extended Bergmann family. In her eighties, Issi Matz (Luise von Arps-Aubert) recalled the pleasure of her visits. Oskar Bergmann always sat at the head of the dining table; beside him sat his three large sons, charming slender wife, and between two and four aunts who always seemed to be staying in the house.

By the end of 1922, Walter Bergmann and Issi Matz were engaged. Issi Matz described it as a wonderful time. 'We were young, engaged and had music that lasted me all of my life.'[10] Initially the couple kept their engagement to themselves, but at the beginning of 1923, against Walter Bergmann's advice, Issi Matz confided in her mother. Neither set of parents were happy about the engagement, once they were all informed about it. Oskar Bergmann asserted that at twenty, his son was far to young to consider getting married, and, as he had no means of supporting himself, let alone a wife, how could anyone believe that his proposal had been serious[11]. It was agreed that there would be a trial period for the engagement involving separation. Walter Bergmann would leave Halle to study law in Freiburg for a year. There was to be no exchange of letters between Issi and himself.

He arrived in Freiburg in the spring of 1923, but it did not feel spring-like due to the parting from Issi, leaving home and the continuing high level of inflation. A loaf of bread now cost astronomical amounts. It was arranged that Walter Bergmann would make an exchange with the son of a professor of mathematics and physics, so that no money would have to exchange hands. Walter Bergmann went to live with the Maurer family and Erhard Maurer went to live with the Bergmanns in Halle. Walter Bergmann reckoned that Erhard Maurer got the better bargain[12]. Professor Maurer was a vegetarian and lived a spartan life. He was a staunch Protestant living in an almost exclusively Roman Catholic town. Daily meals consisted of potatoes and cheese for breakfast and salad for lunch. Although he already had some acquaintances in Freiburg through his Aunt Vera, Walter Bergmann found he had nothing in common with them. He did not enjoy his first term in Freiburg. He made few friends and spent his free time walking by himself.

The second term over the winter of 1923/24 was better, although by 1924 the German currency was worthless. A cousin came to study singing in Freiburg and Walter Bergmann accompanied her. He found a friend with whom he could ski. He enjoyed the winter landscape and felt he had never before seen anything so beautiful. He also was able to hear a significant amount of chamber music, and he twice went to the music festival in Donaueschingen.

Walter Bergmann returned to Halle in 1924 to continue with his law studies, but life was changing radically for the Bergmann Family. Alice Bergmann was seriously ill with cancer. Oskar Bergmann had retired and was hunting for a more suitable flat for his sick wife, eventually finding one in Jena. Issi Matz was working as a housekeeper at Burg Lauenstein and had had second thoughts about getting married. When Walter Bergmann proposed to her again, she refused him. He understood her position. In taking the position at Burg Lauenstein Issi had gained her independence, and she did not wish to lose it.

Walter Bergmann recorded in 1938[13] that his parents' move to Jena had, in retrospect, been very good for him, as it had forced him to become independent and take control of his own life. He remained in Halle and initially found a furnished room to live in, which contained a square piano, the value of which he did not appreciate at the time. He then joined friends in lodgings in Schillerstrasse, from where he took his Referendenexamen, one of the three sets of state exams necessary to qualify as a lawyer. When Walter Bergmann first returned to Halle, his brother Fritz lived nearby. Together they went on bicycle tours, exploring various parts of Germany, including the Thüringer Wald, Spessart and Bodensee. Fritz Bergmann then moved to Freiburg. This marked the final break up of family life, as Hans Bergmann was already living in Dresden.

Alice Bergmann had several operations, and her sister Vera went to Jena to help look after her. All the operations were unsuccessful and Alice Bergmann died in April 1925. The final months were very distressing for her and the family, and her death was a release for them all. Walter Bergmann found it difficult to come to terms with her death[14]. After Alice Bergmann's death, her Mother and sister moved to Jena to live permanently with Oskar Bergmann. Vera König and Oskar Bergmann eventually married in November 1926. The three Bergmann brothers were delighted, but Grandmother König did not approve of the marriage and moved into lodgings. She eventually returned to live with Oskar and Vera Bergmann.

In Halle Walter Bergmann established a new circle of musical friends. By the time he had returned to Halle in 1924, Arnold Matz had left, as had Felix Wolfes. Through Fritz Bergmann, Walter Bergmann met a cellist, Hermann Novak, who was also an excellent pianist. They became close friends, and the friendship continued for many years, with Novak supporting Walter Bergmann through the difficult final years before he left Germany to go to Britain.

There were two homes in Halle where there were regular well-known musical gatherings. Those at the home of Frau Gutzeit were considered the more fashionable and smart, but the participants were apparently more concerned about their appearance and the social aspect of music-making. A large number of young girls participated, and Walter Bergmann felt very uncomfortable in their presence. The other regular musical gatherings were held at the home of the Frankl family, and were of a much more spontaneous and intellectual nature[15]. Walter Bergmann began to get involved with the Frankls in 1925, at the time the family's life and musical activities began to be affected by the serious illness of their son Peter, who suffered from schizophrenia. Walter Bergmann became a close and supportive friend.

Herr Frankl was an art historian who later emigrated to the USA. Elsa Frankl had a coloratura voice. Walter Bergmann had certain reservations about the Frankls' music-making. The music was unplanned, the players never rehearsed, and the participants sometimes played tortuously for hours at a time in front of total strangers[16]. The music performed on these occasions frequently consisted of excerpts from operas and oratorios sung out of context and without the original orchestral accompaniment. Walter Bergmann felt strongly that when arias were sung out of context it was almost impossible to portray the true character and meaning of the music. He also disliked the fashion of playing music by Baroque composers such as Handel and Schütz with lush, refined harmonies. In such arrangements the true vigour, spirit and vitality of the music was lost. Walter Bergmann still acknowledged in 1938[17] that he learnt a great deal through his acquaintance with the Frankl family and experienced much beautiful music, in particular music by Bach and Erbach. In retrospect he felt that he had not perhaps made best use of the opportunities offered to him.

Through the Frankl family's musical activities Walter Bergmann met a number of other musicians. These included a singer, Dr Friedrich Viol. Viol was an enthusiastic and well-qualified bass, who had studied with several eminent singers, but was unfortunately lacking in confidence. Walter Bergmann attributed this to Viol's illegitimate background, and lack of interest or support from Viol's wife. Walter Bergmann and Friedrich Viol worked together a great deal. Viol came to regard Walter Bergmann as 'his' accompanist and Walter Bergmann did all he could to encourage him. Viol enjoyed singing music by Handel and Schütz, but Walter Bergmann felt the singer's voice was much more suited to singing music by Schubert, Schumann and Bach, and that together they gave good concerts when these three composers formed the basis of the programme. Two other musicians Walter Bergmann met through the Frankls were Otto Neumann and Jan Versteeg. Both were professional musicians playing in the Halle Stadttheater Orchestra. Otto Neumann was a cellist who became close friends with Walter Bergmann and they played together for ten years. Walter Bergmann always asked Neumann to play when he needed a cellist.[18] Jan Versteeg was the lead violinist in the Halle theatre orchestra and he also was interested in composing. Walter Bergmann enjoyed his sense of humour and they remained friends for the rest of their lives. The three men played trios together.

It was at the Frankls' that Walter Bergmann first met the singer Marthel Kolb, who became his first wife. Marthel Kolb was an operatic soprano who between 1925 and 1930 performed in and around the towns of Gotha and

Stettin. She originally came from Fürth, near Nürnberg, and was five years older than Walter Bergmann. She held a salaried position at the Landestheater in Gotha and accepted freelance engagements in towns close by, such as Jena, Weimar and Halle. During 1925 Walter Bergmann began to accompany her at public engagements. Over the next five years he became progressively involved in accompanying and rehearsing Marthel Kolb and other singers, as well as pursuing his legal career. In spite of a very busy life, he continued to visit his Father, Aunt and Grandmother regularly in Jena, but with Fritz's marriage in 1926, family ties significantly weakened. Walter Bergmann accompanied his Father to the wedding. It was one of the rare opportunities he had to talk properly with him[19].

Over the next few years, Walter Bergmann felt he was almost living permanently in the theatres of Halle, Gotha and Stettin. He wrote[20] that he experienced lieder and opera to their maximum possibility. He described himself as having been 'married to song'. ('Ich war mit Gesang verheiratet.'[21]) He gained a great deal of experience through organising and preparing for Marthel Kolb's concerts and as acting as a repetiteur for a number of other singers. He believed that one should never underestimate the importance of a repetiteur, who must get the best performance from singers in the most economical time. The repetiteur must lay before the singer all the possibilities of the music, so that each individual singer can select what is suitable for them. 'One must rehearse enough, but not excite them; stretch them without exhausting them; make them concentrate without anxiety and accept their moods and anxieties.'[22] He observed that one must be married to a singer to appreciate truly what the singer can demand from repetiteur, conductor and manager. Walter Bergmann felt that through his work as an accompanist, he gained a greater understanding of song than many operatic directors, and came to understand that opera is drama *through* song, not drama with song. He had first hand experience of a wide range of operas, including works by Mozart, Verdi, Wagner, Mussorgsky, Weber, Strauss, Pfitzner, Rossini and Smetana. Walter Bergmann experienced Wagner's *Tristan* in 1924. He described it as a 'fundamental'[23] piece of music. The two operatic composers he valued most were Mozart and Verdi.

Walter Bergmann had learnt about the production and conducting side of opera from his teacher Felix Wolfes, and from Fritz Hensel, whom he had met through working with Marthel Kolb. Hensel was an actor who became an opera manager. He was an outstanding artist and excellent operatic producer. He had developed a particular method of breathing through which he could achieve an extraordinary range of dynamics. When accompanying singing, Hensel would give up playing if the dynamics reached pp. Walter Bergmann saw Hensel as a brilliant interpreter of Mozart and Verdi and acknowledged that he learnt a great deal from him. Evenings spent with Hensel were lively, stimulating and skillfully directed. Walter Bergman also often accompanied Hensel's wife, Martha Seeliger, who had 'a beautiful, dreamlike alto voice.'[24] Marthel Kolb and Martha Seeliger occasionally gave concerts together, accompanied by Walter Bergmann. They gave such a concert on March 17th 1927, with a programme consisting of songs by Pergolesi, Mozart, Schubert and Dvorak and eighteenth century French songs. Marthel Kolb's standard repertoire consisted of songs by Mozart, Bizet, Verdi and Puccini. Walter Bergmann felt that he was recognised as an able musician in theatrical circles, but only in his association with Marthel Kolb and not in his own right. Professionally he was just a very young junior lawyer earning 150 marks a month.

After passing his qualifying examinations, Walter Bergmann spent six months working in the public prosecutor's office in Erfurt, 25 kilometres from Gotha. During his time there, Walter Bergmann became acquainted with a wealthy family who owned a fine collection of modern art, and he began to develop an appreciation of modern paintings. He was also taken to a nightclub for the first time. He completed his studies in Halle with a lawyer called Justizrat Herold. It was a time of new experiences. He flew for the first time, going on holiday with Marthel Kolb to Joggot. Unfortunately he developed sciatica, for which he eventually had an operation in the autumn of 1928, after which he travelled to Joachimstal in Czechoslovakia for a cure. Walter Bergmann enjoyed the beautiful autumn weather, but he did not feel any better on his return home. The sciatica finally disappeared of its own accord.

Walter Bergmann completed his legal training by working for six months at the Court of Appeal in Jena. He worked with pleasant senior colleagues, but found presenting cases in court an ordeal, particularly while suffering from sciatica. He lacked self-confidence and did not speak clearly enough. Arguments that had appeared methodical and logical on paper did not seem so well thought out when presented in court. In 1921 Walter Bergmann wrote in his diary[25] that his legal personality was only skin deep. He believed that he was not truly a lawyer because he did not think as a lawyer. He finally qualified as a lawyer on January 30th 1930, taking the third state professional examination in Berlin. (He gained his doctorate in 1932, the subject of which was 'Die Verdunkelungsgefahr als Haftgrund im Deutschen Strafprozess' - 'The danger of prejudicing the cause of justice as grounds for arrest in German criminal proceedings'. This was to prove ironic when he himself was arrested by the Nazis.)

On the completion of his professional examinations Walter Bergmann was assigned to become a judge's assistant and sent to Schkeuditz as a trainee. He finally became fully qualified during 1930 and returned to work with Justizrat Herold in Halle. Herold was a respected but elderly lawyer who was chairman of the Halle Anwaltskammer. He had almost lost interest in his legal practice, and there was barely enough work to support two lawyers. Walter Bergmann described[26] Herold as a fine and cultured man and a good colleague. He was left to work on his own in the office, and initially found this quite difficult, as he had previously never worked unsupervised. After a certain amount of reluctance Herold eventually offered Walter Bergmann a partnership.

All through this period Walter Bergmann pursued his interest in opera and song, and his relationship with Marthel Kolb. They married in November 1930. Walter Bergmann was twenty-eight and Marthel Kolb thirty-three. They celebrated their wedding first at the home of the Frankls in Halle and then with Oskar and Vera Bergmann in Jena. The couple went on honeymoon to Weimar, but had to return early because Marthel Kolb was called back to perform in the theatre in Chemnitz.

In November 1930 Marthel Kolb left her position at the Landestheater in Gotha. She gave a farewell concert on November 18th. The programme consisted of arias by Mozart, Puccini, Smetana and Lortzing and songs by Schubert, including *The Trout*. Walter Bergmann noted[27] that she sang beautifully. (It is not clear why she 'retired' at this point; may be she wished to give up singing professionally, or she may have been ill – Dietrich Gerhardt had a vague memory of her having tuberculosis. She did continue to sing after 1930.) Walter and Marthel Bergmann moved into a flat in Halle, in the Fürstenstrasse, which was in a house owned by acquaintances of the name of Jakobsen. Very soon after their marriage there began to be friction between Walter and Marthel Bergmann. Early in 1931 they went together to a costume ball where Walter Bergmann re-met an old acquaintance from the years after the war, Grete Haase. On returning home after the ball, Marthel complained that Walter Bergmann had ignored her and spent far too much time with Grete Haase. She accused him of being in love with Grete. According to Walter Bergmann[28] the matter was blown up out of all proportions. When Dietrich Gerhardt met Walter Bergmann for the first time in 1931, he later recalled[29] that he was aware that the Bergmann marriage was already in difficulties. Walter Bergmann remarked to Gerhardt that it was a little early in his married life for him to be facing a crisis.

As Walter Bergmann's marriage grew more and more strained, his friendship with Grete Haase grew. Grete Haase was the unconventional daughter of a wealthy Halle businessman who owned a starch factory and retail grocery business. She was the second of four daughters, radical in her outlook and considered by her family to be a rebel. She was two years younger than Walter Bergmann and had trained in Munich as a teacher of gymnastics. In September 1931 Walter Bergmann made a conscious effort to repair his marriage and give up seeing Grete. But it was too late; his relationship with Marthel Bergmann was beyond saving. Their life together was stormy and difficult. They quarrelled with the Jakobsens, their landlords, and moved in with the Frankl family on a temporary basis until a new flat was ready for them. Marthel Kolb went on a visit to Paris. On her return she attempted to commit suicide in the new flat.

Elsa Frankl tried to help Marthel Kolb recover and to rebuild the Bergmann marriage. But both Walter and Marthel knew that they could not continue their lives together. In January 1932 Marthel Kolb left for Berlin. Walter Bergmann sincerely regretted the marriage crisis and break-up that his wife had to live through. He wrote in 1938[30] that it was right for him that the marriage ended, but not for her. Throughout his years of association and marriage with Marthel Kolb, Walter Bergmann's circle of musical friends had been broadening and expanding. The 'most significant'[31] introduction Walter Bergmann believed he had through the Frankls music-making was in 1931, which was when he met the young oboist Dietrich Gerhardt. Gerhardt was just beginning his university studies and was acquainted with Friedrich Viol, who invited him to participate in an afternoon of Hausmusik at the Frankls. Viol suggested that Walter Bergmann accompanied the oboist, and Gerhardt went to collect him from his office. He met there a young man who had an abundance of black hair and who proved to be an astonishingly good musician[32]. Gerhardt also discovered that Walter Bergmann had wide knowledge of contemporary music and saw himself as a pupil of Felix Wolfes. On that first meeting they played Haydn's *Concerto Grosso for Oboe*. Walter Bergmann found in Dietrich Gerhardt a technically gifted oboist who he believed had the potential to become a great musician[33]. It was the beginning of a friendship that lasted a lifetime. Dietrich Gerhardt also met Marthel Kolb the same afternoon, as she sang in Haydn's *English Canzonette*.

From their first meeting until Walter Bergmann's enforced departure from Germany the two musicians regularly played together. Walter Bergmann believed that Gerhardt did much to enrich his musical life and particularly admired both his playing and conducting of music by

Bach. Walter Bergmann did not feel that he himself had contributed to Gerhardt's musical development except to recognise his exceptional ability and help strengthen his confidence. Together they played music by Bach, Telemann, Haydn and Mozart. Dietrich Gerhardt also introduced Walter Bergmann to the recorder repertoire, as he was an excellent recorder player. Dietrich Gerhardt in return found Walter Bergmann an extremely competent keyboard player, proficient in realising continuo parts[34]. Gerhardt believed that Walter Bergmann had learnt to realise continuo parts as a teenager. In October 1932 they gave a concert together, which included trio sonatas by Loeillet and Fux. The Loeillet sonata only existed as a composition for piano and the Fux in its original form with an unrealised bass. Walter Bergmann realised both piece of music for the concert. It was an occupation that Walter Bergmann began to spend more and more time on. Other concerts Walter Bergmann and Dietrich Gerhardt gave together included music by Telemann, Bach and Handel, and contemporary works including Walter Bergmann's own compositions. Walter Bergmann wrote two oboe sonatas for Gerhardt, who remembered playing the first movement of the first sonata to Grete Haase in 1932, in an empty flat in Halle.

In 1932 Dietrich Gerhardt introduced Walter Bergmann to two musicians, Rheinhold Heyden and Wilhelm Twittenhof, who were to have a significant influence on his future musical career. They introduced him to a wide range of music from the sixteenth and seventeenth centuries, including recorder music, and to the movement for encouraging amateur music making and adult music education. Heyden had moved to Halle from Berlin to be the musical director of the Volkshochschule (Adult Education Institute). Walter Bergmann described Heyden as an excellent teacher whose work with amateur choirs was outstanding[35]. He did not have as much experience or knowledge in the area of orchestral music and came to rely on Walter Bergmann, Dietrich Gerhardt and their musical circle for help and support. Wilhelm Twittenhof accompanied Heyden to Halle. He was a music theorist with a particular interest in rhythm. Heyden and Twittenhof introduced Walter Bergmann to the music of Rameau, Purcell and W.F. Bach and broadened his knowledge of Telemann through the performance of vocal and chamber music. Their performances included a significant amount of recorder music. For example a concert given at the Volkshochschule on October 19th 1932 included dances by Praetorius, performed by recorders and lute, dances by Hausmann performed by recorders, and choral works by Marenzio, Isaac and Gesius. Walter Bergmann greatly admired the work of the two men, but he acknowledged later that problems were created by their lack of understanding of sixteenth and seventeenth century performance practice[36]. In spite of this, he considered it far more important that early music was performed in a lively fashion and its relevance to amateur players recognised. Dietrich Gerhardt observed[37] that although Heyden and Twittenhof had introduced him to a wide range of music, Walter Bergmann probably had a far deeper understanding of the music than his two 'teachers'. From 1932 onwards his favourite musical occupation was playing continuo.

Dietrich Gerhardt introduced Walter Bergmann into two other spheres of music making in Halle. One was associated with an elderly musician, Carl Boyde, who directed a church choir concentrating on the music of Bach and Handel. Walter Bergmann worked with Boyde for several years, playing both flute and continuo in a number of performances. Concerts with Boyde included J.S.Bach's Cantatas nos. 3, 56, 123 and 93 (17.4.32), nos.

189, 126 and 104 (22.10.33) and in 1934 a Handel concert, which included *The Concerto Grosso No.8* for oboe and strings, with Dietrich Gerhardt as soloist and *The Ode for St Cecilia's Day* (21.6.34). Boyde arduously wrote out all the necessary parts himself, but unfortunately he apparently had little understanding of how to orchestrate or conduct continuo playing or how to conduct recitative. Walter Bergmann still valued his association with Boyde for introducing him to 'the most wonderful of Bach cantatas'.[38] He described Bach cantatas as 'das schönste Gebiet der Musik'[39] (the most beautiful area of music). Gerhardt also gave Walter Bergmann an introduction to an amateur orchestra founded by an acquaintance and conducted by an ex-musical director of the Halle Stadttheater called Roessert. Walter Bergmann belonged as a flautist for a short period. Other musicians he met at this time included Fräulein Steinicke, a music teacher and director of the Halle Children's Choir with whom he played the flute until his separation from Marthel Kolb. He continued to give concerts with Otto Neumann and Jan Versteeg playing such works as the Haydn *Piano Trio No 12 in C major* which they performed at a concert in 1933.

In 1932 Marthel Kolb (who always maintained Kolb as her professional name) issued a petition for divorce. She then halted the divorce proceedings and tried again to persuade Walter Bergmann that they should have another attempt at making their marriage work. It was too late. The relationship between Walter Bergmann and Grete Haase had developed too far. They were expecting a child. Once she knew this, Marthel Kolb issued proceedings for maintenance. Walter Bergmann then began to worry as to how he could support Marthel Kolb, as well as Grete, a baby and himself. Grete Haase temporarily left Halle and Walter Bergmann joined her for a holiday on the Baltic. They were both back in Halle by November, and their daughter Erica was born on December 26th. The immediate impact of Erica Bergmann's birth was the issuing of a notice by Herold to say that his partnership with Walter Bergmann would be dissolved on July 1st 1933.

Life was not easy for Walter, Grete and their baby. Grete Haase's family were not happy with the step she had taken. Her father refused to see her again. Her mother determined to remain in contact, and occasionally managed to visit her daughter and granddaughter and leave a little money behind. A significant number of Walter Bergmann's friends and acquaintances, shocked by the break-up of his marriage, his decision to live openly with Grete Haase and finally the arrival of Erica, gradually disassociated themselves from him. Friedrich Viol had continued to regard Walter Bergmann as a close friend and support him through his marriage problems, but his wife disapproved of Walter Bergmann and his irregular marital situation and the friendship was eventually broken. Walter Bergmann was saddened to hear in 1937 that Viol had died suddenly after a stroke at the age of 47. Rheinhold Heyden remained friendly with Walter Bergmann until he left Halle to take up a position as adviser for youth in Weimar, where he unfortunately died from a brain tumour shortly after. Heyden had had marriage difficulties and was sympathetic to Walter Bergmann's problems. (His friend Wilhelm Twittenhof survived the war years and became involved in music education.) Otto Neumann and Jan Versteeg remained true and supportive friends, both musically and practically. Otto Neumann and his wife gave valuable help and support at the time of Erica's birth, and offered Walter, Grete and Erica a home. Walter Bergmann and his new family became sub-tenants of the Neumanns. He felt immense gratitude for their kindness.

In 1933 Walter Bergmann's musical activities were in the main unaffected by his personal problems, although the influence of the Nazi ideology was already beginning to affect music after Hitler's appointment as Chancellor on January 30th 1933. Both Walter Bergmann and Dietrich Gerhardt were keenly interested in contemporary music, and with a musical historian, Dr Helmutt Wolff, they organised a concert of contemporary music which took place on May 26th 1933. They wished to try to express their opposition to the way in which contemporary music was being diminished by current political thought. Modern music was beginning to founder as Nazi propaganda decreed that little played music was unwanted music. The concert was by invitation only and consisted of piano music by Bartok and Poulenc, chamber music by Helmutt Wolff and Walter Bergmann's first oboe sonata. However it also included a small amount of early music, two ballads by Guillaume de Machaut. Dietrich Gerhardt described the programme as a 'suitable tangled confusion'[40] that seemed to go on forever, but the brave statement somehow 'faded away in the turmoil of the approaching Third Reich'.

Walter Bergmann opened his own legal practice on July 9th 1933. His office was situated in an old merchant's house in Brüderstrasse, Halle, where Goethe was reputed to have stayed. He initially started with a very small amount of work - he was after all only recently qualified as a lawyer and had first handled a public criminal case in the previous year. (He described this case as 'a Gretchen tragedy in Goethe's centenary'.) He gradually built up a small practice. He did not specialise in any particular area of law, but Dietrich Gerhardt[41] remembers him handling a significant number of divorce cases. The combination of his irregular marital situation and the growing power of the Nazi state did not help his career. His income was small and Grete helped the family budget by giving gymnastic lessons at home. Walter Bergmann sometimes accompanied her on the flute. In spite of their limited budget, the family were able to live a reasonably stable and happy life for almost three years, though there were problems for Walter Bergmann's family. The family celebrated Oskar Bergmann's seventy-fifth birthday in November 1934, but following this, Fritz's daughter Alice became seriously ill, as did Vera Bergmann.

Walter Bergmann had a steady flow of cases, many of which arose out of the new sinister effect of Nazism on the law. He acquired a secretary, Charlotte Zimmermann, in 1934. She recalled[42] that although Walter Bergmann had little money, he 'took upon himself the troubles of those who came to him for help'. Walter Bergmann once told Dietrich Gerhardt that he had been told he was an intellectual musician, and that in contrast to this he saw himself as an emotional lawyer[43]. Cases Walter Bergmann handled included arranging a flat for an elderly woman, pursuing a case of sabotage for a considerable period of time until he was able to prove his client innocent and negotiating the release of a woman of Jewish background from the Gestapo. He continued to handle controversial cases even when he began to realise that he could find himself in a precarious position because of his Jewish ancestry. In spite of the scandal caused by the break-up of his marriage and the gradual tightening grip of the Third Reich, Walter Bergmann managed to sustain his legal practice until 1938.

Music with friends continued, especially with Dietrich Gerhardt, Jan Versteeg, Arnold Matz, Hellmuth Wolff and Otto Neumann. On Wednesday afternoons Walter Bergmann closed his office and went home for what became a regular afternoon of music making[44].

There was always a predetermined programme, which was dominated by Baroque music, and the players always included Otto Neumann and Jan Versteeg and other members of the Halle theatre orchestra. Charlotte Zimmermann remembered that after the music, coffee was served, and the assembled company discussed current affairs.

The fall-out from the scandal caused by his marriage break-up and current marital status distressed and depressed Walter Bergmann. He looked for new activities to distract him. In 1934 he took the opportunity to attend the Kasseler Musikfest, where he heard a variety of early music, including performances on old, original instruments and music by Praetorius. (Edgar Hunt also came from England to the Festival, but Walter Bergmann and he were not destined to meet until 1939.) The visit inspired him to begin transcribing a collection of early songs entitled *Reutterliedlein unter Gassenhauerlin*, which dated from 1534, into modern notation. In the same year Walter Bergmann became treasurer and manager of the Halle Handel Verein (Society). The Society's objective was to support prestigious concerts, but the mounting inflation of the preceding years had prevented this from happening. The President of the Society was Professor Rahlwes, from whom Walter Bergmann had received piano lessons as a boy. Walter Bergmann was dismissive of Professor Rahlwes' achievements as President. The Handel Verein was so-called because Halle was Handel's birthplace, but Handel had left Halle at the age of eighteen - a fact the members of the Society tended to overlook. Walter Bergmann once attended a lecture under the auspices of the Society where it was claimed that Halle 'was the town where Handel created his greatest compositions'[45]! During his period of office he was responsible for only one concert, which consisted of chamber music by Bach, Haydn and Telemann. Walter Bergmann succeeded in employing a good flautist for the concert, but apparently the playing standard of the other players meant the concert was not a success. In 1935 the Handel Verein celebrated the 250th anniversary of Handel's birth. Walter Bergmann was not impressed by the amount of research or understanding that went into the performance of Handel's music during the celebrations. Disillusioned, he resigned and apparently did not perform in any public concert again until after he had left Germany.

Until 1936, Walter Bergmann's Jewish ancestry was not of common knowledge, and it had caused him no problems. Indeed in the two years between the coming to power of Hitler in 1933 and 1935, German Jews were relatively free from persecution. In September 1935 this situation was changed by the Nürnberg Laws, which established restrictions on the lives and status of Jews. In particular, Jews were denied German citizenship or the right to fly the German flag, and Jews and non-Jews were forbidden to marry. This should not have been an immediate problem for Walter Bergmann or the Bergmann family. The Bergmanns were outwardly a conventional middle-class German family with a Christian background, although they were not regular churchgoers. All the documents that would have revealed Alice and Vera Bergmann's Jewish ancestry had been destroyed many years previously, when their family name had been changed. The Bergmanns had no reason to believe that they would be considered to be Jewish. The only major problem Walter Bergmann anticipated was the scandal of him parting from his wife and living openly with another woman by whom he had a child. In 1936 Marthel Kolb again initiated divorce proceedings. She also brought a case against Walter Bergmann claiming damages for the trauma of their separation, and she demanded large maintenance payments. Walter Bergmann's lawyer Herr Stegmann succeeded in winning the case, as the damages claimed were excessive, and the amount of maintenance was disallowed as the sum demanded actually exceeded his income. He only had to pay costs. However during the divorce proceedings, Marthel Kolb's lawyer picked up on and made an issue of Walter Bergmann's Jewish ancestry through his mother. This had devasting consequences not only for Walter Bergmann, but also for the rest of the family. The divorce became absolute in March 1936. Walter Bergmann agreed to settle 5000RM on his ex-wife, which Grete Haase's father paid. In May 1936 Walter Bergmann and Grete Haase applied for permission to marry. As Walter Bergmann's Jewish ancestry had been publicly revealed, they now needed a special dispensation to marry. Soon after, Marthel Kolb's lawyer brought charges against Walter Bergmann before the Verband der Anwalte, the professional legal association, which were heard by the Anwaltskammer, the disciplinary body that regulated the legal profession. He accused Walter Bergmann of a breach of professional standards and of falsely denying that his mother was Jewish, this being a crime under the Third Reich. The second accusation was supported by statements made by Marthel Kolb and her brother. The Chairman of the Anwaltskammer, Rechtsanwalt Rabe, who was an honest and conscientious colleague of Walter Bergmann, was troubled by the charges. He did all he could to protect Walter Bergmann, who was allowed to continue practising as a lawyer during the duration of the case, which lasted two years. In October 1937 Oskar Bergmann, now aged seventy- eight, was called as a witness. Two weeks later he died, on October 30th, after contracting a chill. Walter Bergmann mourned his father's death and the distress he had brought to him. He wrote that Oskar Bergmann had been the rock on which the family was built[46].

Walter Bergmann was aware of life becoming increasingly precarious. The cases he handled were often difficult and also liable to being affected by his own personal vulnerable situation. Charlotte Zimmermann recalled such a case[47]. One morning an extremely unpleasant and abusive man walked into Walter Bergmann's office and slammed down some money on the desk in front of Charlotte Zimmermann. She managed to establish that it was a maintenance payment for the man's wife and daughter, which he was reluctantly paying under a court order. The man referred to his wife in derogatory terms and insinuated that the child was not his. Charlotte Zimmermann arranged for the man to regularly deliver the payments so that they could be collected by his wife. After he had left, she made a careful note of the detailed arrangements on the back of a piece of paper she had torn from the office calendar, which displayed the date of the previous day. Due to the unpleasant nature of the man's visit, the incident made a significant impression on her, and after having carefully copied the dates on which he would return, Charlotte Zimmermann filed the piece of paper. On Walter Bergmann's arrival at the office, she recounted what had happened. Walter Bergmann explained that the man wanted to divorce his wife, but she was resisting for the sake of the child. In consequence he had decided make his wife's life as difficult and miserable as he possibly could, and he was prepared to go to any lengths to get a divorce. He had accused his wife of having a relationship with a convicted criminal, but Walter Bergmann had managed to establish that the criminal cited did not know the woman at all. When she arrived to collect the maintenance payments, the wife told Charlotte Zimmermann that her mother in law was also trying to make life difficult for her. After consideration, she decided that she would initiate divorce proceedings against her husband, citing his unreasonable and threatening behaviour towards her. Charlotte Zimmermann agreed to testify on the woman's behalf, as there was no other person who had experienced her husband's abusive behaviour that could be called upon to give evidence.

The husband continued to come regularly to deliver the maintenance payments. Each visit he took the opportunity to verbally abuse Frau Zimmermann, and threatened her with physical violence if she did not tell the truth in court. Walter Bergmann tried to be present whenever he called. When the man realised this, he started to make his visits in his SS uniform to appear more intimidating. He knew that Walter Bergmann had problems relating to Jewish ancestry. In spite of possible retaliation, Walter Bergmann finally threw him out of the office one day when he been particularly abusive. The consequence of Walter Bergmann's action was that the man complained to the Anwaltskammer, adding to the accusations made against him. Walter Bergmann was called before them, and the case was thrown out, but it heightened his vulnerability.

The divorce case came to court, and Charlotte Zimmermann's evidence provided the basis for the marriage being dissolved. This was not however the end of the matter. The husband was determined to exploit Walter Bergmann's, and by association Frau Zimmermann's, increasingly precarious situation. The man was ordered to pay costs as part of the divorce settlement, which he brought in instalments to Walter Bergmann's. On each visit he delivered a very small amount and every time he called he insinuated that Charlotte Zimmermann had committed perjury. He then lodged an official complaint, and Frau Zimmermann was summoned by the police to answer the charge of perjury. She was accused of having lied about the date on which the man had first visited Walter Bergmann's office. The police officer interviewing her had the file containing the papers relating to the divorce case in front of him. Charlotte Zimmermann asked to see the piece of dated paper she had torn from the calendar to make notes on the day the man first visited. As she had expected, the note was in the file and confirmed her evidence so that she was released and the case dropped.

Through 1937 Walter Bergmann's income was slowly shrinking. Often clients either did not or could not pay. What little money he had just seemed to dissappear. Aware of Walter Bergmann's lack of acumen where money was concerned, Charlotte Zimmermann kept tight control of the office petty cash. Although Walter Bergmann earned only a little money, Grete and he had many friends, and an open door to visitors. Music-making with friends continued in private, but no longer in public. Walter Bergmann was also beginning to find that he had time on his hands. He spent more time on his own at home, studying and playing music. He looked at a wide range of music that included Bach Cantatas, Telemann quartets and trios, Purcell fantasias, Haydn's *Sinfonia Concertante*, Haydn and Mozart chamber music for wind, Mussorgsky song cycles and Schubert's *Winterreise*. He sang vocal music 'crossing to and from the women's to the men's musical lines.'[48]. His interest in the recorder increased and he began to regularly play a tenor recorder (with German fingering) that he had purchased several years previously after hearing one of Heyden's groups play. Walter Bergmann initially started playing the instrument because he thought it would be easy to play, as he would be able to transfer the skills he had learnt on the flute, but he then gradually became more interested in the recorder for its own sake. He also pursued his interest in continuo playing and realised many continuo parts. He was introduced to two academics, Professors Lohmann and Schünemann, who were interested in continuo playing, and discussed with them methods of realising continuo parts. Sadly he lost the impetus to compose. By the end of 1936 his compositions included a second sonata for Dietrich Gerhardt (1934), and some choral songs using texts by Meyer and Keller for a Swiss choral competition. He did not return to composition again until he was settled in London.

Walter Bergmann was finally ordered by the Anwaltskammer to appear in court, in the Ehrengericht, on January 29th 1938 to answer the charge brought by Marthel Kolb's lawyer of suppressing the fact his Mother was Jewish. The State Prosecutor called for his dismissal from the legal profession. Judgement was delayed, and Walter Bergmann was allowed to continue practising, although he had only a minimal number of cases. In February 1938 he received a letter from Himmler's office withholding permission for him to marry Grete. The seriousness of the situation in which he found himself was becoming very clear. Walter Bergmann began to worry about the effect it was having on Grete and for the first time he began to think about emigrating and considered whether it would be better for Grete and Erica if he separated from them[49]. Walter Bergmann also received a letter from Marthel Kolb in which she wrote that she had not foreseen or intended the consequences of the divorce case and court action, and that she really regretted the outcome. (Marthel Kolb eventually re-met and married an old acquaintance who was a conductor. According to Fritz Bergmann[50], her lawyer who had instigated the court case against Walter Bergmann survived the war when he was a committed Nazi, and became a Professor of Law.)

In January 1938 Walter Bergmann began to keep a regular diary. In April of the same year he had a short break from confronting his problems, when he travelled to Prague for a couple of days in connection with another divorce case. He noted in his diary that he crossed the border in each direction without any problems. The Germans removed German newspapers from travellers leaving Germany, and the Czechs removed newspapers from those leaving Czechoslovakia, so that newspapers were not confiscated by the neighbouring state! In Prague Walter Bergmann took the opportunity to go the ballet and the opera. At the latter he saw a performance of Dvorak's *Rusalka*. He was also was able to hear the cellist Pablo Casals play. He enjoyed the music he heard and the quality of the performances impressed him. He reflected over the discrepancy between the calibre of the music he was hearing in Prague compared with music that was currently being presented and performed in Germany under the title of 'art'. It also inspired him to think of composing again. He mused about writing a ballet based on a story by Edgar Alan Poe. Walter Bergmann also took the opportunity to look in art galleries in Prague, and he found a picture of Christ playing the recorder. He obtained a photograph of the picture, and this began what became a vast collection of pictures of or including the recorder.

The judgement from the Ehrengericht was delivered to Walter Bergmann on May 14th 1938. He was given a reprimand and a fine of 3000RM, but was not debarred from practising as a lawyer. Both sides appealed against the judgement. Walter Bergmann continued to act for a small number of cases and to employ Charlotte Zimmermann. The cases he handled now carried personal risks for him when they were linked to Jewish problems. Around 1935, Walter Bergmann had become friendly with a wealthy family named Volhard. Hans Volhard was the son of a famous consultant who specialised in internal diseases, and his wife Hilde was the daughter of a wealthy Jewish family called Seelig, who owned a large department store in Halle called Hüth. Dietrich Gerhardt remembered[51] the beautiful house owned by the Volhards in Halle, and that he often met Walter Bergmann there. By the beginning of 1938 anti-Semitic attacks were gradually increasing, although initial boycotts of Jewish businesses, instigated by the Nazis, had not been successful. A list of customer accounts was stolen from Hüth by a caretaker, who sold it to Nazi officials, who presumably wanted the list so that they could put pressure on non-Jewish customers to take their custom elsewhere. Walter Bergmann was asked by the management of Hüth to handle the case and he hired a private detective from Berlin to investigate the matter. The detective managed to recover the list. Walter Bergmann was paid 200RM by Hüth for his handling of the case. Charlotte Zimmermann decided that it would be wise not to retain any paperwork relating to the case. The only item she kept was a copy of the receipt for 200RM.

On the morning of June 11th 1938, Gestapo officers marched into Walter Bergmann's office and demanded to speak to him. They behaved in an intimidating fashion, emptying drawers and kicking the furniture[52]. They forbade either Walter Bergmann or Charlotte Zimmermann from leaving the premises, and Hilde Volhard was brought from her home to the office. The officers then demanded the paperwork relating to the Hüth customer list, which of course did not exist, except for the receipt. The Gestapo took possession of this, and arrested Walter Bergmann. They had obviously been waiting to find another way of silencing him and ending his career, after the failure of the two previous court cases against him. Walter Bergmann was placed in solitary confinement and interrogated. The only crimes they were eventually to accuse him of were that he had overcharged Hüth for the recovery of the stolen list and that he had prejudiced the course of justice. The Gestapo then handed Walter Bergmann over to the jurisdiction of the normal courts of law, and he was placed in custody pending further investigation. This was extremely fortunate, as it gave him protection from disappearing (possibly into a concentration camp), and his family knew where he was. On investigation, the accusation of overcharging was dropped. Enquiries made of other lawyers made it quite clear that no one would have handled the case for less than 200RM. A Berlin lawyer was reported to have said 'I would not stick my nose into such an affair for 200 Marks'[53]. Walter Bergmann was then returned to the custody of the Gestapo, and imprisoned with a collection of people the Nazis considered to be misfits in society, including a Catholic priest, a Jehovah's Witness, a homosexual and a communist.

During his imprisonment Walter Bergmann looked at and thought about his life. He knew there was little chance of his legal career continuing in the foreseeable future. If he survived, his future would have to be as a musician. He took the step of resigning from the Verband der Anwalte. He occupied his time in prison by writing an autobiographical account of his life up to 1938, which included his musical development, experiences and achievements. He assessed where his musical talents lay. He also began to write poetry. (He eventually published a collection of poems privately in 1971.)

While Walter Bergmann was in prison, Grete and Charlotte Zimmermann discussed whether they should maintain the legal practice, or arrange for it to be closed. They both doubted that he would be allowed to continue as a lawyer when (and if) he was released.

His divorce lawyer, Herr Stegmann, who had proved also to be a sympathetic and supportive friend, helped them work through any paperwork from outstanding cases. Stegmann had done all he could to help Walter Bergmann and Grete. In the period immediately prior to Walter Bergmann's arrest, he regularly visited them dressed in his Nazi uniform, aware that his arrival and departure would be noticed by the neighbours, thereby giving some protection to his friends. He continued to visit Grete and Erica after Walter Bergmann's arrest and imprisonment, and he took on any new legal cases that were sent to Walter Bergmann's office. Herr Stegmann used his Nazi contacts to try to establish what would happen to Walter Bergmann. He learnt that the Gestapo were losing interest in him. Grete and Charlotte Zimmermann went together to the Gestapo and asked if he could be paroled so that his legal practice could be wound up. Walter Bergmann was initially given parole of a day to attend to closing his practice, and then finally released at the end of September 1938. He was advised by a Gestapo officer from Berlin to emigrate as soon as he possibly could.

The future in Germany looked totally perilous and bleak. The USA seemed the most attractive emigration proposition for Walter Bergmann, as he had contacts there. Felix Wolfes was living in New York City by 1938. After the rise of the Nazis, he had gone to Paris to work as an accompanist and had found some work with Monte Carlo Opera. In 1938, he left Europe to join the Metropolitan Opera, New York, as assistant conductor. Hearing of Walter Bergmann's imprisonment, he had started to try to organise the support needed to get him an entry visa into the USA. This proved to be extremely difficult. The fact that Walter Bergmann was only partly Jewish probably made it harder to obtain references and a visa. His classification as 'Mischling, Grade 1' put him in a different category to full Jews, who had the financial means to emigrate. He had no problem finding the fare to America, but finding two sponsors appeared to be impossible. In November 1938 Walter Bergmann wrote a letter to the American Consulate in Berlin in which he asked to register a request for a permanent USA visa and stated that if he did not leave Germany in 3 months he would be liable to be re-arrested. He also wrote to Felix Wolfes to say that he would probably leave Germany for another European country, where he would wait for an American visa. The situation for Jews was deteriorating rapidly. In the summer of 1938 all Jewish doctors, dentists and lawyers were forbidden to offer their services to non-Jews, thereby effectively destroying the careers and livelihoods of many professionals. On November 8th 1938 came the terrifying violence on Kristallnacht, when Jewish shops were attacked by Nazi mobs; 91 Jews were killed and 20,000 Jews arrested. Walter Bergmann was frightened of being re-arrested and he left Halle to stay with Arnold Matz in Leipzig. By the end of 1938, Jews were prohibited from managing their own businesses.

When he returned to Halle from Leipzig, Walter Bergmann assessed his financial situation. The firm of Hüth owed him 6000RM for work he had undertaken for them and he wrote to his stepmother Tante Vera and his two brothers to ask if they would together lend him the sum of 1500RM to cover the cost of his fare to the USA and his immediate needs for the journey and initial period of residence. Herr Stegmann undertook to handle and administer the money due to Walter Bergmann. Hüth's assets were frozen due to the restrictions that had been imposed on all Jewish firms, but it was thought there was a reasonable chance that the money due would eventually be released. A substantial part of the sum was to go to Grete and Erica. Walter Bergmann's ex-wife, Marthel Kolb, had agreed to waive any claim to maintenance payments until December 1940 in consideration of the lump sum she had received as a settlement. She would only then claim maintenance if her income was less than 150RM per month, and Walter Bergmann's exceeded 450RM. Herr Stegmann drew up the agreement.

In a letter to Felix Wolfes on November 19th 1938, Walter Bergmann stated that he had an invitation to stay for one month in England. He concentrated on collecting references from his friends and colleagues to support his application for entry to the USA and for a future as a musician. Fritz Hensel, who had become a lecturer at Der Schauspielsschule des Deutschen Theaters (the German Theatre Drama Academy) in Charlottenburg, part of Berlin, gave him a reference, as did Jan Versteeg and Carl Boyde. Dietrich Gerhardt took time on Christmas Day 1938 to write a testimonial in both German and English. All the references recommended Walter Bergmann as a skilled musician and particularly as an accompanist and continuo player.

By February 1939 Felix Wolfes had received one American affidavit of support. The statement came from a Mr Arthur Jameson, who was a friend of Walter Bergmann's König relatives in Berlin. Jameson's statement assured the US authorities of Walter Bergmann's ability to support himself as a musician. A second affidavit of support was not forthcoming, and Walter Bergmann decided to take up the offer to go to England. Through the German Emergency Committee of the British Society of Friends he had obtained a guarantee signed by the eminent Cambridge musicologist Edward Dent, who had vouched for a number of escaping German and Austrian musicians and assured their support in Britain.

On March 13th 1939 Walter Bergmann went to Frankfurt to obtain a visa for Britain. It was issued the next day. On March 15th, German troops invaded Czechoslovakia. He realised he had to leave Germany as soon as possible as the likelihood of war increased. On March 17th, Walter Bergmann made two visits to the Gestapo to obtain an exit visa from Germany. The following three days were spent in saying goodbye to his family and friends. He left Germany on March 21st 1939, taking with him two suitcases, one of which contained clothes, the other was filled with music, including Purcell *Fantasias*, and his flute and recorder.

Walter Bergmann flew from Berlin to Amsterdam. He recorded in his diary[54] that it was interesting to fly over Berlin and in particular to view the Zoo from the air. However the weather for the flight was terrible and he felt very depressed. He had no problems with his papers, but was refused permission to remain permanently in Holland when he requested it. (Later he must have been relieved that he had not been allowed to stay.) Walter Bergmann spent five days in Holland, taking care to avoid the immigration police just in case they decided to arrest him and return him to Germany. On the 22nd, he travelled on to Rotterdam, from where he would leave for England. He took the opportunity to visit art galleries, including the Rijks Museum in Amsterdam, and was impressed by the collections of old masters and modern art that he saw. In his diary he particularly mentions seeing pictures by Rembrandt, Vermeer, Van Gogh, Pissaro and Picasso. He made a point of looking for recorders and flutes in old paintings, and noted unusual features that he observed. For example, one painting contained a recorder that had two holes underneath the windway. In another a flute was being held on the opposite side to normal convention. These entries mark a significant change in Walter Bergman's diaries. Written on March 23rd, they are in Roman script, whereas all previous entries were in

German Gothic script.

Whilst in Holland, Walter Bergmann travelled by train to other Dutch towns, including Utrecht and s'Hertogenbosch. On the journey to s'Hertogenbosch, which lies between Utrecht and Aachen, he had the unpleasant experience of being interviewed by two men in civilian clothes, who were apparently immigration officers. Walter Bergmann showed them his identity papers and his travel documents for his journey to London on March 26th. If these had not been clearly in order, he reckoned that he would have been deported back to Germany. He thought the immigration officials were possibly suspicious of him travelling round Holland, especially as he had been refused permission to remain there. On March 24th Walter Bergmann visited The Hague, where he visited the musical instrument museum and the Museum of Modern Art. He went to the cinema, where he watched an American film and saw a newsreel of Hitler parading in Prague followed by pictures of the British Royal Family greeting the French President. It all seemed dreamlike to Walter Bergmann - a mad dream followed by a dream of hope[55]. He thought of the six year old daughter he had left behind.

On his return to Rotterdam, Walter Bergmann collected letters from Grete and a friend who lived in London, Herr Bonecke. The latter had written to say that he could not offer Walter Bergmann accommodation, but he offered to pay for him to stay in a cheap hotel during his first few weeks in England. Walter Bergmann left Holland to fly to London in stormy weather on Sunday March 26th. He arrived in central London at midday, unable to speak any English.

After Walter Bergmann's departure, Grete tried to get British visas for herself and Erica, so that they could follow him to London. This was to prove extremely difficult. She was not Jewish, and, as an unmarried mother from a 'pure Aryan' background she was viewed from a Nazi point of view as useful 'breeding stock' for the Third Reich. Charlotte Zimmermann did all she could to support Grete through this period. In the summer of 1939 she took Erica and her own daughter to stay with Vera Bergmann, Walter Bergmann's stepmother and aunt, who had left Halle to live in a flat in Heppenheim, which lies south of Frankfurt between Darmstadt and Heidelberg in an attractive area of country known as the Bergstrasse. It had been found for her by Fritz Bergmann, and was well over 200 miles from Halle so that the family's history was not known locally. Grete continued to search for a way to leave Germany for England. In July, through contact with a former gymnastics pupil, she eventually managed to get British visitors' visas for herself and Erica from the British Consul in Hamburg. She travelled to Frankfurt, where she met Frau Zimmermann with the two girls. They said goodbye to each other, and Charlotte Zimmermann returned to Halle with her own daughter, and Grete took Erica back to spend a short time with Tante Vera before leaving for England. They flew to London on July 22nd 1939, taking very few possessions with them, so as not to arouse any suspicions they were intending to leave Germany permanently. Grete had only confided in a few close and trustworthy friends that she was leaving Germany for good, and took with her enough clothes for a week's holiday. She could also only take a small amount of money with her. She did not inform her family she was leaving Germany.

Back in Halle Charlotte Zimmermann, waited until she knew that Grete and Erica had safely left for England, and then went to the Bergmann flat where she met the cleaning lady. Together they emptied the house and destroyed any incoming post.

Hans (a doctor) and Fritz Bergmann (a doctor of chemistry) both survived the war, and were fortunately not significantly affected by the turmoil of Walter Bergman's messy divorce. Vera Bergmann was not so lucky. In spite of relocating away from Halle, someone betrayed her origins. She was warned of imminent arrest and deportation in 1943, and she committed suicide at the age of 65. Walter Bergman's closest friends, Arnold Matz and Dietrich Gerhardt remained in Germany and survived the war. Arnold Matz became an eminent musician in East Germany as a member of the Leipzig Gewandhaus Orchestra and Dietrich Gerhardt pursued an academic career in West Germany.

[1] WB's hand written notes, 1938, p. 31
[2] WB's typed notes, 1938, p. 41
[3] WB's notes for a lecture given in Southampton
[4] Letter from Fritz Bergmann to Erica Bendix, 18.3.89
[5] 'Wir haben offren Ohres des Zeit erlebt, die Man sehr unglücklich die 'atonale' nennt.' WB's typed notes, 1938, p. 8 6 WB's typed notes, 1938, p. 8
[7] see Guy Rickards, *Hindemith, Hartmann and Henze*, (London: Phaidon, 1995), p.48
[8] WB's typed notes, 1938, p. 15
[9] Letter from Frau Luise von Arps-Aubert (Issi Matz) to Erica Bendix, 19.2.88
[10] 'Ja, es war eine herrliche Zeit, wir waren jung, wir waren verliebt und hatten die Musik die mich meinem Leben lang begleitet hat.' Letter from Frau von Arps-Aubert to Erica Bendix, 19.2.88
[11] WB's hand written notes, 1938, p. 27
[12] WB's hand written notes, 1938, p. 35
[13] WB's hand written notes, 1938, p. 42
[14] WB's hand written notes, 1938, p. 49
[15] WB's hand written note, 1938, p. 54
[16] WB's typed notes, 1938, p.21
[17] WB's typed notes, 1938, p.24
[18] WB's typed notes, 1938, p. 35
[19] WB's hand written notes, 1938, p.51
[20] WB's hand written notes, 1938, p. 6
[21] WB's typed notes, 1938, p. 18
[22] WB's typed notes, 1938, pp. 18-19
[23] WB's typed notes, 1938, p. 7
[24] WB's typed notes, 1938, p. 19
[25] 'Ich bin kein Jurist und deshalb habe ich mir unter den juristichen Berufen den unjuristichen; Rechtsanwalt mit Recht ausgesucht.' WB's hand written notes, 1938, p. 62;
[26] WB's handwritten notes, 1938 p.66
[27] WB's handwritten notes, 1938 p.68
[28] WB's handwritten notes, 1938 p.68
[29] Letter from Dietrich Gerhardt to Erica Bendix, 7.3.89
[30] WB's handwritten notes, 1938 p. 69
[31] WB's typed notes, 1938, p.25
[32] Letter from Dietrich Gerhardt to Anne Martin, 29.3.89
[33] WB's typed notes, 1938, p. 25
[34] Letter from Dietrich Gerhardt to Anne Martin, 29.3.89
[35] WB's typed notes, 1938, p.10
[36] WB's typed notes, 1938, p.10
[37] Letter from Dietrich Gerhardt to Anne Martin, 29.2.89
[38] WB's typed notes, 1938, p. 28
[39] WB's typed notes, 1938, p.8
[40] Letter from Dietrich Gerhardt to Anne Martin, 29.3.89
[41] Letter from Dietrich Gerhardt to Erica Bendix, Feb, 1989
[42] Letter from Charlotte Zimmermann to Anne Martin, 9.5.89
[43] Letter from Dietrich Gerhardt to Anne Martin, 29.3.89
[44] Letter from Charlotte Zimmermann to Anne Martin, 9.5.89 Walter Bergmann in 1939
[45] WB's typed notes, 1938, p. 30
[46] WB's handwritten notes, 1938, p. 71
[47] Letter from Charlotte Zimmermann to Anne Martin, December 1989
[48] 'Von den Frauenstimmen war ich zu den Männerstimmen übergangen.'

WB's typed notes, 1938, p.33
[49] WB's handwritten notes, 1938, p. 71 (also referred to in WB's first diary, 1938/39)
[50] Letter from Fritz Bergmann to Erica Bendix 29.3.89
[51] Letter from Dietrich Gerhardt to Anne Martin, 29.3.89
[52] Letter from Charlotte Zimmermann to Anne Martin, 9.5.89
[53] Letter from Charlotte Zimmermann to Anne Martin, 9.5.89
[54] Diary No 1, 1938/39
[55] Diary No 2, 25.3.39 - 10.6.39

Walter Bergmann c. 1923

3. Walter Bergmann in 1939

At the age of thirty-six Walter Bergmann arrived in London to begin a completely new life. He saw his future as a musician and had been encouraged to follow this new career by Dietrich Gerhardt and Jan Versteeg, both of whom believed Walter Bergmann had the ability to become a professional musician. Dietrich Gerhardt writing in 1989[1] said that the one good thing that emerged from the turmoil of Walter Bergmann's life in 1938/39 was his 'opportunity' to give up law and follow a musical career. For Walter Bergmann the greatest wrench in leaving Germany was separation from Dietrich Gerhardt and Jan Versteeg, with whom he had made so much music[2], and the leaving of Grete and his daughter Erica to face an uncertain future[3].

He had begun to prepare for a musical career when he was imprisoned in 1938. His original rejection of a musical life as a young man was because of his unsuitability to be a solo performer. By 1938 he realised that there were other musical possibilities open to him. In his autobiographical notes written in prison Walter Bergmann traced his musical education and experiences. He made an assessment of his musical strengths and weaknesses[4]. He saw his musical strengths as possessing a highly developed perception of intonation and a good sense of rhythm; being a good sight-reader; having the ability to interpret sounds and their relationship to each other, particularly in chamber music; having a good understanding of musical form, harmony and counterpoint and the ability to harmonise at sight; being able to conduct, and he believed he was beginning to develop skills in musical criticism. He thought he probably had the ability to teach. Walter Bergmann believed his weaknesses to be a total lack of singing ability, a poor memory, poor motor skills and his low rate of composition. He found it difficult to assess his compositional skills, as he believed the circumstances of the previous ten years had inhibited his attempts at composition.

By 1939 Walter Bergmann's musical experience was quite broad. Through keyboard and chamber music he was well acquainted with Bach, Handel, Schumann, Haydn, Beethoven, Mozart, Couperin, Scarlatti, Brahms, Chopin and Dvorak. He had accompanied a wide range of Lieder and in particular, songs by Schumann and Wolf. He had significant experience of working in opera and was particularly well acquainted with the works of Mozart, Verdi, Wagner, Mussorgsky, Pfitzner, Rossini and Smetana. His favourite opera was *Cosi Fan Tutte*[5] in its original form (i.e. not as commonly performed in Germany in 1938 with adulterated text). He was well acquainted with the music of modern composers such as Stravinsky, Bartok, Krenek, Schoenberg and Hindemith. Walter Bergmann believed that Hindemith had the potential to become a great composer and he placed a high value on Hindemith's music. He compared Hindemith's craftsmanship and approach to that of Bach[6].

Walter Bergmann had, of course, developed a special interest in the music of the seventeenth and eighteenth centuries, and in particular, an interest in the music of Rameau, Purcell, Telemann and W F Bach. He had made a study of realising and playing continuo music and begun to develop further his greatest interest, Telemann. His experience of choral music was not so extensive, but he was well acquainted with many Bach Cantatas and large-scale works by other composers, such as Beethoven's *Ninth Symphony* and Haydn's *The Seasons*. In his own compositions, Walter Bergmann had concentrated mainly on songs, choral works and the two oboe sonatas. His greatest musical experience was as an accompanist and continuo player and this is where he saw his possible future in the music profession. The testimonials he collected reinforced this aspect of his abilities. Obviously the writers of the testimonials realised how essential it was that Walter Bergmann was furnished with sufficient good references in order to be able to begin a new life and career in another country - i.e. to be seen as a good musician in order to qualify for a visa. All the writers of the testimonials were well-established reputable musicians in Germany whose judgement should be valued. What they wrote tallies with and confirms the musical experience Walter Bergmann recorded in his autobiographical notes written in prison in 1938.

The first testimonial from Fritz Hensel (lecturer at the German Theatre Drama Academy) stated:

I have known Dr Bergmann for many years as a distinguished musician. On countless occasions I have heard him as a good pianist and excellent accompanist and in the last years as a good flautist, recorder player and outstanding continuo player. His pronounced special gift lies in the interpretation of Bach, Handel, Telemann and Haydn.'

Dietrich Gerhardt, who by 1938 was a member of the Reichsmusikkammer and also a teacher and assistant to the state board of examiners, wrote in his testimonial:

In my opinion Walter Bergmann is a born accompanist with an adaptability and sight-reading skill very rarely found. I consider his opinions and work on the practice of continuo playing are epoch-making and indispensable.
His highest achievements are on the one hand the editing of early chamber music, on the other side his ability to direct early music as a continuo player.'

Jan Versteeg, Concert Manager of the Halle Orchestra and long time member of the Bayreuth Festival Orchestra, said of Walter Bergmann:

His gift for chamber music and accompanying is exceptional, his musical education comprehensive. Although Walter Bergmann must be considered through his study of continuo as a specialist player and editor and arranger of music of the age of the basso continuo, nevertheless I consider no less important the musical talent he has for music for other epochs, especially modern music.
Walter Bergmann's gift for sight-reading, even an unrealised continuo part, as well as his pronounced feeling for other instruments, for song and for ensemble playing make him suitable for every performing activity as a chamber musician, accompanist and repetiteur.

Carl Boyde confirmed Walter Bergmann's involvement in performances of Handel and Bach and his value as a musician.

Armed with these testimonials and a belief in himself that he could become a professional musician, Walter Bergmann began to try to establish a life for himself in London. Whether he succeeded would depend on how he managed to continue to support himself. Refugees in London either had to have guaranteed financial support or be prepared in the case of a man to accept a manual job, for example in agriculture, and in the case of a woman, domestic service, i.e. jobs for which there was little British labour available. Initially he would have help from the Quakers and one or two acquaintances.

[1] Letter from Dietrich Gerhardt to Anne Martin, 29.03.89
[2] WB's typed notes, 1938 p. 26
[3] Diary No 2 25.03.39 - 10.06.39
[4] WB's typed notes, 1938 p. 1
[5] WB's typed notes, 1938 p. 23
[6] WB's typed notes, 1938 p. 9

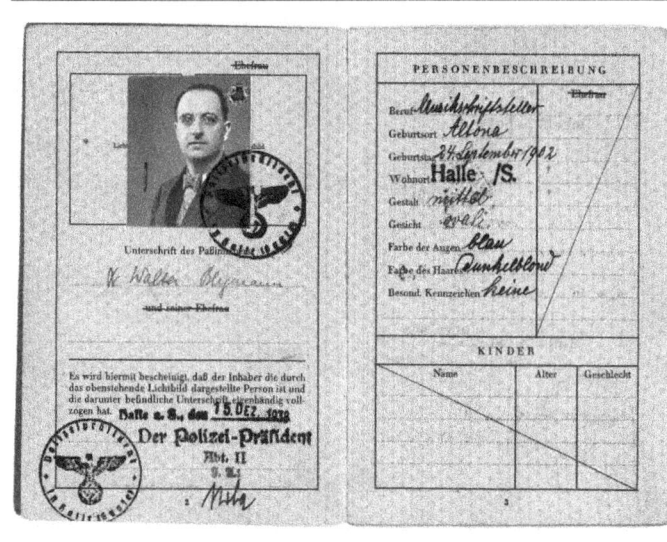

4. The first few months in England

Walter Bergmann spent his first few months in London searching for somewhere to live, exploring the city, establishing new acquaintances and musical contacts, participating in a variety of musical activities and writing letters. Like many German refugees, he was helped and supported by the Quakers and the Christian Council for Refugees from Germany based at Bloomsbury House. Several separate organisations existed under the umbrella of the Council, including the Hospitality Committee and the Refugee Musicians' Aid Committee. Through the Quakers Walter Bergmann was introduced to a number of people who were willing to welcome refugees into their homes for meals and friendship. His entry into Britain had been granted on the condition he did not seek work.

Immediately on his arrival in London, Walter Bergmann booked into a hotel. (The cost for bed and breakfast was 8s 6d.) He then set out to start exploring London. A stranger asked him in English the way to the British Museum. Unable to reply except in German, he discovered that the stranger was also German and they went to the British Museum together. The following morning he had the first 'joyous breakfast of freedom'[1]. After lunch with a couple named Bohringer, he hunted for another, more reasonable hotel. All he visited seemed bad, cold, dirty and expensive. He spent four nights at the Kingsway Hotel, and then moved into moderately comfortable lodgings. Over the next few weeks Walter Bergmann moved rooms several times. He was not at all impressed by English food or the peculiar idea of eating a large cooked breakfast. During the first couple of weeks he visited galleries and museums, such as the Tate, the National Gallery, the Victoria and Albert, the Wallace Collection and the British Museum. In the Tate he was impressed by Turner's paintings. In the National Gallery he particularly enjoyed looking at the Dutch and Italian paintings. He noticed that musical instruments appeared more frequently in the Dutch than Italian paintings, which presumably accounted for recorders appearing more often in Dutch paintings. Walter Bergmann also participated in a variety of activities at Bloomsbury House. These included English classes, attending a concert at which Paul Robeson sang and taking a small part of a waiter, at two days notice, in a play at the Linguist Club. He also visited the House of Commons. He wrote and received letters from Grete, his family, Dietrich Gerhard, Jan Versteeg and the Seelig family, including Hilde Volhard. A new acquaintance he was introduced to was Dr John Edwards, who lived in Green Lane, near Finsbury Park, and played the flute. Walter Bergmann began regularly to participate in musical evenings at Edwards' house.

On April 7th he spoke to Grete by telephone and discussed her possible emigration. It was of course proving very difficult for her to get permission to leave Germany and to enter Britain. They discussed the possibility of her posing as a widow or divorcee, but both ideas were impractical due to the lack of documentary evidence and anyway neither state would have helped Grete to get into Britain.

During April Walter Bergmann ventured outside London for the first time, visiting Dorking and Oxford. He continued to write letters diligently and to seek ways of obtaining money to live on. He made inquiries about entry visas for Grete and Erica and for the Seelig family, who were also trying to leave Germany. His heavy luggage, which had followed after him, finally arrived and he started to play the recorder again. On April 14th he received a reader's ticket for the Reading Room at the British Museum. The first manuscript he examined consisted of twelve violin sonatas by Telemann. He began transcribing and working on the continuo parts of sonatas by both Telemann and Handel. On April 22nd he moved again into accommodation where he began to 'cook' for himself and he went shopping for the first time to buy bread, butter, cheese, ham and tomatoes.

Musical opportunities were gradually increasing, although they were not always very rewarding. Walter Bergmann was invited to play the flute in an amateur orchestra, but at the rehearsal he was not impressed by the standard of playing. A more enjoyable musical experience was playing with Max Rostal, an Austrian-born violinist who had settled in London and had an interest in early violin music. They played three sonatas together for which Walter Bergmann had realised the continuo part, these being two Telemann works and an A major sonata by Handel. Rostal particularly liked the Telemann sonatas (from the *Tafelmusik*). Walter Bergmann accompanied Rostal on a Dolmetsch clavichord built in 1925, which he liked very much. Another memorable event was his visit to Westminster Abbey, where he stood on Handel's grave - and noted that the composer's birth date was incorrectly given as 1684.

On the afternoon of May 3rd Walter Bergmann met Lili Seelig (sister of Hilde Volhard and Erika Seelig) who was passing through London en route from Germany to India. He spent some time each day with her between rehearsals for a concert, before she left London on May 6th. The concert was given by the Modern Symphony Orchestra, the amateur orchestra in which Walter Bergmann was playing the flute. (In his diary[2] he noted that there was really nothing he could say about the concert!) Lili Seelig's departure for India deeply affected Walter Bergmann[3]. It also must have brought home to him that he had to make important decisions about his own life relating to his relationship with Grete, his responsibilities towards his daughter Erica and his friendship with Hilde Volhard.

Walter Bergmann was making strenuous efforts to arrange for Grete and Erica to come to England. He was being helped in trying to obtain permission for them to enter Britain by Clare Soper and Betty Abrahams, who were members of the Quaker Refugee Committee. There was little work open to German immigrants; domestic service was virtually the only opening for women. Before Grete Haase became a teacher of gymnastics, she had studied home economics, and she had experience of working in the kitchens of a first class hotel and as a private housekeeper. Unusually for many of the Germans entering England, she was experienced in domestic work. However Grete and Erica also had the problem of needing to acquire permission to leave Germany. Before leaving Germany himself, Walter Bergmann had become very friendly with the Seelig and Volhard families and had of course kept up correspondence with them since arriving in London. He was particularly friendly with Hilde Volhard. With their Jewish background, leaving Germany would be easier for the Volhard and Seelig families, than it would be for Grete and Erica. Lili Seelig had already left, Erika Seelig was expected to be able to leave soon and Hilde Volhard not long after. The Volhards' marriage was apparently not running smoothly. Walter Bergmann knew there was some doubt as to whether Grete and Erica would manage to leave Germany. Hilde would definitely come to England and he had seriously begun to consider whether he should begin a new life with her in London. On May 8th he visited Clare Soper to try again to obtain visitors' visas for Grete and Erica. He had to wait forty-five minutes and during that time he came to the conclusion that both Hilde and he must make every effort to stay with their respective families, in spite of their strong attraction to each other, otherwise it would be a catastrophe for two sets of children.

Meanwhile Walter Bergmann's circle of acquaintances and friends in London continued to widen and he visited a number of homes to join in a variety of musical activities. At one such evening he heard a Dolmetsch recorder, which he liked the sound of[4]. He noticed that the pitch was a semitone lower than normal. He was also quite frequently invited out for meals - invitations that he was happy to accept with his limited financial resources. (He had opened a bank account on May 5th with £77.) He still had no regular income - he received some money from the Quakers and apparently some from friends.

Erika Seelig arrived in England on May 15th 1939. Walter Bergmann met her and took her to the home of the Blau family, where she was to stay. The following day he visited a solicitor, Siegfried Katz, to discuss his future. Dr Katz told Walter Bergmann that he should look to the Quakers for help and accept any assistance they could offer; any hope of returning to Germany would be impossible in the foreseeable future and he should try to find as much free-lance work as he could that did not require a work permit, including writing articles, accompanying at concerts and approaching the BBC for work. A few days later Walter Bergmann met Edward Dent, who had helped him obtain a visa, in a French restaurant in Charlotte Street. Dent was Professor of Music at Cambridge and had a particular interest in opera. He was closely involved in the revival of Baroque opera, and was also one of the founders of the International Society for Contemporary Music. They had a wide-ranging discussion, and Walter Bergmann noted that they both held similar views on opera and its production[5]. However Dent told Walter Bergmann that he believed there would be no opportunities in England for foreign musicians[6], particularly for a 'true' continuo player, as in England all continuo parts were always fully realised and written out before performances so that any competent keyboard player could play them. Dent recommended that Walter Bergmann should try to go to the USA. Walter Bergmann left the meeting feeling very depressed.

During the next few days he spent time helping Erika Seelig settle in. They went for walks, visited the cinema and ate out together. Hilde Volhard (née Seelig) arrived in London on May 26th. Walter Bergmann, Erika and Hilde all spent a significant amount of time together over the following days visiting London parks and sights. Hilde Volhard then took up a position in Bognor Regis. Walter Bergmann was happy to be reunited with her and still had not resolved what he was going to do about their relationship. At a musical evening at the beginning of June, Dr Edwards gave Walter Bergmann a written invitation for Grete and Erica to stay with him and his family. Walter Bergmann felt himself trapped in a predicament of his own making. On June 12th Hilde Volhard came to London for the day and they tried to decide what to do, discussing the problem of themselves, Hans and Nana Volhard (Hilde's husband and daughter) and her son Reiner, who was already in England, and Grete and Erica, Walter's 'wife' and daughter. The discussion was 'so grave and hopeless'[7]. Walter Bergmann remarked in his diary how much simpler it would be if Grete was married to Hans Volhard and Hilde to himself! Nothing was resolved. The following day Walter Bergmann's spirits were raised by the arrival of a piano from a firm in Barnes. His life continued on the same pattern, with frequent letter writing and musical activities - the latter particularly at the home of Dr Edwards. Edwards especially liked Walter Bergmann's continuo parts for Handel sonatas. Walter

Bergmann was very pleased with his piano and he had also received another reader's ticket for the British Museum Reading Room. He used it over four days to look at a variety of manuscripts, including music by Telemann and Purcell. In the middle of the month he received a letter from his lawyer, Stegmann, in Halle telling him that he must not contemplate returning to Germany. At the end of June a significant event for Walter Bergmann was a concert he organised for a garden party held at the home of Sir Alfred Baker, the first concert he arranged in England. The programme consisted of music by Purcell, folk songs and two suites by Schein. About the same time he also had to register with the police at Bow Street. On June 29th he travelled to Bognor Regis to spend a day with Hilde Volhard.

During the next few weeks Walter Bergmann attended rehearsals for various concerts at which his own continuo parts were sometimes used. The weather depressed him - his diary entry for July 8th, recording a concert rehearsal, stated 'It was raining as usual'[8]. On July 10th Walter Bergmann wrote 'Grete will come'[9]. At the same time as Walter Bergmann received confirmation that Grete and Erica would come to England, Hilde Volhard learnt that her husband Hans Volhard would travel with their daughter to Sweden. On July 12th his diary entry recorded that Walter Bergmann had £35.3s.7d. On the same day he was taken to the ballet at Covent Garden by a friend, Phyllis Smith, which he thoroughly enjoyed. He continued to spend time with Hilde Volhard and Erika Seelig, still apparently fruitlessly discussing with Hilde what they should do about their relationship. Walter Bergmann could not resolve his dilemma and decide what was the best solution for both the adults and for his daughter. He kept himself busy transcribing and realising a Handel recorder concerto, which he then played with a group of friends, writing letters, rehearsing and going out with friends. Among new acquaintances was a composer named Robert Müller Hartmann. He heard again from Grete on July 18th saying she would arrive within the week. He received news from Jan Versteeg saying that he would not be coming to Britain.

On the evening of Saturday July 22nd 1939 Walter Bergmann met Grete and Erica at Croydon Airport. They arrived in the dark and wet at 10 p.m., six year old Erica (known as Dicki, because she was plump) clutching a doll in her arms. The three of them travelled back to Walter Bergmann's room in Glenloch Road, Belsize Park. They spent the next day together, walking over Hampstead Heath and visiting Kenwood and then going to the Edwards family in the evening. Inevitably the future had to be faced and decisions taken. Walter Bergmann noted in his diary[10] that Grete and himself had struggled in Germany for so long for the right to marry - far longer than anyone could normally expect to persevere, and now that it was possible for them to marry, he did not know any more whether it was the right thing to do and he no longer wholeheartedly wanted it. The dream of happiness had gone. He was full of remorse over Erica's joy and pleasure at being together in their 'new' home. Grete was 'marvellous' and optimistic that the future could be sorted out. It was the 'unhappiest day' of Walter Bergmann's life[11]. He fully realised that unless Grete and he married, Erica and herself would probably not be allowed to remain in England. His conscience told him that they also ought to marry for Erica's sake.

Clare Soper who had done so much to help Grete and Erica come to England, was delighted they had arrived. She had already obtained a domestic work permit for Grete, but it had been decided not to send it to her in Halle, because the German authorities would not have given her an exit visa to take up domestic work abroad as she was German, not Jewish. She was not informed of the permit in case her post was opened. The Quakers had accepted Grete's need to leave Germany for Erica's sake, and Grete had arranged for two references to be sent to them, one from Frau Versteeg, the other from Getrud Lasch-Weiss, an ex-speech therapist from Vienna University. Grete immediately took up a post that had been arranged for her with the Nash family at Little Beddow near Chelmsford. Erica was able to accompany her.

After the departure of Grete and Erica, Walter Bergmann resumed the life-style he had established for himself, although he still hoped to be able to emigrate to the USA. On July 28th he went with Dr Edwards to the Fifteenth Haslemere Festival. He noted[12] that the female performers looked as if they had stepped out of old pictures. The programme of the concert they attended consisted mainly of English music and included *Divisions* by Christopher Simpson, a Purcell *Ground and Toccata* for harpsichord and a *Fantasy* by Thomas Weelkes. Walter Bergmann was disappointed in Rudolf Dolmetsch's harpsichord playing, but he described Carl Dolmetsch as a distinguished descant recorder player[13].

Hilde Volhard had returned to London by the end of July. Her son Reiner came to visit her. On meeting him, Walter Bergmann was amazed at his fluent English as the boy had arrived the same time as himself. (Hilde Volhard had heard by this time, that her husband Hans and daughter Nana had arrived safely in Sweden.) On August 9th Grete and Erica (Dicki) came to London to celebrate Grete's birthday with Walter Bergmann. They met together briefly with Hilde and Reiner Volhard. Five days later, Hilde Volhard decided that Walter Bergmann and herself should not continue their relationship. However they still spent time together.

During July and August, Walter Bergmann was fortunate in the support and help he received from new friends and acquaintances. One such new acquaintance was another German musician, Rose Walter, a professional soprano. She had been an established singer in Germany and had sung one of the principal roles in the first performance in 1931 of an oratorio by Hindemith, *Das Unaufhörliche*. She was waiting in London with her husband for a visa to travel to the USA. 'Rose Walter was a very warm-hearted generous lady'[14] who interested herself in Walter Bergmann's problems. She was acquainted with Willi Strecker of the publishers Schott and Co, and she invited Hugh Strecker (who had taken his father's place at Schott during 1939 when war looked inevitable) to her flat to meet Walter Bergmann. Rose Walter told Hugh Strecker all she knew about Walter Bergmann's recent life and Grete and Erica, and asked him what he could do for a foreign lawyer, not qualified to practise in England 'who was passionately interested in music'[15]. Hugh Strecker then discussed whether there were openings at Schott for Walter Bergmann with Max Steffens the Managing Director of Schott London. A couple of days later, Walter Bergmann visited Schott's shop with Hilde Volhard, taking with him some of his recent manuscript realisations. He ostensibly went in to look at and purchase some Telemann trios, but the assistant in the shop noticed his interest in Telemann recorder music and introduced himself as Edgar Hunt. They discussed Telemann and which of his compositions were currently in print. Edgar Hunt showed Walter Bergmann Nagel's latest Telemann edition of a trio sonata for recorder and viola da gamba. He later discovered that one of the manuscripts Walter Bergmann had been holding was his own realisation of the same work in which he had hoped Schott would be interested!

Through another acquaintance of Rose Walter, Walter Bergmann was given two more possible contacts, these being Julian Herbage at the BBC and Rose Standfield at the publisher, Augener. On August 18th he was invited back to Schott to discuss the possibility of publication of some of his manuscripts with Edgar Hunt and Strecker. They were interested in his edition of the Handel recorder concerto, a Telemann cantata, twelve Telemann violin sonatas and a Telemann quartet in F major.

Meanwhile Walter Bergmann could not help but be aware of the significant political events happening in August 1939 and of the ever-growing threat of war. Grete had suggested delaying their marriage plans for 4 - 6 weeks so that they could be certain they were doing the right thing. On August 22nd Walter Bergmann withdrew money from the bank in case of the outbreak of war for Hilde Volhard and himself. In his diary he described the war preparations in London, as all Britain waited on September 1st and 2nd 1939[16]. The diary entry for September 3rd 1939 reads[17]:

11 am England) at war with the
5 p.m. France) Germans.
Germany hasn't replied to the ultimatum.

On September 6th he wrote simply 'marriage'[18]. The decision was made. Grete and he married. Walter Bergmann then remained in London and Grete and Erica Bergmann returned to Essex. Except for two short entries, Walter Bergmann did not write in his diary again until the beginning of October. The first entry recorded the Russian move into Poland on September 16th, and the second stated he was too overwhelmed by events to record them in his diary.

[1] 'Festlicher Frühstück' ; Diary 2 27.03.39
[2] 'Darüber kann ich heute nicht viel sagen.'; Diary 2, 04.05.39
[3] Diary 2, 06.05.39
[4] 'Die Blockflöte klang ausgezeichnet, guter instrument'; Diary 2, 06. 05.39
[5] Diary 2, 22.05.39
[6] 'Mit Musik sei in England für Ausländer nichts zu machen. '; Diary 2, 22.05.39
[7] 'Die Gespräche um Hans, Nana, Grete, Dicki waren so ernst und hoffnungslos.' ; Diary 3, 12.06.39
[8] 'Es regnete wie üblich.'; Diary 3, 08.07.39
[9] 'Grete wird kommen.'; Diary 3, 10.07.39
[10] Diary 3, 23.07.39
[11] 'Es sind die Traurigsten Tage meines Leben.'; Diary 3, 23.07.39
[12] 'Die Frauen sahen aus (auf die Bühne) wie aus Alten Bildern.'; Diary 3, 28.07.39
[13] 'Carl Dolmetsch spielte ausgezeichnet Descant Recorder.'; Diary 3, 28.07.39
[14] Letter from Hugh Strecker to Anne Martin, 24.02.91
[15] Letter from Hugh Strecker to Anne Martin, 24.02.91
[16] Diary 3, 01.09.39
[17] '11 Uhr England J mit Deutschen
5 Uhr Frankreich I in Krieg
D. hat Ultimatum nicht beantwortet.';
Diary 3, 01.03.39
[18] 'Heirat'; Diary 3, 06.0939

5. The War Years

Except for a period of internment, Walter Bergmann remained in London throughout the war years. Grete Bergmann spent the first part of the war in a number of domestic situations outside London. On September 24th 1939 Walter Bergmann celebrated his first birthday in England with Hilde Volhard and Erika Seelig. He was 37. He spoke on the telephone to Grete and Erica in Chelmsford. On the surface, his life continued much as it had done in the previous few months with music-making activities, meetings with Hilde Volhard and other friends, and telephone contact with Grete. However, as was happening for all enemy aliens, the future began to look uncertain. From the first day of the war there was a fear in Britain of the 'unseen enemy' and pressure for internment[1]. The Government was reluctant to order general internment. They therefore decided to set up 120 investigative tribunals, each headed by a lawyer, which would categorise all adult aliens. Aliens were to be placed in one of three categories. Those falling into category A were Germans and Austrians with special knowledge who could damage the British war effort and were to be immediately interned. Category B aliens were those who had lived in Britain for a significant length of time and had not displayed any signs of hostility towards Britain. They were allowed to keep their freedom, but restricted from travelling more than 5 miles from home and could not own a car or a large scale map. Those who could produce references of 'character, associations and loyalty'[2] were put in Category C, as were refugees from religious, racial or political persecution, and not placed under any restrictions. The tribunals began in October 1939 and the results were not always consistent - for example in Leeds all aliens were given the classification B; in Manchester all were classified as C. Walter Bergmann was summoned before a tribunal on October 25th 1939.

Much to his relief, he was placed in Category C, classed as a friendly alien and refugee from Nazi oppression. Dr. Edwards accompanied him to the tribunal, but had to leave before he finally came before the hearing. He had taken with him character recommendations from several supporters including Edwards, and the original invitation of support he had received in Germany from Professor Dent.

A few days later he went to the National Gallery to hear Myra Hess play. He spent time playing with Max Rostal who had decided to include Walter Bergmann's edition of a Telemann *Sonata in A major* for violin in his repertoire. At the end of October, Bloomsbury House guaranteed him £1 a week for 3 weeks. At the beginning of November he went to Chelmsford to visit Grete and Erica. He commented in his diary that Grete had a pleasant employer, Mrs Nash[3]. Erica accompanied him back to London and spent a week with him. He found her to be very independent and easy to look after. After her return to Chelmsford his life continued as before. He was working hard at home, editing music with the hope of publication, as well as participating in as much suitable practical music making as possible. On November 16th he took part in a musical evening with Max Rostal and his wife, the Alexanders, Miete Muthesius, John Edwards and Hugh Strecker and Edgar Hunt from Schott. Max Rostal played the Telemann *Violin Sonata in A major* and Edgar Hunt performed Handel's *Recorder Sonata in F major*. The evening also included a *Quartet in F* by Telemann, two Bach arias with recorder and a Telemann cantata. It was agreed that Schott would publish the Handel recorder sonata with Edgar Hunt's edition of the solo part and Walter Bergmann's realisation of the continuo part.

On November 18th, Walter Bergmann went to hear Carl Dolmetsch play at the Wigmore Hall. He thought

Dolmetsch technically and musically an outstanding recorder player, but he found the performance lacking in warmth[4]. At the end of November, Bloomsbury House again gave him £3 for 3 weeks. In December his musical activities included accompanying the singer Miete Muthesius for whom he became a regular accompanist.

Grete Bergmann had to attend her tribunal on December 11th in Chelmsford. Because of her marriage to Walter, she was classed as a refugee and freed from any restrictions. Walter Bergmann spent Christmas 1939 in Chelmsford with Grete and Erica. He had intended to remain with them only over Christmas and Boxing Day and then leave to celebrate New Year elsewhere with friends. However after a very short time with Grete he decided to remain in Chelmsford for ten days. For the first time he saw and acknowledged how difficult life was for Grete. She had to work as a domestic servant and support and look after Erica. She was fortunate in the positions she found, but her existence was harder and much less rewarding than the life he was leading in London. They both tried to give Erica a typically German Christmas and Walter Bergmann noted that he hoped his daughter would retain the special feeling Germans have at Christmas time[5]. Friends had helped find a bicycle for Erica's birthday on December 26th. Walter Bergmann thoroughly enjoyed the time he spent with Grete and Erica. He wrote that it had re-awakened his feeling for celebrating Christmas. He also began to consciously think about his responsibilities towards Grete and Erica.

At the beginning of 1940 he returned to London. At the end of January the Handel R*ecorder Sonata in F major*, on which Edgar Hunt and he had collaborated, arrived from the publishers. During February Walter Bergmann spent more time in the British Museum and had several discussions with Strecker and Hunt about possible publications. At the outbreak of war Schott had been established in London for over a hundred years as the British outlet of the German music-publishing firm based in Mainz. It had its own retail outlet, but most of its publications were printed in Germany. In the first few months of the war, business had initially gone on much the same as in the pre-war months. However the shop's stock of descant recorders, which had stood at 2000 at the beginning of the war, was gone by Christmas 1939, and the firm was cut off from new publications and re-prints of music. Edgar Hunt realised that he had to find both an alternative source of recorders, and alternative editions of music. He began to prepare editions of music he felt were essential to the repertoire, and with Strecker's support, he discussed with Walter Bergmann what useful editing and arranging he could do for Schott. Hunt commissioned him to write new keyboard parts for the Telemann *Recorder Sonatas* in F and C. They also discussed other possible publications such as the Handel *Recorder Concerto*.

Grete came to London at the end of February to spend a couple of days with her husband. Together they went to tea with Hilde Volhard. On March 1st Walter Bergmann received his first cheque from Schott (2 guineas) for the Handel sonata. During the same week he heard that he would receive no more money from Bloomsbury House, who suggested he joined the Pioneer Corps, worked on the land or found some other means of regular employment. On March 6th he gave a concert with Miete Muthesius and Hilde Alexander (and a violinist named Salinger) in the Friends House in Euston Road. The following day Miete Muthesius sang in a concert given by Carl Dolmetsch at the Queen Mary Hall. Walter Bergmann was delighted with her performance of three Purcell songs on which they had worked together, but sad that he was not allowed to accompany her in the actual concert. Carl Dolmetsch played 'wieder ausgezeichnet' (once again excellently)[6]. Erica came to stay for a night. The following day Walter Bergmann prepared lunch for them both and then they went to the cinema together to see Gulliver's Travels. Grete collected Erica after a visit to the dentist.

At the beginning of April, Walter Bergmann noted that he had been too busy to write in his diary over the preceding weeks. His activities had included participating in a concert at the Friends' Hostel on March 16th. The programme consisted of a Haydn Trio and Scottish folksongs, Mendelssohn songs and the Beethoven *Geister Trio*. The next day he repeated part of the programme with Audrey Toth and Franz Eichbaum in the University Club. The players were then asked out to lunch at an Italian Restaurant. Walter Bergmann returned home very tired after both concerts. A friend rang and suggested that he might enjoy a concert being held at Morley College that evening. Walter Bergmann did not feel enthusiastic about going out again, but finally decided to go. It was fortunate he did, as the evening eventually changed his life. The concert was directed by Michael Tippett. Among the works performed was Tippett's *Piano Sonata*, played by Phyllis Sellick. During the interval Walter Bergmann met Hugh Strecker and sat with him during the second half. Schott had offered Michael Tippett a publishing contract in 1937. Willi Strecker, director of Schott's Mainz had been impressed by the scores of Tippett's *Piano Sonata*, the *Concerto for Double String Orchestra* and the *First String Quartet*. (Because of the war, publication was delayed.) Hugh Strecker introduced Walter Bergmann to Tippett after the concert. They went for a drink together and Walter Bergmann became slightly tipsy and made remarks he later regretted. The next day he looked back at his behaviour and disliked himself for it. However this did not effect the eventual outcome of this meeting.

On March 30th there was another concert at the Friends Meeting House at which Miete Muthesius sang and Walter Bergmann played continuo. The programme included a Vivaldi Concerto and a Bach cantata. Throughout April 1940 Walter Bergmann continued gradually establishing himself as a musician. In his personal life he was concerned about Hilde Volhard, who was very worried because she had lost contact with her daughter in Sweden due to the German invasion of Norway. Erica came to stay again. He paid another visit to the British Museum where he copied out Barsanti's *Recorder Sonata in F major* and was impressed by its form. He felt that in many ways it was superior to the Handel *Sonata in F major*. The Handel sonata had been published and two more Telemann pieces were in preparation. Grete came to London and they spent two days together.

By the middle of May 1940 there had been dramatic developments in the war. Norway was overrun and on May 10th the Germans invaded Belgium, Holland and Luxemburg. On the same day all Class B and C aliens living along the south and east coasts of Britain were detained and all category B males interned. Public concern about a fifth column increased. Anti-alien feelings increased to near paranoia[7]. The British Ambassador from the Hague, Sir Neville Bland warned on his return to Britain[8] that he believed that any German or Austrian servant, even if they appeared charming and devoted, was a grave risk. He suggested that at a signal from Hitler, many would embark on sabotage and attacks on military targets. In spite of the unlikelihood of this being true, Bland's statement profoundly influenced government thought and public opinion. Anyone with a foreign accent became immediately suspect. Walter Bergmann noted all these events in his diary. He was extremely depressed about what was likely to happen. In particular he was worried what would become of Erica if both he and Grete were interned. On May 23rd 1940 all category B women and their children were interned. On May 23rd the Germans reached Boulogne and Walter Bergmann wrote that he could not make up his mind whether he should join the Pioneer Corps. The Home Secretary, Sir John Anderson, issued a warning against panic reaction as a result of Bland's frightening statement, pointing out the major geographical differences between Holland and Britain and that the majority of the 73,000 Germans and Austrians in Britain were refugees from Nazi oppression. They posed no risk to security. But panic overtook reason and from the end of May, the process of rounding up all 'friendly aliens', i.e. Category C, began.

Walter Bergmann waited anxiously. Gradually acquaintances began to be interned. In his diary on May 26th he commented on the beautiful spring day - but observed that it did not compensate for the suffering of thousands of people and the uncertainty of his own future. On June 6th 1940 Grete and Erica Bergmann had to leave the Nashes at Little Beddow, because of its proximity to the east coast. Britain was preparing for invasion. Through a friend of Walter Bergmann, they found a family looking for a refugee companion for their daughter. Erica went to live with the family in Twyford, Berks. It was hard for Grete Bergmann to part with her seven and half year old daughter. She visited her fortnightly and saw her gradually become English. Grete Bergmann stayed in London, looking for a job. Walter Bergmann began to think about trying to leave Britain. He still hoped to eventually get to the USA, but he considered the possibility of emigrating to Brazil with Grete and Erica. At the end of June he collected testimonials and references from Bloomsbury House, Edgar Hunt, Max Rostal and Hugh Strecker to send to the Brazilian Embassy to support his application.

On July 1st Walter Bergmann was in the British Museum again, looking at the Flackton viola sonatas. By this date several hundred Germans and Austrians were being interned daily, Mr Alexander, with whom he had often played, being among them. During the first few days of July a campaign against internment was launched, and Attlee spoke sympathetically about the refugees in a radio broadcast. However on July 9th two officials arrived at Walter Bergmann's lodgings just before 8 a.m.. They told him he had half an hour to pack and they would then return to collect him. He managed to contact Grete Bergmann and Hilde Volhard to tell them he was being interned. There was little time to talk. He wisely made sure he ate some breakfast before he left struggling with his heavy case (presumably filled with music and manuscripts and his flute). He was taken to join around 25 other internees in the cells of Hampstead Police Station. The following day they were taken to Kempton Park Race Course with 150 others; there were eventually around 900 internees at the racecourse. Their belongings were examined and certain items removed such as razors, scissors, knives and any written material, including Walter Bergmann's diary. Each internee was issued with a number (Walter Bergmann's was Group II, No. 3238) and given certain items, including a spoon, a plate and 2 bed sheets. On July 11th the group were ready to leave at 6 am to travel to Liverpool and then on to the Isle of Man. They marched to the station, having been given two pieces of bread, a small piece of cheese and four sheets of toilet paper as their day's ration. After a two-hour wait, they joined the train. Walter Bergmann enjoyed the train journey. The crossing to the Isle of Man was cold and stormy. They arrived cold, hungry and wet in Douglas. They were marched into a large hall, given new numbers and allocated to 'houses' and rooms. The internment camps were set up in holiday accommodation. It was not particularly comfortable. Walter Bergmann was allocated to Room 21, in house number 1, where he was somewhat dismayed to discover he was expected to share a bed.

The first day in internment was long and boring. Walter Bergmann's case had not arrived. He wrote to Grete and took stock of his surroundings. The prison camp consisted of thirty four houses. The internees were taken for walks and sometimes had the opportunity to swim. The windows of the houses were almost completely blacked out, but there was no light in the rooms. During the next few days, Walter Bergmann observed in the new diary he had started, that the internees received an adequate amount to eat, but the food was insipid. He looked forward to a more varied diet. He slept well, but was always tired[9]. The worry over what might happen to them was not over yet for the internees. At a Cabinet meeting on 24 May 1940, Churchill had announced that he was in favour of moving all internees out of Britain. Both Australia and Canada said they would be willing to receive them and in Australia's case, 10,000 prisoners of war and 'dangerous internees' could be accommodated. It was decided to make up the numbers of Category A prisoners to be sent with Category B and C internees. The first boat load left for Canada in June. The second boat of internees was sunk at the beginning of July, en route for Canada. A boat left for Australia on July 10th, and of the 2543 men on board, 2100 were Category C internees. Walter Bergmann worried that he would have to go to Australia and wondered if there were any circumstances which would give exemption from being deported.

Meanwhile he began to investigate the musical life that was developing in the camp among a mixture of amateur and professional musicians (which sometimes caused friction). Apart from the daily roll call the internees were left entirely to their own devices. These were in some way quite remarkable. The number of professional men, artists and intellectuals among the inmates was disproportionate and soon began to influence every day life[10]. Dr Hans Gal, an Austrian-born composer and musicologist, was one of those interned, and some time later Walter Bergmann recounted that in the early days of internment before internees had received music and books, Dr Gal and he used to play together Schubert's opus 160 for flute and piano till they were sick of it, because it was the only music they both knew from memory[11]. Dr Gal gave a concert with a cellist on July 17th. The music included a Bach Fugue, a Beethoven piano sonata and arrangements for cello. Gal played, according to Walter Bergmann, 'without a great deal of technique, but very musically'[12]. Groups of musicians were getting together, although they were not always very well matched. Walter Bergmann found it depressing hearing two musicians rehearse, when the accompanist was, he believed, an inferior player to himself. Initially he found it difficult to establish himself as a serious musician and keyboard player as the 'professional' musicians considered him to be a lawyer, not a musician. He was also depressed because by July 20th he still had not received any letters or money.

He started to play his flute with two musicians called Baron and Markswitz. They played Hans Gal's *Huyton Suite* for 2 violins and flute under Gal's supervision. Baron gave a concert with the pianist Franz Reizenstein. Walter Bergmann considered Reizenstein to be an excellent solo pianist, but a poor accompanist. A new flautist arrived in the camp on July 26th. He proved to be a better flautist than Walter Bergmann, the latter being then thrown out of the group of musicians he had been playing with!

Gradually, however, life began to settle into a pattern, as the internees began to receive their belongings and letters, and to form friendships. Walter Bergmann began to accompany a singer called Dr Pick. On July 30th he telegraphed Grete to make sure she knew he might be sent to Australia and to ask whether she would follow him. The following day Walter Bergmann received a packet from her including chocolate and tobacco. A telegram arrived from Grete on August 1st confirming that she understood the situation regarding Australia. Another packet arrived from her on August 3rd. It was becoming apparent that post could take 3 - 4 weeks to arrive.

During August parcels and letters began to arrive regularly. As well as continuing to accompany Dr Pick, Walter Bergmann began to play with other musicians, although there still seemed to be some conflict between himself and other 'professional' musicians who apparently did not consider him a competent or eminent enough performer to play with them. He rehearsed Purcell Fantasias with two other musicians. He accompanied Dr Pick in a concert of songs by Schubert and Loewe. The internees organised concerts or debates for almost every day. Over the weeks the musicians gradually were sent more music. 'Viel Bridge' was also played[13]. Nevertheless, by the beginning of September, Walter Bergmann was very depressed. War news of the bombing in London was bad. He worried about Hilde Volhard in London and wondered if it had been the right decision to leave Germany. He remembered Dietrich Gerhardt remarking that Hitler's empire-building ambitions would not reach as far as Britain[14]. On September 16th he received a suitcase from Grete, which contained mainly clothes for possible emigration to Australia. During August Walter Bergmann wrote to Grete to discuss whether America or Australia were possibilities.

At the time of Walter Bergmann's arrest, Grete found a job as a cook-general in Shepperton. From there she wrote to the American Consulate to try to find out what had happened to his application to emigrate. The job at Shepperton was not a success for Grete and she found a new job through an advertisement in the *Daily Telegraph* with the Binyon family at Streatly, near Reading (much to the disgust of her current employer). She was able to take Erica to live with her. They met on September 24th 1940 at Reading Station and went together to the Binyons. Grete was very relieved they were together again. On the same day, his birthday, Walter Bergmann received another suitcase that, among its contents, included recorders and music.

Hans Gal was released from the Isle of Man on September 27th 1940 because of serious illness. Walter Bergmann was sorry that he had not managed to develop a closer friendship with him. In October 1940 things did begin to look more hopeful for him. In the camp his relations with the professional musicians seemed to be improving, particularly with Franz Reizenstein. Regarding the situation for internees, public and political opinion was changing. By July 1940 the Home Office had published a white paper listing internees who were to be immediately released. These were those under sixteen (or eighteen if they had previously been living in a family or educational institution) and those aged over sixty-five. The scandal of the internee boats had also reached the British public. In October significant numbers of internees began to be released - for example on October 5th a farewell party was held at the camp for 14 internees. Walter Bergmann was corresponding with Strecker at Schott and working at editing music again. On October 21st the Government announced a new category of internees would be released - all those involved in the arts. As the prospect of release appeared to be an eventual possibility and he had received more music and books, Walter Bergmann felt much more positive. On October 23rd he played continuo in a concert of music by Handel and in the same month he heard from Hugh Strecker that Schott would like to include his realisation of the Handel *Recorder Concerto* in a collection of works for recorder and strings. The entries in his diary became less frequent as he became more fruitfully occupied with music. At the end of November, Schott sent Walter Bergmann the realisation of the Handel *Recorder Concerto* to correct and a cheque for 2 guineas. By the beginning of December he seemed to be well established among the musicians and took part in several concerts. He had become involved with a new group of musicians whom he liked very much and included a young violinist named Nissel. Walter Bergmann noted in his diary that he would be a fine violinist one day. (He of course became a member of the Amadeus Quartet.) On December 11th Walter Bergmann heard that Hilde Volhard had learnt from Robert Müller Hartmann, that Ralph Vaughan Williams had promised to help obtain his release.

Christmas Day 1940 was a miserable occasion 'without wife and child'[15]. Walter Bergmann had been saddened by a letter from Grete a few weeks earlier in which she said that Erica now only spoke English. He was worried they would not understand each other any more. He received a very small amount of Christmas post because of the air raids in Liverpool, but the camp food was better on Christmas Day and he received a card and one food parcel from Hilde Volhard. Two packets from Grete and Erica arrived on December 26th, Erica's birthday. He celebrated New Year with several friends and commented that a frightful year was going out and a yet more terrible year beginning[16]. On January 8th 1941 Walter Bergmann was told he was to be released the following day and he started to pack. He then learnt it was a mistake and a 'Richard' Bergmann was to be freed. The following day he completed six months in captivity. During January he gave a couple of lectures and continued to make music. From Grete he learnt that Vaughan Williams was doubtful of his release. By January 17th 1941 there was still no sign of his release and he was extremely depressed[17]. He was again offered the opportunity to join the Pioneer Corps or work on the land. On January 23rd he learnt for the first time of the mass deportation of German Jews and of their internment in concentration camps. The news was filtering through in letters received by the internees from friends in neutral countries such as Switzerland. Walter Bergmann wondered miserably where Vera Bergmann was. The following day he finally heard that he definitely would be released, and started worrying as to how he would get to London without money. The official confirmation of his release came on January 26th 1941. He was sorry to be parting from the friends he had made, but rejoiced that he would be free. On the next day he received 10/- through the post from Hilde Volhard and a friend lent him £1.

Dr Pick and himself were released together on January 29th. They travelled on the 8 a.m. bus to the harbour where there were formalities to complete with the police. In Fleetwood there were more formalities. He finally arrived in London at around 11 p.m.

Walter Bergmann spent his first night after his release staying with the Alexanders. The following day he registered with the police. During the next few days he attempted to pick up his pre-internment life again. He met Hilde Volhard, and went to Bloomsbury House. He visited Schott and spoke with Edgar Hunt, who was encouraging about more work - in particular Schott wanted him to realise several Telemann trio sonatas. Walter Bergmann then booked himself a coach seat to Reading to visit Grete and Erica and registered for a ration book. He also visited the employment department at Bloomsbury House and experienced his first air raid.

On February 5th Walter Bergmann travelled to Reading by bus, then on to Streatley by train and finally by foot to the home of the poet Lawrence Binyon, where Grete Bergmann was working. He met Erica from school and was sad to find that she spoke no German at all. It still worried him that she had forgotten her native language. However he appreciated that the Binyons' home was a good place for Erica and that they were fine people[18]. Erica was extremely happy as there were always animals and children around, and Grandma Binyon read stories to the children every evening[19]. While he was staying with the Binyons, Walter Bergmann took the opportunity to visit the Bodleian Library in Oxford.

Back in London, Walter Bergmann settled back into his old life. At the end of February, Edgar Hunt played the Telemann *Pastorale* for two recorders with Stephanie Champion and the first movement of the Telemann *C major Recorder Sonata*, both of which had been edited by Walter Bergmann, in a radio broadcast. Walter Bergmann was particularly pleased at how his realisation of the Telemann sonata sounded. (In the pre-war years Edgar Hunt had done a great deal to promote the recorder. His recorder classes at Trinity College of Music, begun in 1935, had to close because of the war, but he had continued to be involved in teaching and broadcasting, and in 1940 he started to produce a news letter that kept recorder players in touch with one another.) Walter Bergmann began to play regularly in concerts again and continued arranging and editing music for Schott and his musical friends. In March 1941 he applied for a work permit to be employed at Schott as a packer. In April he moved to a new address - a furnished room in Orsett Terrace, Bayswater.

April 1941 was a rewarding month. He gave a lecture on 'The figured bass' to the Free German League of Culture. Schott agreed to take his realisation of a Flackton viola sonata. Walter Bergmann was telephoned by the young violinist, Norbert Brainin, a pupil of Max Rostal, who like two other eventual members of the Amadeus, Sigmund Nissel and Peter Schidlof, had become involved at Morley College. Brainin offered to act as a referee for him if needed. He went to Oxford for the conference of the New Education Fellowship. Other activities included visiting Grete and Erica, fire-watching duty, playing the recorder with Max and Stephanie Champion and accompanying Miete Muthesius.

In July Walter Bergmann went to a concert in the Holst Room, the only part of the College that still remained intact after bomb damage. Michael Tippett conducted the Morley Choir in a programme of madrigals. Later in the month he went to a Recorder Society Meeting conducted by Carl Dolmetsch and Stephanie Champion. He liked the sound of a recorder 'choir', remarking that it was 'magical'[20]. The Society of Recorder Players (the SRP) had been found jointly by Carl Dolmetsch and Edgar Hunt in 1937, with the help of Max and Stephanie Champion, with the aim of bringing recorder players together and promoting the recorder.

Max Steffens, Managing Director of Schott also lent his support to the Society.

The following month Erica came to London for a visit. After she had returned to the Binyons, Walter Bergmann spent a couple of days with Dr Edwards, who now lived in Amersham. He observed that Edwards had not been changed at all by the war and was eccentric as ever. He also played with Max Rostal and Sigmund Nissel over the summer. As well as Schott, the publishing firm Boosey and Hawkes had become interested in several of his manuscripts.

In October 1941 Walter Bergmann began to worry seriously as to how he could sensibly support himself. Up until this time he had survived on handouts from Bloomsbury House and friends, and the small amount of money he earned from editing music and giving the occasional recorder lesson. However at last musical opportunities started to open up for him and he began establishing a musical career. On October 23rd he was invited to play continuo at a rehearsal of the Purcell 1692 *Ode for St Cecilia* taken by Michael Tippett at Morley College. He began to play regularly for Michael Tippett's Morley Choir and started to become closely involved with the College. It was the right place to be for his future as a musician in Britain. 'Possibly the most far-reaching influence on post-war music came from a group of musicians who were centred on Morley College South London and included Michael Tippett, Walter Goehr, Walter Bergmann and Matyas Seiber.' (Lewis Foreman[21].) In a tribute to Tippett on his 60th Birthday, John Amis wrote that in the war years 'Morley was a musical refuge for all of us. Elsewhere in those days the repertory was rationed to a severely limited number of classics, but here was Monteverdi, the Elizabethans, Purcell, Purcell and Purcell .... the Bachs and then a big gap until Debussy, Stravinsky, Hindemith... and contemporary British.

'I nearly wrote 'Pritish', for wartime Morley was above all a refuge for the refugees. They brought us much; string players like the as yet unformed Amadeus, the glamorous Maria Lidka .... and a score more beside: and then Matyas Seiber and Walter Bergmann on the teaching staff. Ideas from the continent mingled most fruitfully with the natives like Antony Hopkins, Alison Purves, Anthony Milner, Alfred Deller, Peter Fricker ....

And Michael Tippett was the focal point of all this activity.'[22] Walter Bergmann himself wrote; 'In the dark autumn of 1941, Michael Tippett engaged me to play the piano for his choir at Morley College (or what the bomb had left of it). This started a collaboration of about ten years, he pretending not to know anything about old music and I the opposite, both of us of course being wrong.'[23]

Michael Tippett wrote in his obituary of Walter Bergmann that when the latter came to Morley 'He was already a skilled performer on harpsichord and recorder.' 'His main love was music of the period of Bach and Telemann. But when he came with me to Morley College .... he had to extend his skills and sympathies back to Purcell and even Gibbons. The problem of accompaniment to Purcell's basses fascinated him, simply because Purcell's basses are unfigured, and his idiom contains such un-German problems as 'blues' notes, simultaneous major and minor thirds. His solutions were, in my opinion, very good.'[24]

Although in 1941 the choir and orchestral players Tippett worked with were a mixture of professionals and amateurs, Morley College concerts were recognised for their outstanding success. Under Tippett 'even the most amateurish playing or singing could produce not only tolerable, but highly inspired performances.'[25] The first modern public performance by Morley College of Purcell's *Ode for St Cecilia's Day* (1692) was in a concert on November 22nd 1941. The small choir consisted of approximately 20 women and 8 men; a quintet of strings was led by Jean Layton; there were two oboes and Walter Bergmann played the continuo part on the piano. The solo items where shared between the choir, sometimes sung as a group and sometimes as solos. The concert was reported by Dr Colles[26] in *The Times*, who said that out of the six or so concerts given in London on St Cecilia's Day, that given at Morley was the most appropriate. He particularly commended the singing of Esther Salaman, both in her solo items in the first part of the concert, when she sang songs by English lutenists, accompanied by Walter Bergmann, and in her singing of *Tis Nature's Voice* and *The Airy Violin* in the Purcell Ode, when she demonstrated both the virtuosity required by Purcell and his innate musical genius. He also observed that the pianist knew how to realise a continuo part.

The performance of the *Ode for St Cecilia* obviously caught the essence of Purcell's musical intentions. It was inevitable that the omission of trumpets and drums would be noticed, but the replacement of recorders in *The fife and harmony of war* was apparently remarkably successful. Esther Salaman was the only singer capable of the virtuosity demanded by Purcell, but Colles remarked on how well the Morley College singers had been trained and that their performance brought out the vitality of the music. They avoided making the lively and abandoned music of Purcell sound like music from a Handel Oratorio.

Walter Bergmann wrote of the same concert: 'The oboes played abominably, descant recorders were substituted for trumpets, the strings were out of tune etc. The concert however made a great impression on performers and audience alike thanks to Tippett as a conductor'[27]

As well as the opportunities that were opening up at Morley College, Walter Bergmann found employment at Schott. Initially he worked on an occasional basis, testing and packing recorders. On November 17th he tested 362 recorders and noted in his diary that he could now pay the rent[28]. Edgar Hunt had solved the problem of how to replenish Schott's stock of recorders. Wood was unobtainable, and after fifteen months an acceptable plastic instrument was designed, developed and produced by Schott. It was these instruments that Walter Bergmann was checking and packing. Hugh Strecker writes of Walter Bergmann, 'In those days he had to work downstairs with the other staff which cannot have been easy at first. But I always admired the way he coped with the dry cockney sense of humour and had the impression that he got on very well all round. In fact as 'Dr B' or 'Mr B' he became quite a fixture and always seemed cheerful about their leg-pulling.'[29]

Walter Bergmann began to do other work for Schott, partly through his connection with Michael Tippett. This eventually encompassed both editing and translating. Tippett wrote in a letter to a friend in 1941, 'The man (Walter Bergmann) who played the through bass at Morley for the Purcell is quite a find for me. He knows the period in and out. He's also one of those careful Germans who spot any missing dot a mile off. He's doing the piano reduction of the new work for Hugo (Hugh Strecker) and me. He's so good that I am giving all the oratorio parts and scores to him to collate as a private job. (He's an out of work refugee and an unusually nice one.)'[30]

During 1941 both Hugh Strecker and Edgar Hunt were called up. Edgar Hunt recommended Walter

Bergmann as his replacement. At the beginning of December Walter Bergmann was offered a position at Schott for £3 10/- a week. He accepted and started working permanently for the Company on December 15th. The scope available to Walter Bergmann was limited. Paper was rationed and so the Company was restricted as to how much music it could actually print. However it meant he had a regular, interesting job, which suited his expertise and experience. Max Steffens remained as Managing Director. Virtually everyone else at Schott did any job that was necessary. Walter Bergmann gradually created a niche for himself with recorder music, and through his contact with other musicians.

By the beginning of 1942, he could at last feel he was well on the way to establishing himself as a reputable musician. He was 39 and had been in Britain for almost 3 years. Between the beginning of December 1941 and March 25th 1942, he was too busy to write in his diary. On January 10th 1942 he attended the last meeting of the Society of Recorder Players to be held until after the war. Two new friends he had made through the Society were Freda Dinn and Marylin Wailes, who began to perform with him. During 1942, Walter Bergmann's musical life was divided between Morley College, where he continued to accompany the choir and began to lecture, Schott, and a number of other musical activities. From March to June he gave a series of lectures at Morley, the titles of which included 'Where we stand in the history of music', 'Figured bass' and 'The relation of Society to Music'. He also lectured in Yorkshire. Concerts in the early part of the year, included one for two pianos, which Walter Bergmann gave in Tooting with a Mrs Bond, a performance of the Handel *Recorder Concerto* in which he played the solo part, also in Tooting, and he accompanied Esther Salaman (mezzo-soprano) in a concert. He continued to arrange and edit music. In May 1942 Max Rostal and Maria Lidka (violins) played a Bach *Trio Sonata in C major* for 2 violins at a concert held in the National Gallery using a continuo part realised by Walter Bergmann. (These concerts in the National Gallery had been instigated, after the war had started, by the pianist Dame Myra Hess, and were important regular musical events.) Significantly Walter Bergmann also began to compose again, for the first time in five years. In August 1942 he completed a *Sonatina* for recorder.

With regular employment and income, Walter Bergmann began to plan for the future. By the beginning of 1942 Grete was working and living, with Erica, in Amersham (coincidentally in a house that Edgar Hunt bought after the war). Walter Bergmann regularly visited them. He was still friendly with Hilde Volhard, but knew that his future lay with Grete and Erica. It was decided that in September 1942 Erica (aged almost 10) would go to boarding school and Grete would join Walter in London.

In the summer of 1942, the most important event for Walter Bergmann was the start of his recorder classes at Morley College on August 31st at the invitation of Michael Tippett. Edgar Hunt wrote in his book *The Recorder and its Music* that during the war 'the man who did most to keep the recorder and its music alive at this time was Dr Walter Bergmann, through the classes which he started for recorder players at Morley College in London, and through his work at Schott's where he took over my job'[31] The brief prospectus for the classes at Morley read:-

'*Recorder Playing* The recorder is the easiest serious instrument to learn and group playing is particularly enjoyable. Provision will be made in this class for both beginners and advanced students. As there is a shortage of instruments twelve descant recorders (at 7/6 each) and a few trebles (£2 17s 9d) have been reserved for members of the class.' The class met every Monday from 6.15 to 8.15 p.m. and around 40 students enrolled at the first class. They included Ken Kenworthy who later became closely involved with the Society of Recorder Players. The cost of the classes was 10/- for the session.

These first recorder classes consisted of a very mixed bunch of players. Some were members of the Morley Choir who had heard the recorder being played the previous year. Most were complete beginners, except for a small number who could already play. The interest of the latter was kept by the fact there was almost no other opportunity to play the recorder, and Walter Bergmann was always producing new music[32].

In September Erica Bergmann went to Sherwood School in Epsom, Surrey. She later wrote[33] that the school ' was a co-educational boarding school run on very free lines. We called our teachers by their first names, were able to keep pets and academically it was not successful, but it was the right school for me at the time, not only because I was out of London, but because I was rather unsettled then'. Walter and Grete Bergmann moved into a 2-roomed flat in 30 Belsize Square. Grete Bergmann found work washing-up in a restaurant in Swiss Cottage. (She then progressed to being the vegetable cook and eventually to head chef.) For the first time since leaving Germany, Walter Bergmann began living a more normal family life again. Grete and he tried to create the atmosphere they had established in their home in Halle, where friends were always welcome to make music and enjoy the Bergmann hospitality. Grete Bergmann gained a reputation for being able to make delicious sandwiches out of virtually nothing.

In the autumn of 1942, Walter Bergmann was involved in two concerts which promoted two of his special interests, modern recorder music and Baroque recorder music, in particular the music of Telemann. On September 6th he organised a concert at the Everyman Theatre, Hampstead held under the auspices of the Free German League of Culture. This organisation had been founded in 1938 by anti-Nazis, and its aims included keeping 'alive among German refugees the spirit of free German Culture which once made the name of Germany honoured among the peoples'[34]. The presidents of the Society included Thomas Mann and among its patrons were Antony Asquith, J B Priestley and Ralph Vaughan Williams. The Society's Board had friends and acquaintances of Walter Bergmann's among its members such as Dr Alexander and Max Rostal. The programme on September 6th was entitled 'New Music for the Recorder' and included two works entitled *Sonatina* by Chris Edmunds (written 1940) and Walter Bergmann, and works newly edited by Walter Bergmann. The performers were Miette Hardy (soprano), Antony Hopkins (piano) and Walter Bergmann (recorder). The concert was advertised at the first recorder class at Morley College[35]. On October 10th 1942 Walter Bergmann directed a concert of works by Telemann in the Holst Room at Morley College. The concert again included works edited by Walter Bergmann, such as a *Sonata a 4* for treble recorder, oboe, violin and figured bass and the cantata *Locke nur Erde*. The performers on this occasion included Marylin Wailes (recorder), Norbert Brainin (violin) and Paul Blumenfeld (cello). Throughout the rest of the war, Morley College (or concerts connected with Morley) and the Free German League provided two of the main outlets for Walter Bergmann as a performer. The contribution to musical life these two organisations provided (and of course the National Gallery concerts) was significant in war-torn London.

Towards the end of 1942 Walter Bergmann was again too busy to keep his diary up to date. Erica Bergmann spent Christmas with her parents. Walter Bergmann was pleased to discover that she was musical as she had a good aural sense and was showing an interest in the piano. 1943 was to prove to be an excellent year professionally for Walter Bergmann. As well as a more permanent and stable family life, Walter Bergmann was becoming secure in the professional life he was establishing and in the friendships he had made. He was delighted and flattered when Michael Tippett dedicated his *Second String Quartet* to him. The first performance was in March 1943.

Walter Bergmann was gradually getting more opportunities to lecture. Engagements included a lecture on the recorder to youth club leaders, and one on Schumann to the German Club. For the first time, English entries began to appear in his diary. During 1943 he participated in an ever increasing number of concerts. On March 13th the Morley College Choir performed Purcell's 1683 *Ode for St Cecilia*. This performance was repeated in the National Gallery. The choir also gave a broadcast of three Debussy songs on April 6th.

During the latter part of 1942, Michael Tippett had met Benjamin Britten and Peter Pears. In 1943 they both began to participate in concerts associated with Morley College. For April 10th 1943, Michael Tippett asked Walter Bergmann to direct a concert of sixteenth and seventeenth century music and works by J S and J C Bach, including *Cantata 189*, in which Peter Pears was the tenor soloist. Other performers in the concert included Norbert Brainin (violin), Paul Blumenfeld (cello), Freda Dinn (recorder and violin) and Michael Tippett (percussion). The London Recorder Consort played music by Morley, Wilbye, Locke and Dowland. The recorder consort consisted of Freda Dinn, Helen Wilson, Joan Todhunter, Marylin Wailes and Walter Bergmann, who had formed the group in the autumn/winter of 1942. They made their debut at this concert. Walter Bergmann noted in his diary[36] that they had been rehearsing for six months for this first performance. The whole concert was apparently well received. Walter Bergmann was finding that people were very interested in recorders. The consort gave a successful concert in Lincoln on June 1st. Other engagements for Walter Bergmann included a concert at Morley on May 1st, when he accompanied Esther Salaman singing Dowland. At the end of May she sang at the National Gallery and her programme included Walter Bergmann's arrangement of Arne's *Under the Greenwood Tree* for soprano and string quartet. At the concert, Walter Bergmann was introduced to the mezzo-soprano Elena Gerhardt and the accompanist Gerald Moore.

In 1943, there was a major upheaval at Morley College, caused by the arrest and imprisonment of Michael Tippett. Tippett had become Musical Director at Morley in 1940. He was a pacifist, but was also acutely aware of the plight of Jews and all refugees from Nazi Germany. He made a point of welcoming any refugee musician who came to Morley College. In the autumn of 1942 Tippett was granted exemption from active war service as a conscientious objector, providing he undertook some alternative war work such as agricultural labour or hospital portering. He refused to do so, as he believed that he could give his country far greater service through his musical work at Morley. On June 21st 1943 Tippett was arrested and brought to trial at Oxted Police Court. He was sent to prison for three months. Walter Bergmann noted that June 24th was the first rehearsal 'without Michael'[37]. The conducting of the Morley Choir was shared between Benjamin Britten (who conducted his own music), Peter Pears, Antony Hopkins and Walter Bergmann. Over the summer Walter Bergmann frequently conducted the choir in Tippett's absence. It was not easy as the choir missed Tippett's presence and direction. Walter Bergmann wrote in 1965[38] 'Tippett had two principles, which I admired and later followed myself: never to miss a choir rehearsal (unless one were dead or in prison) and to foster a loyalty among the choir members to the choir but not to the conductor. In spite of the latter maxim the choir adored Tippett passionately and not without reason: his enthusiasm and musical drive were irresistible, in rehearsals as well as in concerts.'

He wrote in his diary in July 1943 that he had had difficult and intense rehearsals with the choir.[39] Walter Bergmann conducted the choir at the Morley College Open Day. He also conducted the first performance of two madrigals composed by Michael Tippett, entitled *The Windhover* and *The Source* at a concert given by the choir on July 17th at the College. (The madrigals were dedicated to the Morley Choir.) On August 12th Walter Bergmann went with John Amis to visit Michael Tippett in Wormwood Scrubs. In the evening of the same day, the Morley College Choir gave a broadcast performance of Seiber's Yugoslavian folksongs. Tippett was released from prison on August 21st 1943.

During August the Bergmanns celebrated Grete's birthday, and Erica spent some time at home. On August 31st Walter Bergmann was interviewed and told that he must find war work. It was suggested that he worked in a munitions factory, for which 20 hours training was required. However he heard nothing further for several months. At Morley College the recorder classes expanded to a Beginners and Intermediate Class for the 1943/44 session. Music played by the classes included a Pepusch *Trio*, a *Little Fugue* by Bach and *Sonata in D* by Daniel Purcell. Over the weekend of October 30th and 31st the first 'Recorder Weekend' was held at Morley College. The weekend consisted of lectures, playing sessions and concerts, starting at 2.30 p.m. on the Saturday afternoon. It was led by Walter Bergmann, Carl Dolmetsch, Max Champion and Freda Dinn. Imogen Holst was to have participated but was unfortunately taken ill at the last minute. In consequence, the programme had to be slightly re-arranged. It opened with a lecture by Max Champion on 'The Recorder in Purcell's Time', which was followed by 'community playing' directed by Stephanie Champion. The final lecture on the Saturday was on playing the recorder for folk dancing. On the Sunday Walter Bergmann lectured on group and class recorder playing, and the Morley College Classes played during the lecture. Freda Dinn talked about the recorder in school, for which some of her pupils played, and finally Carl Dolmetsch lectured on ornamentation. A concert was held each day. At the Saturday evening concert the music consisted of Baroque works for the recorder including a Bach cantata and Telemann concerto grosso. Among the performers were Carl Dolmetsch, the Morley College Choir and the London Recorder Consort. Alison Purves (soprano) replaced Peter Pears who was unable to sing. Walter Bergmann conducted. The second concert on the Sunday was made up of modern works for the recorder such as Hindemith's *Trio* for recorders, and Lennox Berkeley's *Sonatina* for treble recorder and piano, which Carl Dolmetsch played with Joseph Saxby. The concert also included a composition for descant recorder by Carl Dolmetsch. (Carl Dolmetsch had set out to promote the recorder as a virtuoso solo instrument, capable of playing modern music. He had composed music himself to demonstrate the range and character of the instrument. At his first Wigmore Hall recital he played his own composition with the hope it would encourage others to write for the recorder.) Walter Bergmann's *Quintet* for recorders was given its first performance at the weekend Sunday concert. He had completed it one week previously, fifteen minutes before the first rehearsal! Ken Kenworthy recollected[40] that Walter Bergmann was dissatisfied with the work, although the performance appeared to go quite well. The weekend finished on the Sunday with community playing conducted by Carl Dolmetsch. The whole weekend was voted a success by the Morley College Players. The only slight problem during the weekend had been Carl Dolmetsch's lecture, which the participants found too technical. The fee for the whole weekend was 10/-.

In November 1943 Walter Bergmann was continuing to regularly take his turn at fire-watching. He was very concerned that Grete was unwell. On November 13th he conducted a performance of Bach's *Cantata 161* at Morley College. Originally Peter Pears was to have sung, but he had to cancel at the last minute. Michael Tippett then took his place and sang tenor, asking Walter Bergmann to conduct instead of himself. Benjamin Britten played the continuo part. The concert received a good notice in the News Chronicle. Walter Bergmann was well aware of Tippett's generosity towards him and knew how fortunate he had been to work with the composer and musician. In his tribute to Michael Tippett included in the Symposium collected by Ian Kemp for Tippett's sixtieth birthday, Walter Bergmann wrote of Michael Tippett's generosity to himself and other musicians. A 'characteristic of Tippett was the total absence of ambition as a conductor, his generosity in sharing his choir and his concerts with others. One day when there were some cancellations and the concert programme had to be altered, he asked me to conduct a Bach cantata while he sung tenor in the choir and Benjamin Britten played the continuo in my place'[41]. 1943 had indeed been a successful year for Walter Bergmann. The only sadness for him was that he realised during the Christmas holidays that Erica, now aged 11, appeared to have lost interest in music.

1944 saw a continuation of Walter Bergmann's activities at Morley and in other areas. In January he participated in a 'Freie Deutsche Kulturtagung' weekend. He opened each of the two sessions on Saturday January 15th and Sunday January 16th with a concert of chamber music. On February 14th Walter Bergmann was told that he must report for training as a fitter, commencing on February 21st. On completing his training he would have to work regular hours in a factory. He had to leave Schott at the end of the week. He felt extremely miserable.

On February 19th 1944 Walter Bergmann attended a rehearsal, taken by Walter Goehr, of Tippett's oratorio *A Child of our Time*. Walter Bergmann came away disappointed from the rehearsal. In 1943 Goehr had advised Michael Tippett to put the work away for a while. However Benjamin Britten had urged Tippett to let it be performed, in spite of the difficulty of giving a balanced performance in war-torn London. Tippett had begun to compose *A Child of our Time* in September 1939. Through it, Tippett wanted to express his horror of Nazi oppression and persecution, and of the state of the world as a whole. The actual impetus for the work came from the violent pogrom against the Jews in Central Europe at the end of 1938, which resulted from the action of a desperate young Polish Jew aged seventeen who shot a German Diplomat in Paris in revenge for his mother's persecution by the Nazis. The boy became the symbolic hero of Tippett's oratorio.

In spite of Walter Bergmann's pessimism in February, all went well at the first performance on March 19th 1944. Michael Tippett hinted in his obituary of Walter Bergmann, that the two Walters (Bergmann and Goehr) did not always agree. He wrote 'Morley became the scene of intense musicological debate when Walter encountered Walter Goehr ....'[42]. Walter Bergmann was moved to tears by the first performance of *A Child of our Time* conducted by Walter Goehr. He described it as 'very beautiful'[43]. It is understandable that Walter Bergmann was so moved by the work as it related directly to his own experiences. David Matthews writes[44] in his study of Michael Tippett that Tippett saw the death of the boy not so much as a personal tragedy, but as one inevitable event in the turmoil and horror. It was also an event out of which hope could begin to grow.

It is easy to see why all the musical refugees from Nazi Europe felt Michael Tippett understood them and their suffering. After the first performance, Walter Bergmann had a long discussion about the work with Benjamin Britten. In the days following he wrote an article on Michael Tippett for the Freie Deutsche Kultur monthly magazine. In it, Walter Bergmann stated that the events leading to the shooting in Paris and its consequences were for Tippett a warning of the catastrophe that was to follow[45].

Walter Bergmann finally began training as a fitter on March 30th 1944. He had occupied himself in the interim, between leaving his job at Schott in February and starting war work, in writing and arranging. Although he had given up his main employment with Schott, he still managed to continue with most of the rest of his musical activities throughout his period of training and working as a fitter.

On Sunday April 30th a meeting of 'Recorder Players from London and the Home Counties' was held at Morley College from 11 a.m. to 6 p.m. The day consisted of community playing directed by Walter Bergmann and Stephanie Champion, a lecture by Walter Bergmann and a concert. The concert, of chamber music with recorders, consisted of works by Scarlatti, Telemann, Loeillet, J S Bach, Handel, Purcell, Hotteterre and Arne. Three of the works in the concert were 'by request', these being Telemann's cantata, *Locke nur*, Arne's aria *Under the Greenwood Tree* and movements from Hotteterre's *Suite in D*. The performers included Alison Purves (soprano), Freda Dinn (violin and piano), Paul Blumenfeld (cello), Max Champion and Joan Todhunter (recorders). In May 1944 Walter Bergmann was the soloist in a performance of the Handel *Recorder Concerto* at St Martin in the Fields. At the beginning of June a chamber concert was held at Morley College, for which Walter Bergmann rehearsed Pergolesi's *Stabat Mater*. Tippett conducted the actual concert, with Walter Bergmann playing continuo. On June 22nd he directed a concert of music by Telemann for the London Philharmonic Orchestra Arts Club. This organisation was associated with the London Philharmonic Orchestra and held approximately 100 meetings a year. Membership cost an annual fee of one guinea, but concerts were open to anyone at a charge of 1/6d. The secretary was John Amis, whom Walter Bergmann knew at Morley. Due to the restrictions placed by the war on musical life in London, the Club was extremely well supported. Its activities included concerts, record recitals, lectures and talks. In 1944, recent participants included Edith Sitwell, Louis Macneice, Joyce Grenfell, Ninette de Valois, Antony Hopkins, Phyllis Sellick, Reginald Jacques, Peter Pears, Alan Bush, Matyas Seiber and Michael Tippett.

During June 1944 London was badly disrupted

by flying bombs. (Walter Bergmann still continued with fire-watching duties.) On June 27th only eleven players turned up to Walter Bergmann's recorder classes, and the Morley College Open Day was cancelled. Many parts of London were badly affected including the area around the Bergmann's flat in Belsize Square. In July Walter Bergmann wondered what was happening to his family in Germany, in particular to Tante Vera, about whom he was suddenly very anxious. He completed his training as a fitter on July 27th 1944 and on July 31st he took up employment at a factory, Stanleigh's, near London's King Cross Station. He was to work a 47 hour week, 8a.m. - 5.15 p.m. Monday to Friday, and 8.30 a.m. - 12.30 on Saturdays, but on the days he had classes at Morley he was allowed to leave at 5 p.m. (Tuesdays - Intermediate and Advanced Recorders 6 - 9 p.m.; Wednesday Beginners 6.30 - 8 p.m. On Mondays there was the choir rehearsal.) He participated in as much musical life as he could fit round the hours of factory work. He found working in the factory 'deadly boring'[46]. Although he had little spare time, Walter Bergmann still managed to edit and arrange music, and to be involved in concerts at Morley, the London Philharmonic Arts Club and for the Free German League of Culture. He was also pleased to hear that his edition of Arne's *Under the Greenwood Tree* was used at a Dolmetsch concert in Haslemere in August 1944.

On September 4th 1944, he noted that there had been three days without flying bombs, and that it was the first day of the sixth year of the war. The break from bombs did not last long, with the arrivals of the V2s. September was a difficult and busy month for him. Grete Bergmann went into hospital on September 11th and had an operation on September 20th. Walter Bergmann took part in concerts on both September 22nd and 23rd. The concert on Friday 22nd was a recital of music by young English composers, held under the auspices of the Free German League. Walter Bergmann and Antony Hopkins played Walter Leigh's *Sonatina* for treble recorder and piano. On the Saturday, after working at the factory, Walter Bergmann went to the rehearsal for a concert held at 6 p.m. at Morley of Bach and Telemann. Grete Bergmann came out of hospital on October 7th and he was given a week's leave to look after her. On October 17th she went to stay with a close friend, Victoria Kingsley, to convalesce. During this time, Walter Bergmann continued to work with Antony Hopkins, Alison Purves, Norbert Brainin, Paul Blumenfeld and other musicians associated with Morley.

On October 21st 1944 a significant musical event took place at Morley College. The concert was just one of the regular weekend concerts, but among the performers, making his London debut, was Alfred Deller. The evening included a performance of Tippett's *Plebs Angelica*. This was a motet for double chorus, which had been commissioned by Canon Poole for the Canterbury Cathedral Choir. It was completed in 1943 and first performed in 1944 in the crypt of Canterbury Cathedral. Canon Poole mentioned in correspondence to Michael Tippett that he had an outstanding male alto in the choir and he invited Tippett to go to hear him. Antony Hopkins also heard about Deller through a chance meeting and recommended Tippett should go. As well as being a lay clerk in the cathedral choir, Alfred Deller was a conscientious objector, but had been fortunate enough to be able to combine farm work with his singing. He sang Purcell's *Music for a While* to Michael Tippett. Tippett was delighted when he heard Deller sing. He was deeply interested in Purcell and the revival of his music. It was one of the strong bonds between Michael Tippett and Walter Bergmann. Many concerts at Morley had involved works by Purcell including the renowned performance of *The Ode for St Cecilia*. However a very significant number of Purcell's works require a countertenor, and Tippett had doubted that such a voice existed in the twentieth century. In Deller he realised he had been lucky enough to find a true countertenor. The concert at Morley on October 21st included a Purcell verse anthem *My Beloved Spake* for countertenor, tenor, 2 basses, choir and strings and *Music for a While* edited by Walter Bergmann. Deller came to prefer Walter Bergmann's arrangement of this Purcell song above all others. Tippett and Walter Bergmann worked together to edit Purcell's songs and vocal music, inspired by the suitable voice they had discovered. Walter Bergman did a significant part of the editing, taking the results to Tippett for his approval. Tippett was usually happy with the result.

Life continued to be busy for Walter Bergmann, particularly the month of December 1944. Concerts included one in Leicester on December 7th, given by the London Philharmonic Orchestra and the Leicester Philharmonic Society which was conducted by Michael Tippett. Soloists included Peter Pears. The main work was a performance of *A Child of Our Time*. The first half included Handel's *Concerto Grosso Op. 6 No. 6*, in which Walter Bergmann played the continuo part (on an out-of-tune piano[47]). On December 14th he played continuo for a chamber music concert at the London Philharmonic Arts Club, with Maria Lidka, Norbert Brainin (violins), Paul Blumenfeld (cello) and Jani Strasser (bass). The concert consisted of cantatas by Handel and Purcell and three instrumental pieces including a Bach trio sonata. The following Sunday, December 17th, the Christmas Concert was held at Morley. It included *Pastorale* by Pez for recorders, strings and continuo. A week later on December 24th, Michael Tippett conducted the Liverpool Philharmonic Orchestra and Choir in a concert of Christmas Music and another performance of *A Child of Our Time*. Walter Bergmann played the continuo for Corelli's *Christmas Eve Concerto*. On New Year's Eve 1944, he played in two concerts. The first, held at 2.30 p.m. in the Friend's Meeting House in Euston Road, was given by the Morley Choir and Orchestra to a large audience. The programme included *Plebs Angelica* and the *Ode for St Cecilia's Day* (1692). Walter Bergmann wrote the programme notes. The soloists included sopranos Alison Purves and Margaret Ritchie, Peter Pears (tenor) and more significantly, Alfred Deller, countertenor. This was the first time that the music-going public were really aware of Alfred Deller. Walter Bergmann wrote in the programme 'The performance of Purcell's last and greatest ode on St Cecilia's Day tries to follow as close as possible the original performance in 1692 (when Purcell himself sang one of the countertenor parts with 'incredible graces')'. The concert was a great success, for as Walter Bergmann later remarked, 'Suddenly there was Purcell again'. In the evening of December 31st he took part in a concert given by the Hendon String Orchestra at Queen Mary Hall in which he played the recorder in the first performance of his edition of the John Baston *Concerto in F* for descant recorder.

The Bergmanns spent Christmas 1944 quietly at home with Erica. They had a small, pretty Christmas tree and Erica had a new bicycle as a main present. They celebrated her birthday on the 26th with a small party. 1945 began as busy as ever for Walter Bergmann. He was of course still working in the factory. His professional musical life was settling down into three distinct areas of performing, teaching and editing and writing. He also continued to compose. He was developing a dual career of working with both professional and amateur musicians.

His professional work mainly involved continuo playing. In the field of the recorder there were in Britain virtually no professional players and teachers other than Carl Dolmetsch and Edgar Hunt, and Edgar Hunt was of course serving overseas. Walter Bergmann's involvement in establishing good recorder playing in London was very significant. He was in many ways a link between professional and amateur players - as of course Michael Tippett was and, most importantly, Morley College. Walter Bergmann's role as a professional musician and teacher of amateurs came to be reflected in the music he edited. Concerts in the early part of 1945 included 'An Hour of Music' in the Wigmore Hall, promoted by Ibbs and Tillett, on January 16th, in which Walter Bergmann accompanied Deller in *Music for a While*, and played his own arrangements of the harpsichord variations (*Welcome to all the pleasures that delight*) in a performance of the 1683 *Ode for St Cecilia's Day*. On March 3rd 1945 the Morley College Recorder Class, with Victoria Kingsley, guitar, gave a recital at Sherwood School - Erica Bergmann's school. On March 4th Walter Bergmann played continuo in a concert of violin chamber music at Morley, at which Mewton Wood gave the first performance in Europe of Hindemith's *Ludus Tonalis* for piano. For March 17th Walter Bergmann organised a concert of music for voice, strings and recorders. Antony Hopkins (piano) and Neville Marriner (violin) were among the performers. The programme included a performance of Bach *Brandenburg No 4* (second version) with the solo recorder parts played by Max Champion and Joan Todhunter. The concerto was played again at a concert directed by Walter Bergmann at the London Philharmonic Arts Club on April 12th. The programme also contained a *Concerto* in one movement by Antony Hopkins, and the Hindemith Recorder *Trio*. (*An Introduction and Fugue* for recorder by Walter Bergmann listed in the leaflet advertising the concert did not appear in the concert programme.) On May 6th Walter Bergmann accompanied the soprano Margaret Ritchie in a concert at Morley.

Recorder classes were continuing to flourish at Morley. On February 18th 1945 a discussion on 'The Modern Use of the Recorder' was held at Morley College from 11 a.m. - 5 p.m. The meeting was intended for recorder players and for others involved in the teaching and performing of music, in particular;

'Composers -	Recorder Players need modern ensemble music, suitable for amateurs. The lecture and demonstration will show the kind of music which is required.
Conductors -	Recorders are essential for the proper performance of a number of pre-classical works.
Education Authorities -	The Recorder is an ideal instrument for amateur ensembles and for the musical education of children.
Colleges of Music -	The Recorder should be recognised as a serious instrument.'[48]

The day consisted of a lecture by Walter Bergmann, illustrated by Morley College recorder players and a short recital by Carl Dolmetsch. Michael Tippett acted as Chairman for the day. There were opportunities for discussion and playing. The Pipers' Guild was invited to participate and given the opportunity to demonstrate the bamboo pipes. The Guild's magazine reported in April[49] that the 'Recorder Day' had been a notable occasion. In particular it made mention of Walter Bergmann's lecture on the place of the recorder in the musical world and described the high point of the day as being Carl Dolmetsch's playing of Lennox Berkeley's *Sonatina*, the first work in a new series of contemporary works for solo recorder published by Schott.

Walter Bergmann was also editing music in any spare moment he had. Music he completed editing over 1944/45 included *Music for a While* (Purcell), a Handel Suite for recorders and piano, a Handel Cantata *Sei pur bella, pur vezzosa* and a *Quartet* for clarinet, viola, cello and piano by Jean Francois Tapray.

The war was at last drawing to a close. VE Day (Victory in Europe) came on May 8th 1945. Walter Bergmann knew that he was extremely fortunate to be in the position in which he found himself at the end of the war. On July 23rd 1945, he wrote in his diary for the first time since February. He had not had the time or inclination to do so because he was so busy and happy[50]. The music he researched and edited was being performed in public and accepted for publication. His work teaching and with amateur recorder players was becoming well established and recognised. In July 1945 there was another recorder playing day at Morley. The performers at the concert included an interesting representative group of a number of Walter Bergmann's friends, Hilde Alexander, Max Champion, Marylin Wailes, the Morley College Recorder Group and Hilde Volhard. As a performer Walter Bergmann was regularly being asked to play continuo and performing with Michael Tippett, the Morley College Choir and other professional musicians such as Alfred Deller. On July 9th 1945 he took part in a BBC broadcast for the first time, playing continuo for the Morley College Choir.

In his personal life Walter Bergmann was relatively secure in his small family and had made many friends - those at Morley such as Michael Tippett, John Amis and Antony Hopkins; friends he had made on arriving in Britain like Dr Edwards, the Alexanders and Victoria Kingsley; those he had met through the recorder, for example Marylin Wailes, Joan Todhunter and Ken Kenworthy and then there were still friends from the past including Hilde Volhard and Erika Seelig. Hugh Strecker wrote of Walter Bergman's first years in England, 'Looking back, I think Walter's main achievement in those early years in London was how well and cheerfully he adapted himself to the difficult circumstances and surroundings and really made the best and the most of them.'[51]

Walter Bergmann was given a holiday from the factory where he worked as a fitter in the first week of July and finally released from war work on July 14th 1945. Edgar Hunt wrote in his obituary of Walter Bergmann that during his time working at the factory he had taken the opportunity to study 'the British sense of humour and the cockney vernacular'[52].

His contentment at the end of the war was saddened by the news of his family in Germany. He heard via Sweden in June 1945 that Vera Bergmann was dead (she had committed suicide rather than be arrested), and also another aunt, Agnes. Of his brothers, he received no news.

Walter Bergmann returned to his job at Schott on August 1st 1945, thankful for his survival and prospects. He felt he could face the future in Britain with optimism.

1. Barry Turner, *And the Policeman Smiled*, (London: Gould Publishing, 1990),p. 143.
2. Turner, (1990), p.144
3. Diary 3, 04.11.39
4. 'der Flötist technisch ausgezeichnet musikalisch ohne Wärme'; Diary 4, 08.11.3
5. Diary 5, 22.01.40
6. Diary 5, 07.03.40
7. Turner, (1990), p. 144
8. Turner, (1990), p.144
9. Diary 7, 16.07.40
10. Turner, (1990),, p.,148
11. Edgar Hunt to Anne Martin, 28.02.91; see also 'Walter Bergmann, an eightieth birthday tribute.' Edgar Hunt in *Recorder and Music*, Vol. 7 No. 7, September 1982.
12. 'Gal spielt ohne viel Technik aber sehr musikalisch.' Diary 7, 17.04.40
13. Diary 7, 21.08.40 p. 59
14. Diary 7, 09.09.40 p. 66
15. Diary 7, 25.12.40 p. 82
16. 'So ging das furchtbare Jahr aus und kam das noch furchtbarere.' Diary 7 04.01.41
17. 'Ich bin sehr deprimiert darüber.' Diary 7, 17.01.41
18. Diary 6, 05.02.41
19. Erica Bendix to Anne Martin, 26.02.91
20. Diary 6, 26.07.41
21. Lewis Foreman, From *Parry to Britten*, (London: Batsford 1987) p. 222
22. John Amis, 'Wartime Morley' in Ian Kemp (ed.), Michael Tippett, A Symposium on his 60th Birthday: (London, Faber 1965), p. 73
23. Walter Bergmann in Kemp, ed. (1965),p.81
24. Michael Tippett in *Early Music*, May 1988, p319
25. Bergmann, in Kemp, ed. (1965),p.81
26. *The Times*, 24.11.41
27. Bergmann, in Kemp, ed. (1965),p.81
28. Diary 8, 17.11.41
29. Letter from Hugh Strecker to Anne Martin, 24.02.91
30. Michael Tippett, *Those Twentieth Century Blues*, (London; Hutchinson 1991), p.126
31. Edgar Hunt, *The Recorder and its Music*, (London, Eulenberg 1977), p.142
32. Letter from Ken Kenworthy to Anne Martin, 24.09.91
33. Letter from Erica Bendix to Anne Martin, 26.02.91
34. Free German League of Culture, Freie Deutsche Kultur, (London) Oct 1944) p.14
35. Letter from Ken Kenworthy to Erica Bendix, 18.06.88
36. ' 'Mein' Concert in Morley College. Sehr grossen Erfolg.' 'Sehr grosser Erfolg für recorder u. unser Recorder Consort. Wir haben 1/2 Jahr daran geprobt.', Diary 8, 10.04.43
37. 'Rehearsal without Michael', Diary 8, 24.06.43
38. Bergmann, in Kemp, ed. (1965), p.81
39. 'Heftige Proben mit dem Chor. Er ist doch sehr schwierig...', Diary 8, 15.07.43
40. Letter from Ken Kenworthy to Erica Bendix, 18.06.88
41. Bergmann, in Kemp, ed., (1965) p.81
42. Michael Tippett, Early Music, May 1988, p319
43. Diary 9, 19.03.44
44. David Matthews, Michael Tippett, *An introductory study*, (London:Faber 1965), p.33
45. 'Für Tippett war der Schuss von Paris, was ihm vorher ging und folgte, eine Warnung vor der kommenden Katastrophe unserer Zeit, wie sie später in dem zweiten Weltkrieg eintrat.' Walter Bergmann, 'Michael Tippett' in *'Freie Deutsche Kultur* Mai/ Juni 1944, p. 6
46. 'Die Arbeit in der Fabrik ist tödlich langweilig.' Diary 10 22.08.44
47. Diary 10, 07.12.44
48. Morley College Leaflet advertising the meeting
49. *The Piping Times*, Journal of the Pipers' Guild Vol. IV No. 4, April 1945, p.93
50. 'Die Zeit war voll energisch und glücklich für mich in vielen kleinen Einzelheiten.' Diary 10, 23.07.45
51. Hugh Strecker to Anne Martin, 24.02.91
52. *The Recorder and Music Magazine* Vol. 9 No. 5 March 1988, p. 125; Schott & Co.

International
Summer School
Leoben, nr. Graz
1952

Bergmann & Barthel
Summer School
Berlin 1955

6. Post-war years up to the end of 1959

With the end of the war, restrictions on musical life began to be lifted. In July 1945 Walter Bergmann went to concerts given by Casals and Menuhin. He enjoyed the Menuhin concert more than that given by Casals, describing Menuhin as a 'wonderful player' and a 'great classical violinist'[1]. After his release from factory work on July 14th, he spent two weeks at home, trying to get his life in order. From the autumn of 1945 he began to be very busy. Classes resumed at Morley, and at Schott there were 'thousands' of descant recorders to check and pack[2]. Grete and he entertained friends and musical acquaintances. The reality of possible contact with Germany began to appear. On September 7th Erika Seelig left for Germany, returning as an interpreter. Walter Bergmann was busy with concerts and lecture engagements, and he did not have time to write in his diary. Concerts in which he participated between July and the end of 1945 included an evening at the Jordans Music Club in Buckinghamshire with Michael Tippett, Alfred Deller and the Morley College Choir (three ladies from Jordans, a well-known firm making wholesome breakfast cereal, were in the Morley recorder classes), a lunch-time recital in London for the City Music Society with Esther Salaman (mezzo-soprano), Morley concerts, and a concert for the London Philharmonic Arts Club consisting of music by Bach and Telemann and the first performance of Walter Bergmann's *Septet for Two Treble Pipes and Five Treble Recorders* (1945), which was dedicated to John Amis. At the end of October he played the piano at a concert in the National Gallery.

A weekend recorder meeting was held at Morley at the beginning of November, to which bamboo pipe players were invited. Michael Tippett lectured on Purcell, and there was an ensemble competition. During the weekend there were two concerts; the first was given by Alfred Deller, Jani Strasser (bass) and Antony Hopkins (piano) and a number of recorder players. The programme included the new *Septet*, music by Purcell, Blow, Hindemith's *Recorder Trio* and a work by Hopkins for piano and recorder. The second concert included recorder concertos by Baston and Woodcock, the performers including Carl Dolmetsch, Max Champion (recorders), Walter Bergmann (recorder and piano), Delia Ruhm (flute), Paul Blumenfeld (cello) and Thurston Dart (piano).

On Thursday November 22nd Walter Bergmann played continuo at the Wigmore Hall in the second of two concerts organised to commemorate the 250th anniversary of Purcell's death. The programme consisted of music by Purcell and Britten. The Morley College Choir participated, conducted by Tippett, as did Britten himself, Peter Pears (tenor), Edward Armitage (countertenor), Owen Brannigan (bass), Margaret Ritchie (soprano), the Zorian String Quartet and Don Cheeseman (double bass). Walter Bergmann realised all the continuo parts. The concert included the first performance of Britten's *The Holy Sonnets of John Donne*. All the artists donated their services free, and the proceeds went to the India Relief Committee. December found Walter Bergmann back at the Wigmore Hall with the Morley College Recorder Consort, playing in a concert given by Jani Strasser and others, including Antony Hopkins, Leon Goossens (cor anglais), Suzanne Rozsa and Neville Marriner (violins) and Martin Lovett (cello). Eight recorders accompanied Strasser in a Purcell cantata *When Night her purple veil*. The concert was reported in The Times (10.12.45), and the critic remarked that the cantata was a 'fine example' of Purcell's dramatic style. The accompanying octet of recorders was described as blending beautifully with the voice.

December also included two visits to Kent; one to Canterbury to give a concert with Alfred Deller and the flautist Delia Ruhm, and the other to Sevenoaks to give a lecture entitled 'Purcell as seen by a foreigner'. As always he was busy editing and arranging music.

On December 22nd 1945 Walter Bergmann heard from his brother Fritz in Germany for the first time since before the war. He was thankful that both of his brothers had survived. Fritz told him more about Tante Vera's death and that of her brother Georg. Although saddened by the news from Germany, Walter, Grete and Erica Bergmann spent a pleasant Christmas together. On December 26th, the small party for Erica's thirteenth birthday was made memorable because a friend brought a bottle of red wine. Walter Bergmann noted in his diary he had dreamt of a bottle of red wine for years![3]

In 1946 Walter Bergmann continued working with Alfred Deller. He also auditioned for the BBC, playing with the bassoonist Norman Fawcett. The programme included music by Hindemith. (They eventually broadcast together in 1948.) In March Walter Bergmann gave a 9-minute talk in German for the BBC, on Tippett's *A Child of our Time*. In July he accompanied Deller and David Martin for a BBC broadcast. Deller was again one of the soloists at a Recorder Meeting at Morley in April 1946. The concert programme included music by Pelham Humfrey, Purcell, Handel, Schütz, Telemann and a performance of Bach's *Cantata 39*. Other named performers included Alison Purves (soprano), Edgar Hunt, Marylin Wailes and Hilde Volhard (recorders), Norbert Brainin (violin), Pamela Hind (cello), Thurston Dart (figured bass) and Walter Bergmann (conductor). Walter Bergmann was still closely involved with Morley College. In a concert at Westfield College in May, he conducted members of the Morley College Choir in a programme of sixteenth and seventeenth century music given with Antony Hopkins (harpsichord) and Alison Purves. In June Walter Bergmann played the solo descant part in the Baston *Concerto in C* in a concert in Hendon. In July the Morley College Recorders played in the first performance in Britain of Monteverdi's *Vespers of 1610*, at Central Hall Westminster, which was conducted by Walter Goehr. Morley College's reputation was growing after the war and was enhanced by the choir and orchestra's participation in this first complete modern performance of the Vespers. By the 1946/47 session, there were two choirs at Morley, run by Michael Tippett, assisted by Walter Bergmann and Alfred Deller. Entry was by audition.

In spite of a busy schedule, Walter Bergmann found time to compose, and Deller and Delia Ruhm gave the first performance of his *Pastorale* for countertenor and flute in Canterbury in June 1946. Delia Ruhm also played Walter Bergmann's *Sonata* for flute, composed in 1942. The local paper said the two compositions 'took the audience by storm'. 'The *Pastorale* for contra-tenor and flute - a too rare and lovely combination of musical sounds - was extremely beautiful with its enchanting intervals in the melody, its semi-tone of voice against the flute, its untraditional but very satisfying conclusion, and, throughout, its capture of the essence of pastoral music.'

At the end of August 1946 Walter Bergmann spent two weeks in Skye. He thoroughly enjoyed the holiday. On the last day, he contemplated his working life. He decided he always felt so tired because his life was split four ways between his work at Schott, the choir and recorders at Morley, concerts and composing and arranging. Arguments with Goehr and Tippett were also not helping. Nevertheless he started planning the next few months. His immediate tasks were to become naturalised, find music for Christmas and for the resumption of the choir evening class in the new autumn session and write articles. At Schott his work load and position had in fact become easier with the return of Edgar Hunt. Hunt did not return immediately to Schott after he was demobbed in 1945. He did not want to disturb Walter Bergmann's position. However rumours were spread that Walter Bergmann was deliberately keeping Edgar Hunt out of Schott. Edgar Hunt went back to Schott and it soon transpired there was room for both of them. Hunt took over responsibility for the instrument side of the business - a replacement needed to be found for a source of good wooden instruments, as pre-war makers were now situated in East Germany, and there was a need for better plastic instruments that could be mass-produced in the UK. Walter Bergmann continued to be responsible for music publications. Hugh Strecker also returned to Schott as a Director. He did not get on very well with Max Steffens, which did not help the running of the company[4].

By January 1947 Walter Bergmann was still waiting to be naturalised. He dreamt of moving to Germany or Switzerland. At home, Erica was now fourteen and in the middle of difficult teenage years. In February the Bergmanns moved from 30 Belsize Square to 28 Belsize Square. The new flat consisted of the top two floors of the house and gave them much more living space. Walter Bergmann was now in regular contact with his German friends such as Dietrich Gerhardt and Arnold Matz.

During 1947 he worked regularly with Alfred Deller. They worked closely together, each giving the other professional support. In the early years Alfred Deller was grateful for Walter Bergmann's encouragement.

As Deller gained public recognition and acclaim, he was able to staunchly stand by Walter Bergmann and insist sometimes on the latter accompanying him. In January 1947 they unfortunately arrived too late due to snow and ice to give a concert in Leicester. They eventually gave the concert in July. Walter Bergmann accompanied Deller singing *Music for a While* as an illustration for one of a series of lectures given by Michael Tippett, which were broadcast by the BBC.

By December 1947 Walter Bergmann had played seven times in a radio broadcast, mainly harpsichord continuo. These included participation in several other broadcasts given by Tippett and in a group playing a trio sonata to illustrate a talk given by Scott Goddard on 'Music of the Western Masters'. Morley College concerts continued to be successful. Walter Bergmann played the harpsichord continuo for one such concert, given in the Central Hall Westminster in March 1947, which was conducted by Tippett and Walter Goehr and included Bach's *Magnificat* and a Purcell *Coronation Anthem*. Alfred Deller was one of the soloists. Another concert, also held in the Central Hall in November, included the Purcell 1692 *Ode for St Cecilia's Day* and Tallis' motet in 40 parts, *Spem in alium*. The conductors were once again Tippett and Goehr, with Walter Bergmann, Alfred Deller, Peter Pears and Margaret Ritchie among the performers.

In 1947 Walter Bergmann tried to find more time for composing, completing *Five Studies* for recorder. In August he was invited to the Pipers' Guild Summer School who liked the work he had completed in 1945 for pipes and recorders - *The Septet*. Walter Bergmann had submitted this for approval by the Committee for the Promotion of New Music. The Committee were not impressed with either the work or the recorder as a serious instrument. *The Septet* was described as being in 'Berlin 1928 style' and the recorder considered an unsuitable instrument for a fugue. The Chairman, Dr Mosco Carner expressed the opinion that the recorder was 'just like a tuning fork, only a tuning fork is always in tune'![5] With such a view of the recorder it is not surprising that the work was rejected.

Walter Bergmann was by 1947 closely involved with the Society of Recorder Players. He was invited to 'collaborate' with the Society until the rules could be changed to allow for more than two musical directors. By 1947 there were SRP groups in London, Birmingham, Leicester, Manchester and Bristol. In March 1947, the SRP sponsored a concert at the Art Workers' Guild in Queen Square. The performers included the Dolmetsch Family and Joseph Saxby, Freda Dinn, Thurston Dart, Edgar Hunt, Alison Purves and Walter Bergmann. The programme consisted of Baroque music (Loeillet, Pepusch, Telemann, Handel etc.) and English consort music. It was so popular it had to be repeated. Another significant event was the gathering of 400 children for a recorder festival at Roehampton, conducted by Walter Bergmann and Freda Dinn.

Walter Bergmann's work at Schott, editing music and teaching at Morley continued. For the first time since coming to Britain the Bergmanns had a summer holiday together, borrowing a house at Saltdean near Brighton in August 1947. Erica had taken an entrance examination for a local London day school, but it was decided to leave her at boarding school in Epsom. Two other significant events during 1947 for Walter Bergmann were his second meeting in June with Hindemith, 25 years after they had first met, when they discussed Hindemith's *Recorder Trio*, and the visit, later the same month, by Percy Grainger to one of the recorder evening classes at Morley. The latter was apparently enchanted by the sound of recorders.

In 1948 Walter Bergmann was made a Musical Director of the Society of Recorder Players. The Society also began to expand its range of activities. The first 'Recorder in Education' Summer School was held at Roehampton in the summer of 1948. The five founder tutors were Freda Dinn, Walter Bergmann, Thurston Dart, Carl Dolmetsch and Edgar Hunt. The participants were divided into four groups. In the *Recorder Newsletter Number 5*, Walter Bergmann was noted for 'his charming impatience and quick wit'[6].

Walter Bergmann submitted another work to the Committee for the Promotion of New Music, a *Sonata* for pipe and piano. He initially received an encouraging report, but as with the previous submission, the work was eventually rejected although one member of the selection panel commented 'Being for an unusual instrument, I feel that this would make quite interesting hearing'[7]. Walter Bergmann's playing commitments in 1948 included a concert in January of Polish music at the Polish Embassy, with the Morley College Choir and Orchestra, which Michael Tippett conducted. Walter Bergmann played continuo and the trumpet soloist was Philip Jones. In September Norman Fawcett finally played Hindemith's *Bassoon Sonata* with Walter Bergmann in a radio broadcast, and later in the year in November, Walter Bergmann played continuo in a broadcast of Purcell's *Ode for St Cecilia*. In September 1948 he also purchased a harpsichord.

1949 was a busy and significant year for Walter Bergmann. In March he accompanied Alfred Deller making his first recording for HMV. They recorded a number of Purcell songs, including *If music be the food of love* and *Music for a while*, which became Deller's 'signature' tune. In May 1949 he finally received his naturalisation papers.

England was now home. He became Musical Director of the London Branch of the Society of Recorder Players (a position he held until 1968). The SRP was continuing both to expand and gain further recognition. A concert given by the Society in May 1949 attracted an audience of 300, two-thirds of which were non-members. (By this date six evening institutes in London were offering recorder classes.) A Junior Branch of the Society of Recorder Players had been founded with Freda Dinn as Musical Director. In September 1949 a performance of Blow's *Ode on the death of Henry Purcell*, edited by Walter Bergmann, was given at a weekend recorder meeting at Morley College. Antony Hopkins conducted and Walter Bergmann played continuo. Watkin Shaw wrote in *The Listener* of his regret that the concert had not been broadcast. The concert was repeated at St. Martin's in the Fields on December 7th 1949, the 300th Anniversary of Blow's birth. A new activity for Walter Bergmann in 1949 was adjudicating. In June he adjudicated at the Tunbridge Wells Music Festival. He also continued to spend a significant amount of time arranging and editing music. In fact Edgar Hunt became so concerned that his and Walter Bergmann's names dominated Schott's recorder music, that for a short while they both published some editions under pseudonyms, Walter Bergmann's being T. S. Walker.

During 1950 Walter Bergmann was too busy to keep a diary. There was a gap of entries of nearly two years. He participated in all his usual activities. The annual SRP Concert took place at the Royal College of Music, the performers including Alfred Deller, Norman Platt (bass), Thurston Dart, Edgar Hunt and Carl Dolmetsch. There was also a concert for the Junior Section of the SRP, which involved Freda Dinn, Walter Bergmann, Carl Dolmetsch and Edgar Hunt. A significant event for Walter Bergmann in 1950 was a recorder week in Salzburg in July. The week was planned to bring together players from different countries 'so that each could gain a wider vision of the musical life of the others and an insight into their methods and difficulties'[8]. It was organised by Kurt Pitsch, a pioneer recorder player in Austria, and held at the headquarters of the Austro-British Society. Walter Bergmann took a party of British players. During his stay, he gave a lecture on British music at the invitation of the British Council. Erica Bergmann went with her father to Austria, from where they travelled to Ludwigshafen in Germany and met Fritz Bergmann for the first time since 1939. Walter Bergmann also broadcast two programmes for Südwestfunk on music in England, with special reference to the countertenor, then virtually unknown in Germany and Austria. In October 1950 he recorded some more Purcell songs with Alfred Deller.

The Festival of Britain dominated events in 1951. With its growing reputation, Morley College played a significant role in the specially organised events. A Morley College Society had been established with Professor Edward Dent as President and William Walton as Chairman, to promote and give concerts. The Morley College Players performed Shakespeare's *Winter's Tale* at the George Inn, Southwark and Walter Bergmann directed the music. The orchestral players were members of the Morley College Telemann Orchestra and the Recorder Ensemble. (The Telemann Orchestra was formed by Walter Bergmann in 1951.) One of the highlights of the Festival of Britain for Walter Bergmann must have been the performance of the Monteverdi *1610 Vespers* in the newly opened Royal Festival Hall on May 16th. The performance was a revival of the 1946 concert, with Walter Goehr conducting the Morley College Choir, the Philharmonia Orchestra, and the Morley College Recorder Ensemble led by Walter

Bergmann. Ralph Downes played the organ and Thurston Dart the harpsichord. The concert brought Monteverdi's music to a much wider public than the original concert. In June 1951 Walter Bergmann participated in a concert at the Victoria and Albert Museum conducted by Michael Tippett. This concert was one of a series devoted to the music of Henry Purcell. The Morley College Choir and Recorder Ensemble again participated. Walter Bergmann played the harpsichord. The soloists included Margaret Ritchie, Jennifer Vyvyan (soprano) and Alfred Deller. The concert was broadcast by the BBC the following day.

On a lighter note, Walter Bergmann directed the Morley College Telemann Orchestra and Madrigal Choir at the Lambeth Festival in a concert entitled 'Vauxhall Gardens 1851'. The programme was made up of pieces of music that would have been heard in the gardens in the few years just before their closure in 1851. Another unusual opportunity for Walter Bergmann in September 1951 was his involvement in a production of *The Tempest* at the original Mermaid Theatre.

The Mermaid Theatre opened at the home of Bernard Miles in 1951. The Miles family had bought Duff House in St John's Wood in 1945. The building had been a school with a well-proportioned hall, although by the end of the war it was in a derelict state. Bernard Miles saw the possibility of turning the hall into a small theatre. The dramatic soprano Kirstin Flagstad, who was a family friend, was persuaded to try out the acoustics of the room. She immediately agreed to come to sing there if the theatre conversion was made. The Miles' suggested she came to sing in a production of *Dido and Aeneas*. Bernard Miles and his wife Josephine Wilson became very excited about the new project. They created an Elizabethan stage for a short season of music and drama during the Festival of Britain and obtained the backing of Ivor Novello. Twenty performances of *Dido and Aeneas* and twenty of *The Tempest* were planned to be performed before a privately invited audience. The performers gave their services free. Maggie Teyte (soprano) and Thomas Hemsley (baritone) joined Kirstin Flagstad to sing in *Dido and Aeneas*. Both Flagstad and Teyte had international reputations for their operatic roles. Thomas Hemsley made his operatic debut at the Mermaid. Bernard Miles played Caliban in *The Tempest* and his wife Josephine, Miranda. Walter Bergmann arranged the incidental music for *The Tempest* and directed a small ensemble group from the harpsichord (lent by Robert Salkeld). The musicians consisted of a small group of strings, a serpent and six recorder players. The whole venture was extremely successful.

Walter Bergmann's involvement with recorder players and the recorder movement in general was continually growing. At the end of July 1951, for a second year running, he took a party of players abroad, this time to a summer recorder meeting in Innsbruck. Erica Bergmann once again accompanied her father. This second gathering of recorder players gave German, Austrian and British players another opportunity to play together and exchange ideas. The Austrian players included Hans Ulrich Staeps. Walter Bergmann recorded in his diary[9] that he recognised that Staeps was a good player, but he did not like his use of vibrato. Walter Bergmann also thoroughly disagreed with Staep's suggestion that school children should first be taught to play on the recorder in D.

Most of the first week of the Innsbruck course was devoted to preparing a concert of seventeenth century and modern music to be played at the British Council. The programme included solo works by Walter Leigh and Herbert Murrill, played by Staeps and a pupil of Carl Dolmetsch, Michael Walton, and the *Sonata a 7* for recorders by Johann Schmelzer, an Austrian composer (c 1630 - 1680). The Schmelzer sonata was re-introduced back to Austria through this performance. The manuscript had been discovered in the library of Uppsala University in Sweden. Schott (London) published an edition by Ernst Meyer in 1948. Considering the overall standard of recorder playing on the course, Walter Bergmann observed that the standard of individual playing was higher among the German and Austrian players, but the British standard of ensemble playing was higher.

From Austria, Walter and Erica Bergmann met with Fritz Bergmann and his wife Anneliese, this time in the German town of Mittenwald, just across the border from Austria. While in Innsbruck Walter Bergmann visited the Hofkirche and remembered his previous visit in 1913 during a family holiday spent in Mayrhofen in the Zillertal. The memory of the holiday in the comfortable security before the First World War must have seemed totally unreal.

On his return to England, Walter Bergmann went to the Roehampton Summer School. The Sunday of the course was devoted to Telemann; a Telemann 'orgy' according to J. Tadman in the 1951 December edition of the *Recorder News*[10]. Walter Bergmann lectured on Telemann and two Telemann concertos were performed.

As ever Walter Bergmann was arranging, editing and writing. This included music for Schott, Morley College, the Society of Recorder Players and school children; keyboard realisations and writing programme notes for concerts (sometimes for Michael Tippett). In November 1951 he gave a lecture at Downing College, Cambridge on 'The Continuo, problems in our time'. During 1951 he also joined the Performing Rights Society.

By 1951 Walter Bergmann had worked at Schott for ten years, but things were not running particularly smoothly. He was not always an easy man to get on with and he often found it easier to talk to women than men. There were other individuals at Schott who were also not particularly easy to work with! Throughout his life Walter Bergmann did not always feel secure in either the work relationships or friendships he made. He was also unsure of his ability to be successful. Michael Tippett[11] writes in his autobiography that Walter Bergmann never got on well with Howard Hartog who was responsible for the publication of modern music at Schott. Hartog 'was not in sympathy with recorders and early music and thus never saw eye to eye with Walter Bergmann'. As well as finding problems at Schott, Walter Bergmann felt Morley College activities were also not running as they had during the war years. From 1949 onwards Michael Tippett had begun to reduce his involvement with the College as he devoted increasing time to composition. He finally resigned from his post at Morley in June 1951. By this time Walter Goehr had already taken over most of Tippett's commitments. Walter Bergmann was not completely happy with the new organisational arrangements under Walter Goehr.

Walter Bergmann had worked closely with Michael Tippett editing Purcell. By 1951 Tippett was devoting virtually all his working time to compositions, and both the working relationship and friendship between himself and Walter Bergmann were not as close as they had been in the 1940s. They still came into professional contact with each other at Schott. Walter Bergmann found Tippett's teasing and off-hand manner hard to cope with and took it very personally. On October 9th 1951 he wrote to Michael Tippett deploring the latter's attitude towards a score they were working on together. He complained about Tippett's apparent lack of consideration towards himself to the extent of ignoring him and missing an appointment. Walter Bergmann stated to Tippett 'there is no choice for me but to end our collaboration'[12].

The following day Walter Bergmann also wrote a strongly-worded letter to Schott's Managing Director, Max Steffens. From the letter[13] it is apparent that Walter Bergmann felt he was being unfairly criticised at work. He had obviously been reprimanded by someone, for receiving private telephone calls during office hours and for having an untidy desk. In his letter to Steffens, Walter Bergmann criticised the lack of formal organisation at Schott. He expressed the opinion that his special talents were underused and not appreciated as he had to waste his time doing mundane tasks others could do. He believed that apart from Edgar Hunt, there was no musician in a position at Schott to be able to develop an overall policy for the publication of music. Some areas were being neglected, for example schools' publications. In his letter, Walter Bergmann set out proposals for the reorganisation of the recorder department of Schott. He asked for reassurance from Steffens that he would be a member of any reading panel formed to select and publish music composed before 1800; he asked that a secretary should be available for his use and that his salary should be a minimum of £10 per week. He also informed Steffens that he had ended his collaboration with Michael Tippett. As to his own health and prospects, he was very pessimistic. He wrote: 'I must know where I stand. I am in a productive period and have not very long to live.'

Michael Tippett's reaction to Walter Bergmann's letter was genuine concern. He had been pulling Walter Bergmann's leg and had fully intended keeping the arranged appointment to discuss their joint editing. He wrote to Walter Bergmann[14]

'Your behaviour is as mystifying to me as mine to you.' Tippett acknowledged that he was not an easy person to collaborate with, but pointed out that his own priorities were composition and earning enough money to support himself so that he could continue to compose. Earning money for its own sake was of secondary importance to him. Although his collaboration with Walter Bergmann was not of first importance to him, Tippett wrote that this in no way affected their friendship, 'My affection for you remains unchanged.' He expressed his concern that Walter Bergmann was too over-sensitive, which he suggested was often a problem of those who are artistic. Tippett pointed out that he must come to terms with this or have continual problems in his working life. Tippett was perhaps aware that Walter Bergmann was not finding working relationships at Schott very easy.

Financially life was by this time easier for the Bergmanns. Grete Bergmann had purchased a restaurant, The Dorice, with a partner, although after a year she sold out, following a disagreement. With the money from this sale, bank loans and the help of friends she bought another restaurant, 'The Cosmo', where she had worked in the latter part of the war (in Swiss Cottage). Hugh Strecker was a sleeping partner. The work was extremely hard, often 8a.m. to midnight. Erica who had by now left school, worked there as well. With Walter Bergmann's earnings the Bergmanns' income was reasonably sound and secure - though Walter Bergmann was never a very good businessman. In June 1951 he purchased the manuscripts of two sonatas by William Flackton (nos. VII and VIII) and presented them to the British Museum. He was aware of how important his access to manuscripts had been in his early years in Britain and in helping him make a career for himself. England had provided him with a new life and a musical career for which he was extremely grateful - even if he sometimes could not fathom the English and their way of thinking! In the Spring of 1952 he was called for jury service at the Old Bailey, bringing home to him that he was now truly a British subject.

One organisation Walter Bergmann found very difficult to understand was the BBC. A significant professional engagement for him in August 1951 was his involvement in the broadcast of the Telemann cantata *Locke nur, Erde*. He had edited the work and he played continuo in the broadcast performance. Apart from involvement in schools' broadcasts, (and his *Pastorale* was broadcast on New Zealand radio, an alto singing the counter tenor part) this was the only broadcast work of any consequence in which he participated during 1951. During the year, Walter Bergmann started writing to the BBC to try to establish what he regarded as fair treatment for, and professional recognition of, specialised harpsichord continuo playing. In a letter written in July 1951[15] he asked Herbert Murrill why editors of keyboard realisations of figured basses were not acknowledged by announcers, or listed in the Radio Times, while on some occasions arrangers of other music, perhaps involving less skill, were acknowledged. Walter Bergmann pointed out that he had not received fees when his realisations were performed by other musicians in radio broadcasts. Regarding the matter of fees, Herbert Murrill replied[16] that as a member of the Performing Rights Society (which of course Walter Bergmann had only recently joined) he should receive appropriate fees. On the matter of acknowledging editors of music, Murrill stated that it was difficult to find time and space to include them, and also problematic to work out criteria for deciding which editors' work justified recognition.

Exactly what was a 'continuo part' and what was a 'harpsichord accompaniment' was proving difficult for the BBC's musical bureaucracy. Walter Bergmann found himself in further correspondence with the BBC in connection with Alfred Deller. The BBC were keen for Deller to give a solo broadcast, which he had not done by 1951, in spite of his enormous success. He wanted to use Walter Bergmann as his harpsichord accompanist, particularly as he wished to sing songs using Walter Bergmann's realisations. At the end of 1951, the BBC refused to allow Walter Bergmann to accompany Deller on a solo broadcast. Perplexed, Walter Bergmann wrote to Denis Stevens at the BBC, sending him manuscript examples of his realisations and pointing out that he was a specialist in this field. Denis Stevens acknowledged the manuscripts, making no reference to Walter Bergman's letter except to say he would bear them in mind for future broadcast performances[17]. The confusing nature of the BBC's attitude towards Walter Bergmann was increased by a letter to him in February 1952 inviting him to practise on the BBC's newly acquired harpsichord. In March Walter Bergmann wrote to Denis Stevens again[18], pointing out that he was a specialist continuo player and that he had sent the manuscripts to illustrate this, not as materials for future programmes. With the letter he included examples of three programmes Deller and he could perform, these being: 1.Purcell Songs; 2. Blow's *Ode on the Death of Henry Purcell*; 3. Music by Christoph Bernhard (1628-1692) and Dietrich Buxtehude (1637- 1701). In reply, Walter Bergmann received another non-committal letter from Denis Stevens.

By September 1952 still no progress had been made on a broadcast for Deller, and Walter Bergmann wrote to Norman Carrell, the BBC's Music Booking Manager, requesting an explanation. As a regular accompanist to Deller he wanted to know why the BBC were reluctant to use him and he pointed out to Carrell that the 'attitude of the BBC would be detrimental not only for my activity there but also for my artistic career altogether'[19]. In his answer, Norman Carrell at last explained why the BBC would not employ Walter Bergmann to accompany Alfred Deller. He was on the BBC's books as a harpsichord continuo player and a recorder player, but not as a pianist. In the eyes of the BBC anyone who was a professional accompanist played the piano. Therefore Walter Bergmann was not eligible to act as an accompanist to a solo singer, i.e. Alfred Deller. Carrell wrote[20].

'The reason why our Programme Builders were unable to accept you as pianist to Alfred Deller is that you are not on our official list of accompanists.'

Yet again Walter Bergmann wrote back to the BBC explaining that Alfred Deller wanted him as an accompanist precisely because he was not a pianist but a harpsichordist! He asked for an appointment with Norman Carrell. The matter was finally resolved after a meeting with Carrell in November 1952. Walter Bergmann at last received a letter stating,

'Further to our recent meeting, your point regarding 'continuo' as opposed to 'accompaniment' has been discussed with the Artists' Committee and it has been agreed that a figured or unfigured bass line which has to be realised by the performer constitutes a continuo even though it is in support of one solo instrument or solo voice only'[21].

This change in the attitude by the BBC, achieved by Walter Bergmann, was significant for the burgeoning early music movement in Britain. From the 1950s onwards there came the emergence of a new group of musicians who could be described as 'performing scholars' or 'scholarly performers'[22]. Along with other more well known musicians such as Thurston Dart, Denis Stevens, Karl Richter and Raymond Leppard, Walter Bergmann was one of this new breed of post-war musicians. During the first part of the century, those interested in Early Music fell mainly into two camps, the musicologists on one hand, and the performers on the other. Amateur musicians also played a significant role in the performance of early music. One significant exception to this division into musicologists and performers was of course Arnold Dolmetsch. Arnold Dolmetsch's pioneering work in England was of great importance in laying down the beginnings of a serious Early Music Movement in England. He established an internationally recognised workshop for the manufacture of early instruments and in 1925 an annual festival of early music, The Haslemere Festival. He linked performance, scholarship and craftsmanship. Arnold Dolmetsch did not however collaborate with many other musicians other than those who had studied with him. His technical restrictions in performance and sometimes suspect scholarship led to a slightly ambivalent attitude in the fifties and sixties towards his achievements. His status was also affected by his apparent association with amateur musicians. The new breed of performers after the Second World War wanted to get away from this. They did not want early music to be linked with amateur musicians. They aimed to move the performance and practice of early music firmly into the realms of professional musicians.

Both Walter Bergmann and Thurston Dart (each continuo specialists) saw the importance of establishing respect for the performance of early music. During the war and in the years directly after it, musicians such as Michael Tippett at Morley with Walter Goehr and Walter Bergmann, performed and encouraged the performance of previously forgotten treasures of Renaissance and Baroque music by composers such as Monteverdi, Purcell and Telemann. They had established a respect and growing interest in such music that could be developed and built on. In 1954 Thurston Dart published a book entitled *The Interpretation of Music*, which significantly affected the performance of early music in Britain[23]. From his base at Cambridge, Dart was in a strong position to influence many aspiring musicians.

Walter Bergmann's fight with the BBC was important because it led to recognition by the BBC of new types of musician that did not fall into their previously neatly designed categories. The BBC was playing a significant role in the early music revival and therefore its attitude was important. The Third Programme, which began broadcasting in 1946, reached a specialist minority, but a significant minority. It provided one of the main sources of performance of early music. By the 1950s, the broadcast repertoire reached back to include medieval music, and music by composers such as Dufay, Dunstable and Tallis[24]. Music written before 1700 made up a significant portion of weekly broadcasts in 1953. Walter Bergmann realised that it was important to his status as a musician that he be eligible to perform for the BBC. However unlike some of his contemporaries he valued the contribution of amateur players to musical life. His experiences at Morley and later through the Society of Recorder Players taught him both the enjoyment of working with amateurs and what could be achieved with good amateur players. All through his working life he worked equally with professional and amateur musicians - a situation which unfortunately was sometimes to his disadvantage when working with and being evaluated by some professional musicians.

The first half of 1952 continued with the usual mixture of work for Walter Bergmann. In April he lectured at Morley on recorder music. In the same month the London Branch of the Society of Recorder Players presented a concert in London. The performers included Carl Dolmetsch and Edgar Hunt, Joseph Saxby (harpsichord), Gerald English (tenor), the Oriel Recorder Consort (Audrey Abbott, Doris Ford, Ron Plowman and C. Kenworthy*), the Taylor Recorder Trio (Christopher, Richard and Stanley Taylor) and the Telemann Orchestra conducted by Walter Bergmann - a gathering together of probably all the best recorder expertise in England at the time. In May Walter Bergmann had lunch with Imogen Holst to discuss a collection of folk tunes, and he took two recorder classes for Edgar Hunt at Trinity College of Music. However a significant change in his life was about to happen. On 10th June Walter Bergmann resigned from his teaching at Morley College, something he 'thought would never happen'[25]. The atmosphere had changed considerably at Morley College since Michael Tippett's departure and Walter Bergmann was no longer happy working there. He was extremely sad to hand on his recorder classes to someone else. (Robert Salkeld succeeded him.) In July the Bergmanns held a party for the Morley Recorder Ensemble and Walter Bergmann gave each member a copy of the miniature score of Hindemith's *Recorder Trio*. Hindemith had given Walter Bergmann permission to transpose the trio up a minor third from its original key so that it could be played comfortably on C and F recorders, having originally been written for A and D instruments. This new edition was published by Schott in 1952. Five days previously Walter Bergmann began teaching at the Mary Ward Settlement with three classes - a cantata choir, a beginner recorder class and the Telemann Orchestra, the one class he brought with him from Morley. He took over the recorder teaching at Mary Ward from Freda Dinn. The summer saw another visit to Austria for the International Summer School, this time held in Leoben, near Graz. The participants included Austrian, British, Danish, Dutch and German players. The final concert of the course was given

---

* The Oriel Consort was formed in 1950 by Audrey Abbott, Doris Ford, Ken Kenworthy and Ron Plowman, all members of Walter Bergman's Morley College Recorder Class. Theo Wyatt replaced Audrey Abbott around 1952.

jointly by the recorder players and the Leoben Chamber Orchestra, directed by Walter Bergmann, Kurt Pitsch and the orchestra's conductor Rupert Doppelbauer. The concert included music by Purcell, Arne, Gibbons and Schmelzer and a performance of Bach's *Brandenburg concerto No 4* in its original instrumentation with two recorders. As in previous years, Walter Bergmann also taught at the Roehampton Summer School.

1953 began for Walter Bergmann with a concert in Birmingham with Alfred Deller. The Society of Recorder Players' Annual Concert was also held in Birmingham in the Central Hall in June 1953. The review in the *Recorder News*[26] stated, 'A special mention must be made of the versatile Walter Bergmann who appeared as conductor, harpsichordist and recorder player.'

By 1953 the Society of Recorder Players had a membership of 656. Its structure was established in a form that was to last for several years. Carl Dolmetsch, Freda Dinn and Walter Bergmann were Musical Directors, Edgar Hunt, the Society's Chairman, Dr Percy Scholes its President and Joyce Tadman the Secretary. C. (Ken) Kenworthy was the Editor of *Recorder News*. Benjamin Britten succeeded Dr Scholes as President in 1959 (who in turn was succeeded by Michael Tippett in 1976 and Peter Maxwell Davies in 1998). *The Recorder News* offered Walter Bergmann a regular outlet for articles and reviews of music and concerts.

As the number of recorder players grew, Schott's market for recorder ensemble music expanded. Two series were now being produced, these being the 'Archive of Recorder Consorts' and the 'Recorder Library'. The editors and arrangers for these collections included Dolmetsch, Dinn and Bergmann.

In the summer of 1953, Walter Bergmann found himself involved in three summer schools. The Recorder in Education Summer School (now organised by the Dolmetsch foundation for the SRP) expanded its activities in 1953 to cater for players as well as experienced teachers, giving the opportunity of ensemble playing with some coaching. The SRP teacher's certificate had been introduced the previous year with seven successful candidates being awarded the certificate. Edgar Hunt, Carl Dolmetsch, Freda Dinn and Walter Bergmann were the course tutors. On the conclusion of the course, Walter Bergmann flew to Berlin, where he was a musical director of the Berliner Blockflötenwoche with Rudolf Barthel and Ernst Genth. Barthel had established a recorder orchestra of about players at the Volksmusikschule in Neukölln Berlin[27]. The course culminated in a concert, the participants including Barthel's recorder 'choir', Hans Conrad Fehr from Switzerland and Dietrich Gerhardt, Walter Bergmann's friend from pre-war days who was establishing a successful career as an oboist. After the course, Walter Bergmann made two broadcasts, one with Radio Basel, the other from Baden-Baden. On return to England he then went to teach at the summer school held by the University of Birmingham's Extra Mural Department at Attingham Park near Shrewsbury. The course was directed by the Department's Staff Tutor, Wilfrid Mellers (who became Professor of Music at the University of York). Music of the 17th and 18th centuries formed the basis of the course and it was the first year that recorder tuition was offered, for intermediate and advanced players. Other lecturers and performers included Alfred Deller, Hilda Hunter (oboe and recorder), Gervase de Peyer (clarinet) and Edmund Rubbra, who lectured on composition. There were eighteen recorder players on the course. The inclusion of recorder teaching reflected a growing acknowledgement of the recorder as a serious instrument.

Family-wise, Walter Bergmann met his brother Hans during his visit to Germany. In September 1953 his nephew Rolf Bergmann came to stay with him, while Grete Bergmann went on holiday to Hamburg for ten days. In October 1953 Erica Bergmann left for a year in Israel. Both her parents were anxious and concerned about her going, especially as she was only partially Jewish, (through Walter Bergmann's mother), and not from a practising Jewish family. Walter Bergmann was worried as to how Grete would cope with the separation. The year Erica spent away was not made easier by the fact that from 1954 Walter Bergmann began to be dogged by ill health, which lasted for several years. 1953 ended well enough - one of his last engagements that year was accompanying Ilse Wolf in Schubert's *Der Hirt auf dem Felsen*, on a piano dating from Mozart's time, in a lecture-recital entitled 'The Fortepiano' given by Antony Hopkins in the Recital Room of the Festival Hall on December 10th. Peter Hawes played the clarinet. Life was busy for Walter Bergmann although he was having problems with his eyes. In his diary he noted[28] a remark made by a friend Dora Head, 'If you get old, never sit back.'

1954 opened with uncertainty at Schott and concern about his eyes. In the middle of January he was diagnosed as having a detached retina, needing immediate surgery. He travelled to Utrecht in Holland for the operation, remaining there in hospital for three weeks. He finally returned to work at Schott on March 1st. Life then appeared to return to normal. Fritz and Anneliese Bergmann came to England for the first time and stayed for 2 weeks. Over the summer Walter Bergmann was as busy as ever. He spent 3 weeks in Germany, partly working and part on holiday. He had discussions with Schott in Mainz and saw various relations and acquaintances, notably his brothers and Hildemarie Peter, a leading German recorder teacher who in 1953 published a thesis entitled *The Recorder, its traditions and tasks*[29]. He re-visited Freiburg, finding it more beautiful than he remembered and once again explored the Black Forest, visiting Höllenthal and Titisee.

The Roehampton summer course of 1954 was extremely successful. The visitors included a number of distinguished international recorder players; Hans Ulrich Staeps from Vienna, Ferdinand Conrad and Hildemarie Peter from Germany, Joannes Collette from Nijmegen in Holland and Kurt Pitsch from Austria. Walter Bergmann was again not impressed by Staeps, writing in his diary that he gave a poor lecture[30]. Others were not impressed by Walter Bergmann's recorder playing and teaching, including Brian Bonsor, who, on his first visit to the Roehampton course, was disappointed with Walter Bergmann's tone, articulation and overall level of skill on the recorder, although he clearly recognised his other musical skills. Walter Bergmann later admitted that he took a while to develop as a good teacher.

He was impressed at Roehampton by the recorder playing of Joannes Collette, and his wife's singing voice. They were accompanied by Franz Reizenstein. Conrad also played well. This gathering of international recorder specialists was not without problems. Walter Bergmann felt it was important that British players, both professional and amateur should be aware of other traditions of recorder playing. In particular he felt Carl Dolmetsch should be aware of other expert players and recognise that there were alternative ways of playing to the Dolmetsch tradition. This he felt should enhance Carl Dolmetsch's knowledge, not threaten it. The Dolmetsch family were however worried by the predominance of other players and needed careful handling. It was a problem that was to continue for many years.

In October 1954 Erica Bergmann returned home fit and well. At the beginning of 1955 she travelled with Walter Bergmann to Holland at the start of what looked like being a successful and healthier year for him. In Holland he gave a radio broadcast with the Collettes. Back in London, problems at Schott were still rumbling on, but Max Steffens was adamant that he did not want to lose Walter Bergmann. He was busy again with concerts and professional engagements, which although not quite so prestigious as in previous years, were varied and interesting and often outside London. These included concerts with the Wolverhampton and Staffordshire Technical College under the direction of Dr Percy Young, and a performance of the St John Passion with the Amersham and Chesham Bois Choral Society conducted by Edgar Hunt, for which the soloists included Josephine Veasey (contralto) and Maurice Bevan (bass). In all of these concerts Walter Bergmann played the harpsichord. In February 1955 he gave the second of two One-Day Recorder Schools at Birmingham University. In June 1955, with Professor Ian Parrott, Professor of Music at Aberystwyth University, he conducted a concert of music for voices, recorders, oboe and strings at Gregynog in Wales. The performers included Edward Bor (violin) and Hilda Hunter (oboe). In London the London Branch of the SRP gave its annual concert in March at the Mary Ward Settlement. Among the players were the Oriel Consort, Layton and Christine Ring (keyboard and flute), Freda Dinn, Carl Dolmetsch, Joseph Saxby and Walter Bergmann. A concert given by the Oriel Consort (Ronald Plowman, Theo Wyatt, Doris Ford and C Kenworthy) in the Salle Evard in London on April 29th attracted a large audience. The concert finished with a performance of John Blow's *Ode on the Death of Henry Purcell* edited by Walter Bergmann. The soloists were Alfred Deller (countertenor) and Wilfred Brown (tenor). In March of 1955 Alfred Deller and Walter Bergmann finally attended an audition for the BBC in the Albert Hall.

In June 1955 Walter Bergmann returned to Holland again and then travelled on to Hanover and Berlin for the summer school in Charlottenberg. For the first time since childhood, he revisited Bremen. He stayed overnight with Grete Bergmann's sister Liselotte, and they talked about acquaintances they both had had in Halle.

In July 1955 just before the Roehampton Summer School, Walter Bergmann was taken seriously ill, this time with a duodenal ulcer, again necessitating immediate surgery. During his prolonged stay in hospital he received letters and flowers from many recorder players. Grete Bergmann was always at the hospital whenever Walter Bergmann was at his most ill, often visiting twice a day. Other regular visitors included Erika Seelig and one of his pupils Dr Silbiger. On leaving hospital he went to convalesce in Bognor Regis. He was back at work at Schott on October 10th. One engagement he managed to fulfil before the end of 1955 was the SRP's annual concert, held in November in King's College, Newcastle upon Tyne. The concert was a combined effort by the North-eastern Branch of the Society, the Music Department of King's College Newcastle and the Newcastle Bach Choir Society. Walter Bergmann shared the conducting with Dr Chalmers Burn, the Choir's conductor. The concert consisted of a varied programme including a performance of Britten's *Alpine Suite* (published in 1956). The soloists were Carl Dolmetsch, Edgar Hunt, Layton Ring and Walter Bergmann. The concert rehearsal was attended by 335 schoolchildren. The concert audience was over 500 and the gross takings were a record for the hall. The concert involved high costs and travel expenses, but still made a small profit of £11.

Although he was still not fully recovered, life had resumed its usual shape for Walter Bergmann by the beginning of 1956. He performed in and directed a number of concerts, particularly at the Mary Ward Settlement, where his evening classes continued. The music of Telemann featured prominently in the 1956 concerts, for example as in a concert given at Fenton House in Hampstead in February with Ilse Wolf (soprano), which included three new Telemann editions made by Walter Bergmann. The concert also included his new edition of the *Sonata in D minor* for cello by William Flackton, played by Jennifer Ryan. By 1956 Walter Bergmann was recognised and respected for his editing and scholarship. As well as his Telemann editions, he was acknowledged for his work on Purcell through his collaboration with Michael Tippett. Another concert, devoted to Telemann, using Walter Bergmann's editions and programme notes, was given by the New English Consort on March 23rd in the Great Drawing Room of the Arts Council in London. The group included Marilyn Wailes, friend of Walter Bergmann and an editor of recorder music.

Walter Bergmann worked regularly as an accompanist during 1956 with Ilse Wolf, Gerald English (tenor) and Norman Platt (bass). Gerald English and Norman Platt both took part in the SRP annual concert held in London in March 1956. The concert included five modern recorder works, among these Britten's *Alpine Suite*, Michael Tippett's *Two Inventions* for recorder duet and a new *Suite* for three recorders by Peter Racine Fricker. The Fricker piece was played by Edgar Hunt, Elli McMullen and Walter Bergmann.

In 1956 the BBC decided to record a performance of John Blow's *Ode on the Death of Henry Purcell* using Walter Bergmann's edition, with Alfred Deller as soloist, to be broadcast in April. Deller requested Walter Bergmann as harpsichordist. After all the correspondence he had had with the BBC in 1951 and 1952, Walter Bergmann believed he was on their panel of performers. He had received the letter from Norman Carrell confirming this in November 1952. However he now heard from the BBC that their panel of harpsichord players had been reviewed in 1953 and his name had been removed! The BBC would not re-employ him unless he could produce fresh recent evidence of his proficiency as a harpsichord continuo player and accompanist. This of course was difficult for Walter Bergman, as his illness over the preceding years had affected his professional engagements. Ironically the BBC were willing to broadcast reasonably recent records Walter Bergmann had made accompanying Alfred Deller. However the BBC did eventually agree to Walter Bergmann performing. The programme, consisting of the Ode, and Blow's *Venus and Adonis* was finally broadcast on July 1st 1956. Alfred Deller and John Whitworth sang the countertenor parts, the recorder players were Carl Dolmetsch and Edgar Hunt and Desmond Dupré played viola da gamba. Walter Bergmann directed from the harpsichord. After the broadcast, the *Musical Times*[31] stated, 'Of more than historical interest were performances of two works by John Blow, the second being the *Ode on the death of Henry Purcell* under the scholarly direction of Walter Bergmann'.

The BBC implied they might allow him to perform again as a harpsichordist and they continued to use him as a recorder player, particularly in schools broadcasts, as for example on April 29th, when he played *Sellenger's Round* and *Greensleeves* in a talk given by Gordon Reynolds. One broadcast in which Walter Bergmann did not participate was a performance of Purcell's 1692 *Ode for St Cecilia's Day*. In May 1956 he met Tippett to discuss a possible broadcast performance. Walter Bergmann had of course played continuo and helped edit the music for the first revival performance under Tippett in 1941. He had played the continuo part in other subsequent performances, such as one given by the Amersham and Chesham Bois Choral Society in November 1954, conducted by Edgar Hunt. He was greatly saddened not to be asked to play in the broadcast performance when it finally happened in November 1956. However by this time, Walter Bergmann had been ill yet again. He did have the consolation of seeing his work as editor acknowledged in the *Radio Times*.

In May 1956 Walter Bergmann gave a concert at the University of London Institute of Education as part of a Conference on Recorder Playing. The concert contained a varied programme, which showed the range of music incorporating recorders, and included a Telemann trio sonata, Chris Edmunds *Sonatina* (1941) for descant recorder and piano, and J.S.Bach's aria, *Sheep may safely graze*, with Ilse Wolf as the soprano soloist. In the same month, Walter Bergman had the shattering experience of finding his pupil and friend Dr Silbiger dead in his home. Silbiger had failed to turn up at Belsize Square for his regular lesson, so Walter Bergmann went to his flat to see what had happened. With the night porter, he found Silbiger dead in his bedroom. Walter Bergmann had not seen Dr Silbiger often, mainly just for his regular lesson, but he had enjoyed his company and found him a good friend, who had visited him regularly in hospital the previous year. The death greatly disturbed Walter Bergmann, particularly as his own health was deteriorating again. He was fortunate to have managed to perform in the broadcast of the Blow *Ode* in July. Three days later on July 4th, he had a hernia operation. On leaving hospital, he once again went to convalesce in Bognor Regis.

He returned to London in time to teach at the Roehampton Summer School. Norman Platt collected him from Bognor by car. On the way back to London they called to see Marie (Mary) Dolmetsch, Carl Dolmetsch's wife. The Dolmetsch marriage was in difficulty and the problems affected the organisation of the Recorder Summer School. The actual summer school ran successfully without any major hiccups. Performers at the concert in 1956 included Carl Dolmetsch, Natalie Dolmetsch, Joseph Saxby, Joyce Tadman, Freda Dinn, Layton and Christine Ring, Brian Bonsor, Walter Bergmann, Edgar Hunt and Herbert Hersom - most of whom were to make a significant contribution to the practice and recognition of the recorder in performance or education over the following years.

Walter Bergmann continued to tirelessly promote the works of Telemann. In the October 1956 edition of *Recorder News* he published a list of Telemann's music for recorder. In February 1957 he presented a concert at the Mary Ward Settlement, partly aimed to 'answer some recent distinguished critics of Telemann's works'. He was incensed at Telemann being dismissed as an unimportant composer. Yet again, the soloists included Ilse Wolfe, Gerald English and Norman Platt. Norman Platt also sang in the London SRP Branch's 1957 annual concert. The SRP's National Concert moved to Bristol for its 1957 venue. It was given in March before a large audience, which included the Lady Mayoress and the Sheriff, in the Bristol Museum Lecture Theatre. The concert was extremely successful in spite of last minute illness. Enid Hunt, Edgar Hunt's sister stepped in to replace Freda Dinn. Once again the concert was a collaboration, this time between the Bristol SRP Branch, members of the Bristol Madrigal Society and string players from the

Bristol Music Club. Edgar Hunt conducted the concert, and the soloists were himself, Carl Dolmetsch, Walter Bergmann and Enid Hunt. As usual there was a varied programme, which included a Telemann Concerto with Carl Dolmetsch as soloist and Walter Bergmann's recently published arrangements of *Country Dances from the Apted Book*. Walter Bergmann returned to Bristol at the end of June to conduct 1000 children in the Colston Hall. They played his arrangement of *Men of Harlech*.

Engagements gradually began to pick up again during 1957. In March he accompanied Hildemarie Peter and Johannes Colette in a performance of the Purcell Chaconne on Radio Berlin. In April he participated in a light-hearted 'April Fool's' Concert in Liverpool promoted by Fritz Spiegl. Walter Bergmann contributed an arrangement of *The First of April* from the Apted Book. This consisted of variations for 9 recorders, strings, harp and percussion. Walter Bergmann played all the recorder parts! The concert was sold out, and the other performers included Gerald Hoffnung, Thomas Helmsley, Denis Matthews, John Pritchard and Fritz Spiegl. Denis Matthews, dressed as a 'Wonder Boy' in velvet shorts, played a piano concerto for one note. Gerald Hoffnung was Tubby the Tuba. Several newspapers including the *Daily Express* reported the concert. Walter Bergmann's friends and pupils knew of his wit and sense of humour. The Liverpool concert brought his humour to a wider audience, as did the publication of his 'Golden Rules for Ensemble Playing' in the *Recorder News* of June 1957.

'Many times I have been asked to publish my Golden Rules and music dealers have from time to time received orders for them. I would still keep them from the public eye, if not from the public ear, in order to preserve my copyright and to make myself indispensable, but recent publication in foreign journals has distorted these wise rules so much that I feel obliged to publish them, or at least some of them, in order to protect them from further deterioration. Recorder players are strongly advised to observe or not to observe them. They have originated in the happy experiences of more than fifteen years of recorder teaching

WALTER BERGMANN

1. Play the same piece.
2. Repeat marks are repeat marks and not places for discussion.
3. Rests are difficult, especially on the recorder.
7. Tune before playing then you can safely play out of tune the whole evening.
19. Take your time in turning over. You can always catch up later.
27. An ornamentation should be an embellishment and not a catastrophe.
59. Your conductor has been paid for. You waste your money if you don't look at him.
61. Aim at the highest n.p.s. (notes per second).
79. A right note at the wrong time is a wrong note.
132. My foot my tutor? (Prospero was presumably a Desert Island Recorder Player.)
147. Spare the breath and spoil the tune.
151. If all are wrong and you are right, follow the wrong.
163. Forte and piano marks, slurs, dots above and behind a note, etc., are not to be observed. They are only decorations for the eye made by frustrated engravers.
167. Thou shalt not play the little bit left over at the end.

In June it was Grete Bergmann's turn to be ill. She was operated on for the removal of gallstones; then she too went to convalesce in Bognor Regis. On June 2nd Walter Bergmann recorded twelve Purcell songs with Alfred Deller. The summer of 1957 found him, as usual, at Roehampton. On August 10th the Bergmanns celebrated Grete's birthday with a party, the guests including Hilde Volhard and Erika Seelig. The following day Walter Bergmann flew to Hamburg. On arrival he travelled to Bremen to meet Dietrich Gerhardt and then to Frankfurt to visit Schott. From there he went to Basle, where he accompanied Ilse Wolfe singing Schubert and four English songs (in translations by Walter Bergmann), for a radio broadcast. He then travelled on again to spend a few days in Austria. He particularly enjoyed a weekend staying at the home of the Flatz's in their ancient tower house in St Jakob. Prunella Flatz was English and an old friend. (Erica Bendix remembers her drawing an amusing picture of the Bergmann move to 28 Belsize Square in 1947.) On his way home to London on September 1st, Walter Bergmann managed to meet Dietrich Gerhardt again. He also met briefly with his nephew Rolf. Fritz Bergmann, who had recently had an operation and wanted to accompany his son to see Walter Bergmann, fortunately did not come. He had a relapse and only just survived.

Walter Bergmann found himself in hospital yet again at the end of September 1957, this time with jaundice. He was hospitalised for five weeks and missed three concerts. He took the opportunity to read in hospital, but the time passed very slowly. His reading included Adison's *Essay on Musical Expression* and a biography of Rameau. In November after his return home from hospital to recuperate further, Walter Bergmann wrote in his diary 'Old age is not the loss of teeth but of illusions'[32]. He also noted that Grete Bergmann's restaurant 'The Cosmo' was going through difficulties. A more cheerful event was the arrival of his new small harpsichord. He continued to be depressed, especially by the fact that Schott were putting together a recorder catalogue without him. In the same diary entry he noted that he had been re-elected to the executive committee of the Galpin Society and that there was also possibility of more reparations money from Germany on top of the 300 DM he had already received. (An old friend Eva Zilling, who had helped Grete Bergmann when she was pregnant with Erica, had sworn an affidavit for the Reparations Committee, confirming how Walter and Grete Bergmann's life and livelihood had been affected under the Nazis. She described to the Committee the suffering and problems they had experienced, leading eventually to their departure for England.)

By the beginning of December 1957 Walter Bergmann was feeling well enough to work at home preparing and editing music for Schott. He visited the British Museum on December 7th and finally returned to work at Schott on December 9th. Everyone was pleased to see him. On December 11th he was fit enough to conduct the community singing at a concert held at Mary Ward.

Walter Bergmann was determined that he was going to be healthy in 1958. On January 4th 1958 he wrote in his diary 'My resolutions for 1958. To be healthy for 5 years. To be gentle even in anger. To be kind to everybody (except or even myself?)'. However good health still eluded him and he had to cancel a concert with Norman Platt on doctor's advice. He gradually improved and by February was well enough to fulfil engagements again. He accompanied Norman Platt and Ilse Wolf at a concert at the Mary Ward Settlement on February 8th. In March the Society of Recorder Players gave its annual concert in the Queen Mary Hall, London. Walter Bergmann shared the conducting with Edgar Hunt. Norman Platt sang in the concert. A significant musical event in March was the German premiere of Tippett's *A Child of our Time*, the text had been translated by Walter Bergmann. The review in *Die Welt*[33] remarked on Walter Bergmann's careful translation.

In spite of his resolutions, Walter Bergmann found himself back in hospital again, this time with pneumonia. He spent five weeks in New End Hospital, returning to the same ward. Yet again he had to give up engagements, including a lecture course in Newbury. During his period in hospital he was grateful for his regular visitors, Grete and Erica Bergmann, Erika Seelig, Hilde Volhard and Norman Platt. Five days after his discharge from hospital he flew to Wiesbaden. He spent two weeks visiting Schott and seeing family and friends. This included the Versteeg family, the pre-war friends from Halle.

On his return home Walter Bergmann gradually began to pick up his regular routine of work. This of course included his work at Schott, concerts, conducting meetings of the Society of Recorder Players, arranging and editing, work with children, teaching and lecturing. He was invited to play the recorder in a concert given at Cecil Sharp House to celebrate the Diamond Jubilee of the Folk Song Society. Peter Pears and Benjamin Britten participated and Imogen Holst conducted the Purcell Singers. Walter Bergmann played the recorder with Elli McMullen and Leonard Lefkovitch in a performance of *Bonny at Morn* arranged by Michael Tippett for unison voices and recorders. The critic in *The Times* the following day did not like the arrangement.

At the end of June he was back in Germany. From 23rd –28th June 1958 he was in Köln, attending the seventh congress of the International Musicological Society. The congress was well-organised and included 128 lectures. Seven hundred musicologists attended. One of the main concerts was given by Cappella Coloniensis with the Deller Consort, and included *Canzoni* in 12 and 15 parts by Giovanni Gabrieli. The concert 'was one of the best' that Walter Bergmann had ever heard[34]. After the conference he accompanied Alfred Deller in recitals in Mainz and Münster. Walter Bergmann found working with Deller extremely tiring. He had to spend a whole day transposing Deller's songs, because the singer's voice had dropped by almost a tone and a half. In Mainz they gave a broadcast recital together, and Walter Bergmann was anxious about the accompaniments, which irritated Deller. Walter Bergmann noted in his diary[35] that the singer was unaware he was difficult to accompany. They gave a successful evening concert of songs by a variety of English composers including Campion, Dowland, Parsons, Blow and Purcell at the Mainz Staatliches Institut für Musik. The concert received a good review the following day in the *Allgemeine Zeitung*. Both singer and continuo player were praised. The countertenor voice was still rarely heard in Germany. In Münster they gave a concert on July 1st with Dietrich Gerhardtt and five string players. Walter Bergmann accompanied Alfred Deller, and played the recorder in a Loeillet trio sonata with Dietrich Gerhardtt playing the oboe. The audience was packed with students, who were extremely enthusiastic. Walter Bergmann spent three enjoyable days with Dietrich Gerhardt. While in Germany he also took the opportunity to discuss the possibilities of future publications with a representative from Bärenreiter and Moeck. He met his brother Fritz but not, as he had hoped Hans, for whom he left a gift of 2000 DM with Fritz Bergmann. (Hans Bergmann returned half the money).

On returning home he resumed his usual summer activities, including the Roehampton Summer School. By September Walter Bergmann was hopeful of remaining fit, and celebrated his birthday with Grete, Hilde Volhard, Erika Seelig, Ilse Wolf, Norman Platt and two nurses from New End Hospital with whom he had become friendly during his five week stay. (On September 20th he had given a concert in the nurses' home with Ilse Wolf, Sylvia Cleaver (violin) and Jennifer Ryan (cello).) Now that Walter Bergmann had fewer problems himself, he found himself acting as a listener for other friends' marriage problems, in particular Norman Platt and Marie Dolmetsch. In October he was at last able to accompany Norman Platt (bass) in two postponed concerts of music by Pelham Humphrey, Blow, Peerson, Purcell and Schubert. He also conducted a concert at Mary Ward on the 250th anniversary of John Blow's death. It included Blow's *Ode on the Death of Henry Purcell*. The performers included Alfred Deller, John Whitworth (countertenors), Gerald English (tenor), Norman Platt (baritone), Freda Dinn, Theo Wyatt (recorders), Kitty Wyatt (violin), Jennifer Ryan (cello) and Ian Kemp (harpsichord). On November 22nd there was a St Cecilia's Day Concert involving some of the same musicians and Ilse Wolf.

One major undertaking Walter Bergmann began was the establishing of a Telemann catalogue. He also saw Denis Stevens at Schott in connection with a continuo part for some Monteverdi. He was not impressed by Steven's realisations, and irritated by the fact that Stevens had in the past rejected his continuo realisations on behalf of the BBC.

The year 1958 ended well. He had seen many of his friends (Dietrich Gerhardt and his wife came to stay in October), work was building up again and he was fit enough to travel to various engagements. After a hospital check-up in November he was told to return in six months.

1959 was a busy and healthy year. At the end of January Walter Bergmann went to Belfast to give a weekend course on 'The recorder and its music' and he was invited to play in the Queen's University regular Monday recital. The programme included the Handel *Concerto for treble recorder and strings* and Telemann's *Concerto Grosse in A minor* for two recorders and strings. The annual SRP concert was held in Edinburgh on March 14th. As usual the performers included Walter Bergmann, Freda Dinn, Carl Dolmetsch and Edgar Hunt. Arne's *Under the Greenwood Tree* for soprano, sopranino, strings and figured bass edited by Walter Bergman was one of the items in the concert. The concert received a good criticism in *The Scotsman*. *The Scotsman* also reviewed one of Walter Bergmann's concerts at the Mary Ward Settlement in an article entitled 'The Music Makers'. 'There was (more) Purcell to be heard at a concert at the Mary Ward Settlement under the loving and intelligent direction of Walter Bergmann. Mr Bergmann taught for many years at Morley College under the aegis of Michael Tippett, with whom he has published many fine editions of works of the time of Purcell. On this occasion there was to be heard a concert performance of *Dido and Aeneas*, chiefly distinguished by the outstanding singing of Ilse Wolf as Dido.'[36] Walter Bergmann was extremely lucky that an artist of Ilse Wolf's calibre was willing to work with him frequently.

Another favourable review was in the March edition of *Music in Education* on Alfred Deller's recording of Purcell songs (HMV TEP 7068); the review mentioned 'fine phrasing' by Deller and 'unobtrusive accompaniment' by Walter Bergmann. Later in the year, a recording of Purcell's *Ode on St Cecilia's Day 1683* also received good reviews. It was coupled with the Blow *Ode on the Death of Henry Purcell*. The soloists were Alfred Deller (countertenor), April Cantelo, Eileen McLaughlin (sopranos), Gerald English (tenor), Maurice Bevan (bass) and John Whitworth (second countertenor in the Blow Ode). Walter Bergmann played the harpsichord and the recorder players in the Blow were Christopher and Richard Taylor (Bach Guild: BG-590). In his assessment of the Purcell Ode, the reviewer for *Musical America* described the extended interlude for harpsichord as a 'perfect gem' and Walter Bergmann's performance as 'magical', which made the record well worth buying.[37]

1959 was the 200th anniversary of Handel's death, and Walter Bergmann received an invitation to return to Halle for the Handel Festival held in April. He travelled via Hamburg to visit the Gerhardts and then on to Berlin to collect a visa for East Germany. He continued via Dresden and Leipzig, where he met Arnold Matz. It was his first trip back into what had become East Germany and he managed to meet a good number of past friends including Charlotte Zimmerman (his ex-secretary), Otto Neumann and Helene Stegmann. It was twenty one years since Walter Bergmann had left Halle as a lawyer in unhappy circumstances and he was returning as an eminent musician and musicologist. One great source of amusement to Walter Bergmann was the menu at one of the hotels he stayed at. This was in three languages, German, Russian and English, and it extolled customers to 'Please choose you from the abundant offer of fares!', which included 'Roasted Plates', and contained the explanation that 'The waiters are permitted to catch their bills at once'!

Back in London Walter Bergmann played the harpsichord in a concert at the German Institute to commemorate Handel, accompanying April Cantelo (soprano), Sylvia Cleaver and Lucy Moor (violins), Joy Hall (cello) and Neil Black (oboe). 1959 was also the 300th anniversary of the birth of Henry Purcell, and there was a combined Purcell-Handel Festival in London. On Tuesday June 6th, Sir Arthur Bliss unveiled a glass plaque in Purcell's honour in the Royal Festival Hall and this was followed by a concert of Purcell's music given by the Philomusica of London, with two choirs directed by Martindale Sidwell and including among the artists, Alfred Deller, Kenneth Bowen (tenor) and Walter Bergmann (harpsichord).

During 1959 Walter Bergmann's interest in working with children and teachers was still growing. In June, 850 children in Bristol sang and played his arrangement of *Marching through Georgia*. It was not a particularly good performance, but he was moved by the concert. As well as teaching at Roehampton he was involved in two other summer schools. At the Attingham Park Summer School he accompanied Alfred Deller. Immediately after he taught with Hilda Hunter at the summer school at Matlock Training College arranged by the Music Teachers' Association. Hilda Hunter was an oboist and recorder player who had become a family friend.

In August 1959 Walter Bergmann was at last feeling happy and well. He wrote in his diary[38] that, since his illness in 1955, he appreciated every day and each night went to bed thankful. He noted that his daughter Erica was more content and making use of her abilities. Grete Bergmann passed her driving test in August.

In September both Grete and himself travelled separately to Germany. Walter Bergmann went to Wiesbaden and to Mainz to visit Schott. He visited Fritz and Anneliese Bergmann. Gabrielle, his brother's daughter, who was almost twelve, was causing great concern to her parents. She was obviously unwell as she was always tired, drained of colour and lacking any energy, but the family did not know what was wrong with her. Walter Bergmann felt Fritz was looking older (he was just sixty).

October was a busy and rewarding month. Walter Bergmann taught on a government sponsored recorder course in Ipswich with John Horton. He also now had a recorder class at the London College of Music. Fourteen players attended on the evening of October 13th. He found teaching them very rewarding.

On October 23rd a letter arrived from Fritz saying that Gabrielle had been diagnosed as having acute leukaemia. All the family were shaken and saddened by her death on November 29th. She had been the much-loved younger daughter - a second family born after the war. Walter Bergmann flew to Germany on November 30th for the funeral, returning on December 6th.

On a more positive note a concert in November directed by Walter Bergmann had been a significant occasion. Given by the Cantata Choir at Mary Ward to commemorate Purcell's death, it included the first modern performance of two works newly edited by Walter Bergmann, Jeremiah Clarke's *On Henry Purcell's death* and Henry Hall's *A Piece of Music on Mr H Purcell's Death*. The concert was expected to be the last but one given by the choir before the Mary Ward Settlement closed the following year.

1959 ended on a cheerful note for the Bergmanns with Erica Bergmann's engagement to Peter Bendix. Both Walter and Grete Bergmann liked Peter Bendix and were in favour of Erica marrying him.

So in spite of a few bad years, by the end of 1959, at the age of 57, Walter Bergmann could be well satisfied with the career he had established over the preceding twenty years - although he was still always very critical of himself and his abilities. He was fortunate enough to still be performing as a keyboard accompanist, and sometimes as a continuo player on a number of occasions. His best engagements were usually through working with Alfred Deller, but he was still regularly accompanying Ilse Wolf and Norman Platt. He was making recordings with Deller, although not for the BBC. In Europe there appeared to be less problem about him accompanying on radio broadcasts. He had broadcast in Germany, Austria, Holland and Switzerland with Deller, Ilse Wolf and the Collettes. As a recorder player, Walter Bergmann's main performance outlet was through the SRP, but he also had opportunities to perform during lectures and in a few recitals, where he sometimes played solo concertos. The BBC also occasionally still used him as a recorder player, particularly for BBC schools programmes.

He was writing regularly for journals such as *Recorder News* and the Galpin Society journal and for other publications, for example *Music in Education*. He was also frequently asked to write programme notes for concerts, and was recognised as an authority on Purcell and Telemann and, to a lesser extent, Handel. He was recognised in Germany as a musicologist, continuo player and recorder teacher.

He had the security of his job at Schott, although it was not always a happy environment for him. His diary entry for July 14th 1959 noted that he was very unhappy at work, particularly as Hartog would not co-operate with him. Walter Bergmann felt they could have achieved a great deal if they had managed to work together. It was a definite clash of personalities.

All through the 1950s Walter Bergmann had continued to consistently arrange and edit a variety of music. This included substantial works such as the *Odes on Henry Purcell's death* by Blow, Hall and Clarke, and sonatas and chamber works; ensemble works, mainly for amateurs, such as music for the new Schott 'Recorder Ensemble Series' for which, for example, he arranged Purcell's *Music to Distressed Innocence* and made a free arrangement of *Greensleeves*, both for recorder quartet. Then there were arrangements for school children such as *Marching through Georgia* and *The Common Cormorant* for voices and recorder. Walter Bergmann's interest in children had increased during the 1950s. He had started to visit schools where the recorder flourished such as Ambler School, where Herbert Hersom taught recorders and music and Bridge Road School, Neasden, where Eileen Downer taught.

Walter Bergmann's involvement with the SRP had grown over the years, as had the Society itself. The London branch had a membership of around 150, and meetings reached a regular attendance level of a hundred or more. Walter Bergmann often visited SRP branches outside London. He taught on courses organised through the Society and other organisations, and did a little private teaching. He was also a Vice President of the South-East London Music Association.

By the end of 1959 Walter Bergmann's income was secure. For example, in September 1959 he received £500 of royalties from Schott. He had his regular salary from Schott and income from teaching, lecturing and a little from performing. There was no need for Grete Bergmann to work so desperately hard. Erica Bergmann's future looked secure and happy. At long last Walter Bergmann was leading a normal, healthy and stable life. He had many friends both in Britain and Germany, with regular contact with his family and old friends. The Bergmanns had also acquired a dog (in the early 50s'), called Muschi, from the Battersea Dogs' Home. Walter Bergmann had been invited back to Halle as a respected musician to a mixture of sad and happy memories, which were now well in the past. London and England was definitely his home.

[1] 'Herrlicher Spieler', 'grosser Klassischer Geiger'; Diary 10, 10.07.45
[2] 'tausende von descant recorders zu prüfen und zu verpacken.'; Diary 10, 05.12.45
[3] 'mein Wunschtraum seit Jahren'.Diary 10, 26.12.45
[4] Edgar Hunt to Anne Martin, March 1994
[5] Recorder News No. 5 1947 p. 12., Society of Recorder Players
[6] *Newsletter Number Five*, September 1949, The Society of Recorder Players.
[7] Lawrence Leonard (Secretary of Committee for the Promotion of New Music) to Walter Bergmann, 16.04.48
[8] *Newsletter Number Two*, New Series October 1950, The Society of Recorder Players.
[9] Diary 11, 28.08.51.
[10] *The Recorder News*, New Series No. 5, December 1951.
[11] Michael Tippett, *Those Twentieth Century Blues*, (London; Hutchinson 1991) p. 160
[12] Walter Bergmann to Michael Tippett, 09.10.51.
[13] Walter Bergmann to Mr Steffens, 10.10.51.
[14] Michael Tippett to Walter Bergmann, October 1951
[15] Walter Bergmann to Herbert Murrill, 25.07.51
[16] Herbert Murrill to Walter Bergmann, 03.08.51
[17] Denis Stevens to Walter Bergman, 03.01.52
[18] Walter Bergmann to Denis Stevens, 02.03.52
[19] Walter Bergmann to Norman Carrell, 21.09.52
[20] Norman Carrell to Walter Bergmann, 10.10.52
[21] Norman Carrell to Walter Bergmann, 17.11.52
[22] See Harry Haskell, *The Early Music Revival*, (London; Thames and Hudson 1988) p. 161
[23] Haskell (1988), p. 161
[24] Haskell (1988), p.122
[25] 'die mir niemals glaubt'; Diary 11, 10.06.52
[26] *Recorder News*, New Series No. 9, Summer 1953
[27] See H. Fischer (ed.), Handbuch der Musikerziehung, Vol 1, (Rembrandt 1954)
[28] Diary 12, 09.12.53
[29] H. Peter, *The Recorder, its tradition and tasks*, 1953, trans.

Gedman, (Lichterfelde 1958)
[30] Diary 12, 12.08.54
[31] *Musical Times*, August 1956, p.420
[32] Diary 13. 07.11.57
[33] *Die Welt*, 13 .3.58
[34] *Recorder News*, 1958 p.10
[35] Diary 13, 06.07.58
[36] *The Scotsman*, 03.04.59
[37] *Musical America*, October 1959
[38] Diary 14, 23.08.59

Walter Bergmann being congratulated by Benjamin Britten.
Aldeburgh. June 15, 1960

7. The Sixties

At the age of fifty-seven, many people are thinking of retirement, but not Walter Bergmann. Over the Nineteen-sixties, the emphasis of his career shifted from performing towards directing, teaching and lecturing, but the amount of work he undertook did not diminish. 1960 began with a visit to Norwich for the ISM (Incorporated Society of Musicians) Conference. The death of his niece Gabrielle was still on Walter Bergmann's mind, and he was preoccupied in considering composing something to remember her by that could also be played at his own funeral. The following week, Walter Bergmann attended a conference on music in schools at the Royal Academy. By 1960 he was regularly visiting and listening to recorder groups in a growing number of schools - an experience he did not always find enjoyable!

February 1960 was an enjoyable and rewarding month. Walter Bergmann felt he was becoming an experienced conductor of amateurs and that he had learnt how to get the best playing result from them. Of an SRP meeting on February 13th he wrote, 'the best session of amateur conducting I have done'[1]. His published articles in 1960 included 'Conducting a recorder class' (*Recorder News* Nov/Dec 1960) in which he discussed the role of the conductor of recorder groups and classes, and defined the differences between amateur and professional players. Of the conductor he wrote, his job is 'to train his players to become musicians, to understand and to be able to execute music without him; he has to teach them real ensemble playing with the intention of making them independent of him'[2]. He defined an amateur as a player who does not play for other people who 'aims at the emotional and artistic experience of music he chooses and likes'. The professional 'is the player who plays to and for others'. 'The professional may love the music he plays, but he plays for money: the amateur may love money but he plays for the music.' In his article, Walter Bergmann also acknowledged the rising standards in recorder playing. Twenty years previously he had defined the difference between amateur and professional players as follows:- 'an amateur is a player who has practised a work for six months but when he stands on the platform he gives the impression he is sight-reading. The professional on the other hand has never seen the music before, but on the stage he gives the impression that for the last six months he has done nothing else but practise this piece of music.' Restating this definition in 1960, he added, 'Today, however, I know from experience that in this respect also, recorder amateur musicians can behave professionally'[3].

On February 25th 1960, Erica Bergmann married Peter Bendix at a quiet registry office ceremony followed by a lunch attended by the newly married couple, Walter and Grete Bergmann and three other guests. Walter Bergmann noted in his diary that he was happy for Erica and Peter, but sad for themselves, as Erica would no longer be with them. He wondered how Grete would cope with this separation.

Walter Bergmann's contentment continued into March. On the seventeenth he directed a concert at the Mary Ward Settlement as part of the St Pancras Arts Festival. The programme consisted of music from the seventeenth and eighteenth centuries, including cantatas by Bach and Telemann, Jeremiah Clarke's *Music on the Death of Henry Purcell* and three Purcell songs. The soloists included Alfred Deller, Norman Platt, Laura Sarti (contralto), Ilse Wolf and Edgar Hunt. The Mary Ward Cantata Choir participated. The orchestra was led by Sylvia Cleaver, and included Francis Baines (double bass), Leonard Lefkovitch and Kitty Wyatt (violins), and Jennifer Ryan (cello). The concert was a great success, and although Walter Bergmann was not happy with his continuo playing, he considered it the best concert he had directed[4]. At the end of March his old friend, the violinist Arnold Matz visited. Walter Bergmann thoroughly enjoyed the two days they spent together.

In April he played continuo in a performance of Bach's *St John's Passion* in Waltham Cross. In May he played for a performance of *The Mass in B minor* in the Kingsway Hall, conducted by Donald Cashmore. The soloists included Helen Watts (contralto) and Richard Standen (bass). The organist was John Birch. The chorus was the Kingsway Choral Society. (the Society's Secretary was Herbert Hersom, who was also a recorder player and SRP member.) Walter Bergmann considered Bach's *Mass in B minor* to be the most beautiful piece of music he knew[5].

In May Walter Bergmann ran a recorder weekend at Belstead House with Theo Wyatt. June 1960 was an exciting month. At the beginning of the month, he enjoyed a visit by LaNoue Davenport, an American professional recorder player, who was touring Europe with the early music group, founded by Noah Greenberg, the New York Pro Musica. Davenport was also President of the American Recorder Society, and came to the London SRP Branch Meeting. He complimented Walter Bergmann on his conducting. The most significant event in June for Walter Bergmann was a concert at the Aldeburgh Festival, given by twenty members of the London SRP Branch. Walter Bergmann directed the concert, and Josephine Murphy (soprano) also participated. The group played in the late afternoon in the walled garden of Eaton House. The programme included the Schmelzer Sonata a 7, Dances by Susato, *Five Pieces* from Bartok's *Mikrokosmos* arranged by Imogen Holst and Benjamin Britten's *Alpine Suite*. Britten was in the audience. The acoustics in the garden were good and the weather kind.

Walter Bergmann thoroughly enjoyed the three days he spent at the Festival. On his first evening, he played in a concert of medieval sacred music conducted by Imogen Holst. (Imogen Holst was one of the three Artistic Directors of the Aldeburgh Festival, Benjamin Britten and Peter Pears being the other two.) On the evening of June 25th, after the recorder concert, Walter Bergmann attended the second performance of Britten's opera *A Midsummer Night's Dream*. This had been specially written for the 1960 Festival and the reopening of the Aldeburgh Jubilee Hall, which had been improved and upgraded, although it was still very cramped. Until 1967 and the opening of the Maltings Concert Hall, events at the Festival were restricted by the available venues. Other than local churches, the Jubilee Hall was the only venue for the more important concerts and operatic productions. At Aldeburgh, Walter Bergmann enjoyed meeting and talking to people, some of whom he had met before or worked with. These included Britten, Alfred Deller, Jennifer Vyvyan, April Cantelo, Peter Pears and John Amis.

In August Walter Bergmann was worried by arthritis in his knee and hip, but his doctor was optimistic about it improving. It did not curtail his normal summer school activities at Matlock, with Hilda Hunter on the Music Teachers' Association course, and at the Recorder Summer School at Roehampton. At Roehampton he lectured on the three *Odes* written on the death of Purcell, and Clare Walmesley and Norman Platt sang for him. LaNoue Davenport also visited the summer school.

September 1960 brought the news that Hans Bergmann, at the age of 64, had moved from East to West Germany with his family. They were not allowed to take anything with them. In October, Walter Bergmann embarked on a week's 'mini-tour' of Scotland.

He conducted SRP Branch meetings in Aberdeen and Edinburgh. In Glasgow, he lectured on Barsanti, and directed a concert devoted to the composer's music. He also lectured on the recorder at the Royal Scottish Academy of Music. After a wet two-day break in the Trossachs, he travelled to Manchester, via Carlisle, where he gave a lecture at Forsyth's, the Manchester Music Shop.

November 1960 was a busy month. Concerts included one in Birmingham with Sylvia Cleaver and Ilse Wolf, (who replaced Joy Hall), at the City Arts Gallery. The evening was the first of the new concert season and well received. It consisted of music by seventeenth and eighteenth century composers, Buxtehude, Festing, Bach, Purcell and Haydn. In London, Walter Bergmann gave a concert at the New End Hospital with Clare Walmesley (soprano), Laura Sarti (contralto) and Norman Platt (bass). The music included songs by Purcell, Blow and Mozart. The same performers were joined by Paul Hamburger (piano), for a concert a week later on November 29th in St Martin in the Fields, for a programme of Purcell, Blow and Mozart, and other arias sung by Laura Sarti. Walter Bergmann noted in his diary that the BBC had not accepted Laura Sarti after they had auditioned her. He thought they were idiots not to do so[6].

At the beginning of November Walter Bergmann went to a production of Stravinsky's Oedipus Rex at Sadlers Wells. He was very impressed by the work. In the middle of the month he lunched with Alfred Deller. Deller had created the role of Oberon in the first production of Britten's opera *A Midsummer Night's Dream* at Aldeburgh in June 1960. The opera was now to be staged at Covent Garden, but Britten had engaged another countertenor, an American, Russell Oberlin, to replace Deller in the role of Oberon. Deller was very bitter and Walter Bergmann did all he could to console him.

The Cantata Choir, which Walter Bergmann conducted at the Mary Ward Settlement, was just about managing to survive, although the attendance fluctuated each week and was often very low. At the beginning of December the choir gave a concert at Mary Ward, with a group of strings led by Sylvia Cleaver, members of the recorder group Walter Bergmann had started to run at the London College of Music, Clare Walmesley, Laura Sarti, Norman Platt, Pamela Weston (clarinet) and Elli McMullen (harpsichord). The programme consisted mainly of seventeenth and eighteenth century music, but it also included the first London performance of a *Nonet* for five recorders, clarinet, two violins and cello by Martinu. Walter Bergmann was very pleased with the concert. A few days later he went to Maidenhead to lecture to forty recorder teachers. During December he began working on the translation into German of Tippett's new opera *King Priam*. The libretto (as with that for Tippett's previous opera *The Midsummer Marriage*) was Tippett's own. The year ended with a quiet, but enjoyable family Christmas with Erica and Peter Bendix, and Hilde Volhard and Erika Seelig and their mother.

January 1961 saw changes at Schott, with the retirement of Max Steffens. His successor appointed as Managing Director was Peter Makings. Steffens had worked for Schott for a long time and he had given a great deal of encouragement and support to the publication of recorder music, and to the Society of Recorder Players. He had given Edgar Hunt his job at Schott in 1937. Walter Bergmann was aware that there might now be significant changes at Schott. Peter Makings was an accountant (originally employed by Schott's accountants) who had major plans for the firm.

The year began as usual with his attendance at the ISM Conference. On January 5th, he was invited to lecture on 'Basso Continuo' for the Royal Musical Association, at Trinity College of Music. Walter Bergmann was very apprehensive about giving the lecture and dreaded failing to present his subject - or himself- competently. The lecture went well, and he received help and support from the RMA Chairman, Sir Jack Westrup (who had just received his knighthood). He could justifiably feel he was recognised as a musicologist by the musical establishment. He attended other lectures given at the ISM Conference. He found one given by Peter Maxwell-Davies the most interesting[7].

Walter Bergmann had also begun to have driving lessons. He decided to postpone his driving test - it was not easy learning to drive at the age of fifty-eight! He was travelling around the country on a regular basis, and wanted to be able to drive himself. On January 14th he went to Cambridge at the invitation of Miller's Music Shop, to participate in the second meeting of Miller's Junior Music Club, which had been founded by Mr H. Woolfenden. The daylong session concentrated on wind and brass instruments, particularly recorders and the French horn. Walter Bergmann took the morning session and talked about the recorder to around one hundred children. He played to them, the music including his *Variations for 9 Recorders*. He then conducted the children playing his own Handel arrangements and Viennese classics. Walter Bergmann obviously enjoyed the session, which was reported in the *Times Educational Supplement*. Their correspondent wrote[8], 'With a winning combination of enthusiasm, charm and easy authority, Dr Bergmann took this large ensemble through music by Handel, Haydn and Mozart spending enough time and care on each short item to produce pleasing results, but not so much as to risk boredom.' He gave a lecture recital in which he played 'a number of well- chosen light, descriptive pieces with gentle artistry'. In the afternoon, Guy Woolfenden gave a lecture-recital on the French horn.

Walter Bergmann's recorder class at the London College of Music was proving to be quite successful, with twenty pupils participating. On January 18th 1961, he was invited to put proposals before the College Board for an Early Music Department. On the following Saturday, the Dolmetsch family came to play at the London SRP meeting. Walter Bergmann was impressed with how the Dolmetsch children played - he felt it was the first time he had really heard them play musically together[9]. Although separated, both Carl and Marie Dolmetsch came with the children. Walter Bergmann had lunch with Marie Dolmetsch a few days later.

David Bendix, Walter Bergmann's grandson was born on January 24th 1961. In the evening, Walter Bergmann went to a concert at the Festival Hall, where the programme included Hindemith's *Concerto for Orchestra* Op. 38, which he had first heard in Erfurt in 1926, a year after its composition. It was a memorable day for him. He visited his daughter Erica and his new grandson for the first time on January 29th.

At the end of the month Walter Bergmann had a meeting with Archie Harradine, a theatrical producer, to discuss an idea that he and Norman Platt had been thinking about for several months. The proposal was for a Purcell cabaret, and Walter Bergmann invited Harradine to produce it. Archie Harradine was extremely interested and Walter Bergmann sent him a draft programme at the beginning of February 1961. They met again to plan further. Walter Bergmann was very keen to establish this new venture. February also saw a brief opportunity to meet Dietrich Gerhardt at Heathrow (he was en route for Harvard). He had lunch again with Alfred Deller, who was still depressed by Britten's choice of another countertenor to sing Oberon.

Walter Bergmann was enjoying participating in another of Britten's works, *Noyes Fludde*. *Noyes Fludde* is a one-act play set to music, which was first performed at the Aldeburgh Festival in Orford Church in June 1958. It was written so that the majority of the parts could be played by children. The cast was designed for three adults and ninety children. The orchestral parts were written for a mixture of professional and young amateur players. The professional group requires one solo treble recorder player, and the amateur group, descant and treble recorders. Altogether the work requires one hundred and fifty-six actors and instrumentalists to perform, plus audience participation. The West London Mission presented the production at the Kingsway Hall London in February 1961, the acting participants being drawn from the organisations associated with it, and local primary schools. Owen Brannigan, the bass, who had sung Noah in the original production, sang the same role in the Kingsway production. The voice of God was Donald Soper. Walter Bergmann played the solo treble part and led members of the London Branch of the Society of Recorder Players playing the recorder parts. In his diary he described the music as 'brilliant Britten'.

In March Walter Bergmann saw the realisation of his idea for a 'Purcell' cabaret. Described as 'A new entertainment with music of the 17th and 18th centuries', and entitled 'Musical Pills to purge Melancholy', the first two performances, produced by Archie Harradine, were given at the Mary Ward Settlement on March 17th and 18th as part of the St Pancras Arts Festival. The singers were Ilse Wolf, Laura Sarti, Clare Walmesley and Norman Platt, the actors Geoffrey Hedger and John Masters. They were accompanied by an instrumental and choral ensemble directed by Walter Bergmann. The items included music by Purcell, Hook, Blow and Biber and a scene entitled 'Bach in Potsdam' written by Walter Bergmann. The evening's entertainment would, it was hoped, 'add to your Pleasure, divert your Hours, when your Thoughts are unbended from the Times, Troubles and Fatigues'. This quotation prefaced the programme and was taken from Thomas D'Urfey's dedication of *Wit and Mirth: or Pills to Purge Melancholy*. It was a great success and well attended, with the Saturday night full. Walter Bergmann noted that the performance had weaknesses that could be improved, but he was very encouraged with the initial reaction. The 'Musical Pills' became one of his most successful ventures and one that gave him enormous satisfaction. The performance was reported both in the local *Kensington News and West London Times* and in *The Scotsman* in an article on London Music. The local paper praised the performances by Ilse Wolf, Laura Sarti and Clare Walmesley, and Walter Bergmann's direction of the instrumentalists. It was not complimentary about the 'Bach in Potsdam' scene. *The Scotsman*[10] described the evening as 'a sort of high-class cabaret'. The article was complimentary to Walter Bergmann, describing him as 'an expert on the art of the continuo (he gave a fine lecture on the subject recently to the Royal Musical Association), a first-rate musical editor, a scholar and a practical musician capable of playing quite well on piano or harpsichord, and composing a witty set of variations, all of which he played himself.

'As well as this, we had some naughty songs of the seventeenth century and a whole host of interesting pieces by Blow, Purcell, Tapray (a fascinating 1783 *Quartet*), Hammerschmidt and others, some of them staged by Archie Harradine, some of them just played or sung by musicians or choir.'

On March 22nd the participants, excepting the actors, met at the home of Norman Platt to evaluate the success of the 'Musical Pills'. They were critical of their performance - in particular, it was felt that words had not been enunciated clearly enough. However it was agreed that the performances had been well received, and plans were made for a second production in June 1961.

Two SRP 'annual' concerts were held in the spring of 1961. The first was in Leeds, and organised through Anthony Rowland-Jones, who was a Leeds University Lecturer and a recorder player. He ran an evening class in Leeds, from which a small group helped organise the concert. The performers were Carl Dolmetsch, Edgar Hunt, Walter Bergmann, Freda Dinn, Anthony Rowland-Jones, Alfred Deller and three string players, Walter Jorycz, Peter Denny, Etain Lovell and a small number of players from Rowland-Jones' evening class including Mary Hargreaves (Bonsor). The music was from the seventeenth and eighteenth centuries with the exception of Francis Baines' *Quartet* for two treble and two tenor recorders (1960). The concert was held in the Great Hall of the University. The concert was reviewed[11] in the *Yorkshire Post*, the correspondent of which was obviously not an enthusiast of the recorder and Baroque music! The recorder was dismissed as 'a limited and somewhat inexpressive instrument' that 'nonetheless commands a growing allegiance'. The content of the programme was described as 'music much alike in general texture and generally of the kind that provides more fun for the players than the listeners'. However the critic did find the Baines' *Quartet*, and songs and arias by Purcell, Bach and Handel more interesting listening. The concert was hoped to be a springboard for forming a branch of the SRP in West Yorkshire.* The second concert was held in the Bluecoat Hall, Liverpool. Some items from the first concert were repeated, but this time the performers did not include Alfred Deller. The soprano soloist was Olive Brunning, and members of the Merseyside Branch of the SRP participated in the concert. The music included arias by Handel, Bach and Arne with recorder obbligato. The concert was well received by the local press. The *Daily Post* wrote 'A packed Bluecoat Hall bore evidence to the widespread new interest in the instrument' (recorder) 'and four of the Society's directors (Carl Dolmetsch, Freda Dinn, Walter Bergmann and Chairman Edgar Hunt) joined forces with members of the Merseyside branch in presenting a programme of unusual artistic merit, delightfully performed'. 'Telemann's *Concerto Grosso in B flat* for two treble recorders, two oboes, strings and continuo made a fitting climax to a most successful concert. Given a few more programmes like this, the public might soon be able to forget, if not forgive, the shrill whistle of the badly-played school descant.' The *Liverpool Echo's* correspondent voiced his surprise that there were enough interested adults in Merseyside to fill the concert hall. Carl Dolmetsch's playing was 'the high spot of the evening'. The article observed that 'the recorder is an easy instrument to play - after a fashion - but obviously it has inherent possibilities that require a high degree of artistry to reveal'. Obviously the SRP decision to hold concerts in the northwest and Yorkshire were valuable in changing attitudes to the recorder! It is interesting to look in the programme for the Liverpool Concert and see how many music publishers were publishing recorder music by 1961. The advertisers of published music included Universal, Heinrichsen, Boosey and Hawkes and Oxford University Press, and there was also an advertisement of

---

* This did indeed happen, the West Riding SRP being founded by A. Rowland-Jones and Mary Hargreaves.

recordings made by Carl Dolmetsch and the Dolmetsch Ensemble for HMV (EMI).

The concert given by the London SRP Branch at the end of April was not so successful. The London Branch seemed to be declining in membership. April as a whole was a month of failures and successes. At the beginning of the month, Walter Bergmann completed translating the first act of Tippett's *King Priam*. On April 13th, he failed his driving test. The following day he arranged to participate in a BBC broadcast for the first time since 1956. The end of the month found him in a reflective mood. He wrote his epitaph, 'A musician whose hobby was music', and contemplated about God. He wrote in his diary[12] that he was an atheist who talked every night with God, and wondered why.

In May 1961 the decision was made to end the recorder classes at the Mary Ward Settlement. The Choir would continue, while Walter Bergmann would transfer his recorder teaching to the Marylebone Literary Institute. Sadly for Walter Bergmann, he did not receive an appointment at the London College of Music, in spite of the fact he had been taking a recorder class there. He was very disappointed that Robert Salkeld was eventually appointed Professor of Recorder (in June 1961). May 18th saw another performance of the Blow *Ode on the death of Henry Purcell*, this time in St Margaret's Westminster, as part of a concert given by two choirs, Pro Musica Sacra, conducted by Bruno Turner and the Elizabethan Singers, conducted by Louis Halsey. The two counter tenors were John Whitworth and Grayston Burgess. Walter Bergmann played the harpsichord. The performers also included Ian Partridge (tenor) and Archie Camden (bassoon). At the end of May Walter Bergmann had lunch with Basil Lam from the BBC. This was as a result of further correspondence Walter Bergmann had had about harpsichord continuo parts and their performance.

At the beginning of March, Charles Spinks had accompanied Alfred Deller singing Purcell songs for a broadcast on the Home Service. For the performance for the two songs *Music for a while* and *I attempt from love's sickness to fly*, Charles Spinks had hired the editions edited by Michael Tippett and Walter Bergmann from Schott. During the performance he did not adhere to the printed continuo. Walter Bergmann wrote[13] to William Glock at the BBC to discuss 'artistic, personal and legal' questions, which the broadcast raised. Eric Warr (Assistant Head of Music Programmes) replied on behalf of William Glock. He assumed, presumably because of the previous wrangle over whether Walter Bergmann could accompany Alfred Deller, that Walter Bergmann was questioning Charles Spinks' competence. It took several letters to sort out the situation. The BBC seemed unaware that Mr Spinks had hired copyright material, and pointed out that if the editor of a particular realisation is not acknowledged by the *Radio Times* or the announcer, a continuo player is under no obligation to adhere to a particular edition. In a letter dated May 7th 1961, Walter Bergmann eventually managed to convince Eric Warr that there was need for discussion, and that as well as discussing copyright material, he would like to raise the issue of why editors of particular editions were not acknowledged when the scholarship was of decisive importance. Eric Warr finally answered[14] 'I do understand the points you are making.'

The meeting was arranged with Basil Lam (who had been in charge of the broadcast), to try to answer Walter Bergmann's questions. Walter Bergmann was pleased with the meeting over lunch (at Walter Bergmann's expense), which resolved the problems. He noted in his diary 'BBC me!'[15], referring to the invitation he had made.

The beginning of June saw another performance of 'The Musical Pills' at Morley College, this time with the support of the Arts Council. The soloists and actors were the same as in the original performances, but some alterations were made to the original material. The overall number of items was reduced from seventeen to fifteen and the programme order altered. The instrumental ensemble was larger and there were no choral items. Again the evening was successful and received a favourable criticism in the *Times Educational Supplement*. It stated

'With Dr Bergmann as chief dispenser the pills were bound to be colourful. He constructed an imaginary dialogue between John Sebastian Bach and his son Carl Philip Emmanuel, on the comparative difficulties of being cantor at Leipzig and being harpsichordist for Frederick the Great. The rise of opera and the obsession which the King had for flute concerti were well brought out. In an evening where everything was smoothly organised this dialogue and the following item were particularly well-knit. Carl had suggested to his father that the latter should make a present to the king of a new composition. The six-part *Ricercare* for *The Musical Offering* began as he pondered upon this idea.

'The simultaneous translation spoken by Mr Platt to *Kusslied* by Hammerschmidt (1611-1675) proved most amusing, and it is hoped that similar prescriptions will be available again at Morley College.'[16] The making of revisions to the original material had definitely benefited the performance.

During June Walter Bergmann was working hard at completing an article on Barsanti and continuing to translate *King Priam*, in spite of the diversion of his five month old grandson coming to stay. He went with Norman Platt, Clare Walmesley and Laura Sarti to the Arts Council to ask advice about making a Scottish tour with the 'Musical Pills'. They received helpful and positive advice, and decided to go ahead with the plan. They also made the decision to ask Ilse Wolf to join the tour, although this would mean a financial loss. On July 8th, Walter Bergmann participated in a concert given by the London SRP at Roehampton for the Froebel Institute, in aid of the Froebel Institute Building Fund. The other performers included Carl Dolmetsch, Edgar Hunt, Joseph Saxby and Clare Walmesley. Later in July, Walter Bergmann attended the opening concert of the Haslemere Festival. He was not impressed. He enjoyed one or two items, but found the overall standard poor, and felt that the recorder playing had mainly been of an 'impossible amateurish standard'.[17]

Walter Bergmann took his driving test again in July and much to his annoyance, failed a second time. He obviously felt he should have passed! He wrote in his diary 'The Chief Examiner was a swine - I think I did very well'. Others weren't quite so sure of his driving capabilities!

At the end of July 1961, an unexpected professional engagement arose. Alfred Deller had worked with the lutenist Desmond Dupré since 1948. Unfortunately Dupré was taken ill and Walter Bergmann stepped in to accompany Alfred Deller in a concert at University College, Oxford during a summer school for singers, founded by Margaret Ritchie. He enjoyed the concert, though he had to play from a difficult manuscript, which required him to improvise some of the continuo parts. In August came the usual round of summer schools. First came the Recorder Summer School at Roehampton. Afterwards he wrote in his diary that he needed to be delivered from the sins of 'generalisation, lust of power, immorality and vanity'.[18] (By immorality he meant not taking a balanced view of one's advantages in relation to someone else's disadvantages.) After his regular visit to the summer school at Matlock, Walter Bergmann was invited to the summer school at Dartington Hall, Devon. He lectured on ornamentation and bass continuo. He enjoyed being with respected professional musicians, who included among their number some with whom he had worked in the early years of their careers before they had established themselves professionally. These included members of the Amadeus Quartet, who by 1961 had been established for thirteen years and become an internationally recognised string quartet. Walter Bergmann had of course known the two violinists, Norbert Brainin and Sigmund Nissel, since his early days in Britain. Norbert Brainin played for both Walter Bergmann's Dartington lectures, and the soprano, Jennifer Vyvyan, whom he had also known in the early stages of her career, sang for his continuo lecture. (Jennifer Vyvyan had achieved recognition through the roles she had created in Britten's operas, for example that of the Governess in the first production of *The Turn of the Screw* in 1954.) Walter Bergmann was pleased to be asked by Brainin to edit a Handel sonata for him, which they might present together to the BBC. Later in 1961, Walter Bergmann sent Jennifer Vyvyan some of his editions of Purcell songs and when she wrote to thank him, she mentioned how much she had learnt from his continuo lecture[19].

Walter Bergmann spent just over a week in Devon. For most of it, he stayed in a hotel in Chagford. He enjoyed the scenery of Dartmoor and its villages. He visited Clare Walmesley at home, accompanying her while she learnt music from *Der Freischütz*. It brought back memories from almost forty years previously. He still found it beautiful music[20]. The few days away gave him plenty of time to think. He had not been well while staying in Matlock, and he had lost his voice. His imagination ran away with him and he began to imagine he had cancer. He spent time thinking about his will. He wanted to be on his own, then found he was depressed and miserable by himself. He did manage to work at the *King Priam* translation.

Walter Bergmann returned briefly to London and then spent a few days in Bexhill on Sea with Grete and Erica, Peter and David Bendix. He was back at Schott on September 4th, where things were not going well (he had had an argument with Hartog in August). He started driving lessons again. On September 19th, he visited a primary school in Willesden, where there was an excellent recorder teacher called Eileen Downer. Among the players he heard was a young girl called Evelyn Nallen, who impressed him with her musical potential and ability.

At the end of September, Walter Bergmann began teaching the recorder at the Marylebone Institute. His two classes consisted of a small beginners' class and fourteen players of intermediate standard. October saw him at last passing his driving test. In November he finally finished the *King Priam* translation two days before the deadline. At the beginning of December, Walter Bergmann heard a group of around 100 children, conducted by Herbert Hersom, play his Christmas Carol arrangements. It was the first time he had heard them played by children. He noted[21] in his diary that he felt he had reached 'maturity' in his continuo writing and arranging. On December 16th Walter and Grete Bergmann flew to Germany. They went first to Marburg, where they visited Hans Bergmann in hospital, and then the Versteegs, his old musical friends from pre-war days. Jan Versteeg was now 79. Walter Bergmann also visited the publisher Bärenreiter to discuss his editing of Telemann quartets. After a difficult parting from Hans and Daisy Bergmann, they travelled on to Wiesbaden and then separated for a few days. Walter

Bergmann travelled to Basel and Schaffhausen. He met a friend from his student days whom he had not seen for thirty one years. Travelling to Basel reminded him of his student days in Freiburg, when he had been packed off to be separated from Issi Matz. In Schaffhausen he met Herr Küng, the respected Swiss recorder maker, to discuss recorder problems. He returned north to meet Grete in Karlsruhe, where she was visiting relatives, and then they went together to Ludswighafen to Fritz and Anneliese Bergmann. They spent Sylvester (New Year) with Grete Bergmann's two sisters in Hamburg, joined by other friends including the Gerhardts. Walter Bergmann then tried to fly home, but snow in London cancelled all flights. He ended up returning by train and boat via Harwich, anxious to get back for the ISM Conference in Bristol. Grete returned a week later.

In the September of 1962, Walter Bergmann was sixty. However there was no diminution of his activities. His diary for 1962 was as full as it had ever been. In fact his range of commitments seemed to be growing, not getting smaller. Teaching and adjudicating were playing a larger role in his life than before. During the year Walter Bergmann travelled widely throughout Britain to adjudicate; the venues included Brighton, Portsmouth, Norwich, Watford and Bury St Edmunds. He could of course now drive himself to engagements. A new venture for him was the start of his involvement in Summer courses at the Orff Institute in Salzburg.

One of his first engagements for 1962 was participating in a conference on 'Teaching the Recorder' at the University of London Institute of Education, which was sponsored by Schott. Around two hundred people attended. The conference was opened and closed by members of the Institute's teaching staff. Freda Dinn, Edgar Hunt and Walter Bergmann gave three short lectures. Freda Dinn lectured on the educational value of the recorder, Edgar Hunt talked about the recorder itself, and Walter Bergmann presented a lecture on teaching materials for the recorder. Throughout 1962, Walter Bergmann lectured to teachers and visited schools.

He participated in a number of concerts in 1962. In February he again took part in two performances of Britten's *Noyes Fludde* at the Kingsway Hall. On March 2nd, Walter Bergmann conducted a concert he had organised for the St Pancras Arts Festival in St Pancras Town Hall. This was a rewarding and fulfilling experience for him, as the concert went extremely well. The music consisted of four works: Clarke's *Music on the Death of Henry Purcell*, a Telemann *Concerto Grosso in B flat*, Purcell's music for *Timon of Athens* and his *Ode for St Cecilia's Day 1692*. The solo singers were Ilse Wolf, Clare Walmesley, Laura Sarti, Alfred Deller, Gerald English, Maurice Bevan and Norman Platt. The instrumentalists included Carl Dolmetsch, Edgar Hunt, and Neil Black (oboe), and the orchestra was led by Sylvia Cleaver. The choral parts were sung by the augmented Mary Ward Cantata Choir. All the music was edited by Walter Bergmann. (The *Ode for St Cecilia* was co-edited with Michael Tippett.) The concert received good reviews in *The Times*, *Music and Musicians*, and the local Hampstead paper. The Times was complimentary about the rarely heard programme content and described the evening as stimulating, making particular reference to the intelligent and lively performance of *Timon of Athens*. The Hampstead News wrote that the concert 'was one of those rare occasions where everything went off extraordinarily well, providing an evening of unalloyed pleasure. Most of the credit must go to the conductor Walter Bergmann, who secured delightfully unaffected performances from start to finish.'[23] Walter Bergmann was delighted with the success of the concert and public recognition of his competence. He was at last receiving recognition for his work and achievements.

There was, unfortunately, one sad aspect to the concert. Walter Bergmann and Alfred Deller fell out with each other over the concert rehearsals, and Deller told Walter Bergmann that it was the last time he would sing for him. They had argued over which rehearsals Deller should have been expected to attend. Walter Bergmann was angry that Deller was not prompt in attending rehearsals and did not come even when he was free to come. Deller argued that too much was expected of him and that Walter Bergmann had made conducting mistakes. Walter Bergmann noted in his diary that it was the end of twenty years of friendship[24]. Gerald English also had problems attending rehearsals, which Walter Bergmann did not like.

On Good Friday 1962, Walter Bergmann played continuo in a performance of Bach's *St John Passion* in the Kingsway Hall, conducted by Donald Cashmore. In June he played in one item for Imogen Holst in a concert at the Aldeburgh Festival. At the end of September there was another performance of the 'Musical Pills', this time in Newmarket. The participants were restricted to four singers (Ilse Wolf, Clare Walmesley, Laura Sarti and Norman Platt) and Walter Bergmann. The programme changed to suit the different circumstances.

On May 29th 1962, Walter Bergmann attended the premier of Tippett's *King Priam*, which was performed at the 1962 Coventry Festival to celebrate the completion of the new cathedral. The theme of the Festival was 'Peace'. As with Britten's *War Requiem*, the other major work premiered at Coventry in 1963, *King Priam* dealt with war and the possibility of reconciliation. Erica Bendix drove Walter Bergmann to Coventry with Grete and Clare Walmesley. Walter Bergmann was not sure about the new cathedral. In some ways it appealed to him, but there were aspects about he disliked, and he found it sentimental. In June he went to Glyndbourne to a performance of Mozart's *Cosi fan tutte*, one of his favourite operas, which he enjoyed very much indeed.

In July 1962 Walter Bergmann taught at what became a regular annual recorder weekend at Belstead House in Ipswich. There were three groups of players. Walter Bergmann took the advanced group. A few days later he travelled to Salzburg to the Orff Institute, with the objective of becoming both involved in Orff's Schulwerk, and in the publication of English editions of the Schulwerk. He visited the different classes and had discussions with Carl Orff. He also became acquainted with Margaret Murray, who had worked for some while with Orff and would be the editor of the English editions of Orff's work. They arranged to meet in London for further discussions. The following month Walter Bergmann enjoyed the annual Recorder Summer School at Roehampton. In particular he found pleasure in working with Brian Bonsor. At the Tutor's Concert, Walter Bergmann conducted Bonsor's *Tango* for recorders and piano. During the week he appreciated Brian Bonsor's skilled and sensitive piano playing.

His sixtieth birthday celebrations were low key. During September he had problems with ill health again, this time with his gall bladder. He was well enough to travel with Grete at the end of the month to attend a conference in Kassel. He found it very tiring. There were two operas performed, by Strauss (*Frau ohne Schatten*) and Gluck (*Orpheus and Euridice*), neither of which he enjoyed very much as he thought they were badly conducted and unimaginatively produced. They must have been an enormous contrast to the Sam Wanamaker production of *King Priam* a few months earlier. He did enjoy the company of Margaret Murray, with whom he attended the lectures and performances, and had formed a strong friendship, which lasted until his death. Before leaving Germany, he visited Fritz and Anneliese Bergmann, and went to Schott in Mainz. Back in London in October he wrote in his diary,[25] 'I am sixty, but I only look forward, and not back.' A week later, Imogen Holst offered him a contract to play the recorder at Aldeburgh the following June.

Work at Schott was going reasonably well. He had a great deal of music to edit, and responsibility for the English editions of the Orff work. Makings had made a discreet start at Schott. In June Walter Bergmann had come to an agreement with him that he, Bergmann, would arrive later at work, and go earlier on some occasions.

As usual, his SRP activities and work with children had continued during 1962 - although conducting amateur adults and children was not always an enjoyable experience! For example in October he conducted a recorder meeting in Wakefield. It was a long afternoon, the playing was appalling and he was offered no tea. 'It was hell.'[26] (No-one had any tea because there was no access to the kitchen, something WB probably did not appreciate.)

By October 1962, the rift between Alfred Deller and Walter Bergmann had begun to heal. Alfred Deller asked Walter Bergmann to accompany him in a BBC broadcast of Purcell songs (which the BBC accepted). Recorded on October 12th 1962, the programme was broadcast on the Third Programme on November 24th. On October 16th Deller and Walter Bergmann gave a concert in Maidstone with William Bennett (flute), Sylvia Cleaver and Desmond Dupré under the name of the Amphion Ensemble (which had not existed for fourteen years). The music, mainly edited by Walter Bergmann, consisted of Telemann, Purcell songs, including *Music for a While*, and songs by John Dowland (1563-1626) and Thomas Campion (1567 - 1620). Alfred Deller was obviously trying to make amends, support Walter Bergmann and settle their differences.

At the end of the year Walter Bergmann had his first engagement in connection with his new association with Orff School Music and Margaret Murray. He conducted a concert at Wykeham County Secondary School. The programme included the first English performance of Carl Orff's *The Christmas Story*, translated by Margaret Murray. The choir for the performance was drawn from primary schools in the Willesden area, and the actors from Willesden Grammar School. The first part of the concert consisted of music for recorder and strings. The soloist in the *Siciliana* from Sammartini's Concerto for descant recorder was Evelyn Nallen, aged ten. The second half of the concert consisted of the Orff work. Among the instrumentalists playing the accompanying parts for Orff instruments was a young girl who later became known as Twiggy when she developed a highly successful modelling and acting career. The concert was reported in the January edition of the *Musical Times*, who described it as 'delightful' and complimented Walter Bergmann on his 'sure and spirited direction' resulting in 'a memorable account of the music'. The reviewer remarked 'What a change this made from the carol concerts and Gilbert and Sullivan routines that, year after year, glut the end-of-term market'[27]. Also in December Walter Bergmann was delighted that his *Pastorale* was performed in a concert entitled 'New Music for Old Instruments' given in London. The performers were Carl Dolmetsch and Brian Brockless.

1963 started with a significant occasion for Walter Bergmann - the German premier of *King Priam* in Karlsruhe, using his translation. He flew to Germany on January 23rd, noting in his diary[28] that his car would not start and he had had to hurry to Heathrow by underground, which made him aware of his age. The opera was well received in Germany. However *The Times* critic felt the overall production was not as appealing as the English production and that the producer had laboured over his interpretation, a point also echoed by the *Frankfurter Allegemeine Zeitung*. The latter praised the musical quality of the performance and the quality of Walter Bergmann's translation[29].

During 1963 Walter Bergmann had several good engagements. On Friday March 8th he conducted 'An Evening of 17th and 18th Century Music' for the second year at the St Pancras Arts Festival. The programme consisted of music by J S Bach, Telemann, Blow and Purcell. The singers included Walter Bergmann's 'regulars' such as Ilse Wolf, Norman Platt, and Alfred Deller. The solo instrumentalists included William Bennett (flute), Neil Black (oboe) and Philip Jones (trumpet). Margaret Murray played the harpsichord. The augmented Mary Ward Choir sang the choral parts, and the orchestra was the Telemann Orchestra. The concert had a large audience and received good criticisms in *The Times*, the *Daily Telegraph* and the *Financial Times*. David Cairns, critic of the *Financial Times* complained about the length of the concert[30]; he wrote that 'Purcell's superb *Music and Masque to Dioclesian*, practically a concert in itself, was preceded by a Bach cantata, Telemann concerto and ode by Blow. Only the stern call of duty dragged me away before the end of the Purcell.' He praised direction of the concert and the orchestral playing. 'Walter Bergmann's conducting more than made up in zeal, warmth and understanding what it lacked in decisiveness of beat. The admirable orchestra was alert and vigorous and sensitive.'

On May 17th 1963, Walter Bergmann conducted another concert of eighteenth century works, edited by him, in the Wigmore Hall. The music included Haydn's *Arianna a Naxos*, a cantata for soprano and piano, and two works by Telemann. Ilse Wolf was the soprano soloist, and the instrumental soloists again included William Bennett, Neil Black, and Jennifer Ryan. Walter Bergmann played the keyboard. The concert was quite well received by the critics, although the reviews in the *Daily Telegraph* and *The Times* disagreed, one liking the performance of the Haydn cantata, the other not. Although apparently still having doubts about Telemann's worthiness as a composer, *The Times* critic praised the 'stylistic expertise' shown in the Telemann works.

May 1963 also saw the first edition of the new re-launched *Recorder and Music Magazine*, a joint venture between the Society of Recorder Players and Schott, which incorporated the SRP journal *The Recorder News*. The Editor was Ken Kenworthy and the Assistant Editor, Ronald Corcoran. The editorial board consisted of Walter Bergmann, Herbert Hersom, Anthony Rowland-Jones and Richard Noble. The first edition included an article by Walter Bergmann on Telemann's *Wedding Divertissement* for descant recorder and piano, and a photograph of Carl Dolmetsch, taken by Walter Bergmann, to accompany an interview given by Dolmetsch to John Thomson for the magazine. Photography was a growing interest for Walter Bergmann.

In the June of 1963, the 'Bergmann Recorder Consort' played in two concerts devised and directed by Imogen Holst at the Aldeburgh Festival. The two concerts were entitled 'Dowland and His Contemporaries'. The first consisted of music by William Byrd, the second of secular music. Both concerts were recorded by the BBC. The Consort, consisting of Walter Bergmann, Elaine Kaye, Margaret Murray and Theo Wyatt, played a Byrd *Fantasia* arranged for four recorders in the first concert, and five instrumental pieces in the second concert. The reviews were not very good, although the *Guardian* stated[31] that the recorder consort had contributed 'agreeably' to the programme. Also in June 1963, Walter Bergmann played the harpsichord in two concerts at the Stour Music Festival, the brainchild of Alfred Deller. Both Walter Bergmann and Alfred Deller were happy to work together again. The first concert was devoted to Bach, consisting of *Cantata 106*, the Brandenburg *Concerto no. 4* and the *Magnificat*: the second was a concert of music by Purcell including *Music for a While*. The recorder soloists in the Brandenburg Concerto were John Beckett and John Southcott.

Walter Bergmann had a number of lecturing and teaching engagements during 1963. These included lecturing on the recorder at Girton College Cambridge in April, attending a conference on the recorder in Newcastle in May, teaching on a course for teachers in Wakefield in September and two lectures at University College Londonderry on 'The History and Repertoire of the Recorder'. He adjudicated at a number of music festivals and visited a variety of schools. He started two recorder classes at the City Literary Institute, one intermediate and one advanced class. The first evening was not a great success. 'It was frightful'[32] he wrote in his diary. Sadly, only four singers registered for the Mary Ward Choir in September 1963, and he reluctantly decided to give up the choir and his association with Mary Ward. He had worked there for ten years. 'I am very sad' he wrote in his diary.[33]

In December 1963, Walter Bergmann and Ian Kemp became Directors of Eulenburg for an annual annuity of £400. The Eulenburg Company published miniature scores. Dr Kurt Eulenburg brought the company to London in 1939, occupying a room on the top floor of 48 Great Marlborough Street, the home of Schott and Co. Schott became the owners of the firm in 1957, but it retained its operating independence. By 1963 Kurt Eulenburg was still running the firm at the age of eighty-four. Walter Bergmann had lunched with Dr Eulenburg in February 1963, who told him he would like him to be involved in the running of Eulenburg. (Kurt Eulenburg finally retired in 1969 at the age of 90!)

On December 31st Walter Bergmann went to Chester to lecture on the famous collection of old recorders in the Chester Grovesnor Museum. The Chester collection included a matching quartet of instruments, particularly important because they include double holes for the lowest semi-tones, this being the outstanding improvement to recorders in the eighteenth century. The instruments were actually owned by Carl Dolmetsch, who prior to the lecture, brought four instruments to London for Walter Bergmann to examine and play. They were made by Bressan, who was considered by many to be the finest recorder maker of around 1700. Walter Bergmann immediately insured the instruments for £1000 for the two weeks he had possession of them. Margaret Murray and Robin Read joined Walter Bergmann in Chester to play illustrations for the lecture. While in Chester, he spent time examining and photographing the other Bressan recorders in the collection.

During 1963 plans had been made for more performances of the 'Musical Pills', with a new producer Douglas Craig, who was a friend of Laura

Sarti and Norman Platt, and a Resident Producer at the RCM Opera and Drama School. He had experience of producing small-scale opera productions. Musical Pills needed to be produced with a minimum amount of scenery and maximum effect. The first revised production took place in Salisbury in February 1964, the performers being Clare Walmesley, Laura Sarti, Margaret Murray and Walter Bergmann. Margaret Murray joined Walter Bergmann to augment the instrumental forces, playing recorder, cello and harpsichord. The revised programme included 'The Interrupted Serenade' by Mozart, 'Mad Bess' by Purcell and five pieces from a *Wedding Divertissement* for recorder and harpsichord by Telemann. A slightly shorter and re-ordered performance of the programme was given at the Stour Festival in June 1964.

Walter Bergmann again contributed a concert of seventeenth and eighteenth century music to the Tenth St Pancras Festival held in February 1964. This concert was one of the most successful that he directed ever. The second part of the concert was devoted to a work by Telemann, his cantata *Ino*. Walter Bergmann had revived *Ino* and directed the first English performance at the Mary Ward Settlement in April 1953. The work was written for solo soprano, and Ilse Wolf was the soloist at both the original revival and in the 1964 performance. The original performance, coupled with Telemann's opera *Pimpinone*, had been well received by the audience but not the press. In 1965 the reaction was very different. Attitudes towards Telemann had begun to change. The critics were unanimous in their praise of the work and its performance. *The Times* critic considered[34] that one of the most important contributions of the St Pancras Festival made to London's musical life was in providing the opportunity to hear little known works, and Walter Bergmann's concert did just this, with the performance of *Ino* being a revelation.

The Financial Times stated[35] '*Ino* is a magnificent piece. Telemann was perhaps the most prolific composer who ever lived; some of his music is certainly dull and one is inevitably suspicious of so fluent and futile a craftsman who once boasted he could set a play bill to music. But in this work, composed in 1766, when he was 85, there is inspiration. It is a tour de force for solo soprano, whose only point of rest during 35 minutes of the most varied and dramatic music is a *Dance of Tritons*.' The paper commended Walter Bergmann on his championship of Telemann and his conducting of the Telemann Orchestra. Ilse Wolf was also commended for the dramatic style she brought to the music. Overall 'the whole concert was enjoyable, being made of music that was choice, mainly unfamiliar, and affectionately performed - and being not too long.' (The latter comment perhaps made with thought of the previous year's concert!)

The *Musical Times*[36] wrote 'Two years ago Bergmann produced an exciting minor masterpiece in Jeremiah Clarke's *Music on Henry Purcell's Death*, published it and has seen it completely neglected ever since. This year's revelation was Telemann's solo cantata *Ino*. It is a most imaginative score. Violently dramatic, the music, after Ino's inspired header into a calmer world, approaches the suave elegance of Telemann's younger contemporaries.' 'Ilse Wolf sang the enormously taxing solo part with resplendent tone and dramatic fire. Ranging through a gamut of emotions she scored a notable personal triumph in which she was handsomely supported by conductor and orchestra. The conductor, if he has not been discouraged by the fate of his Clarke piece, should publish his edition of *Ino*. And somebody should certainly ask Ilse Wolf to record it."

Music and Musicians also praised the performance[37], and pointed out the historical significance of the work. When Telemann wrote the work, 'Haydn was already 34 years old, and *Ino* belongs much more to the 'galant' world than to the baroque period.' Walter Bergmann was very pleased with the concert.

In March 1964 Walter Bergmann noted in his diary that he had been in England for twenty-five years. In June he wondered whether he should write his diary in English or German. He could he felt express himself better in English, when writing about music. He decided he would write in English in future, except where he could express something better in German. However after just over a page the journal resorts back to German except for a few English words!

Walter Bergmann's age was beginning to concern him. On visiting an acquaintance he wrote[38], 'He is 8 years younger than I, I thought the reverse. That is because I do not see myself. My age starts worrying me. In 2 months Grete will draw her first old age pension! The financial future is dark, but we don't worry, though my bank account is always near the red.'

In June 1964, Walter Bergmann was heavily involved in the Stour Music Festival. The music included the first performance of a work for countertenor and harpsichord by Rubbra. Alfred Deller and Walter Bergmann began rehearsing the work in May. All the rehearsals had gone reasonably well. Alfred Deller told Walter Bergmann he preferred his harpsichord playing to that of anyone else[39].

On the evenings of June 26th and 27th, performances were given by the Deller Consort and the Philomusica of London of music by Locke, Handel, Purcell and Arne including Arne's *The Masque of Alfred*. Walter Bergmann played continuo. Among its performers, the Philomusica included Alan Civil (horn), Neil Black (oboe) and Francis Baines (bass), (whose *Recorder Quartet* was published in 1960). During the afternoon of June 27th, Alfred Deller and Walter Bergmann gave the first performance of Rubbra's new work *Salve Regina*, for countertenor and harpsichord, which was followed by J S Bach's *Mass in B minor*. The solos in the *Mass in B minor* were sung by members of the Deller Consort, Honor Sheppard (soprano), Robert Tear (tenor) and Mark Deller, Alfred Deller's son who was also a countertenor, and had sung for Walter Bergmann in his 1964 St Pancras Concert. The Festival Choir was conducted by Alfred Deller. Walter Bergmann played continuo. In the late evening of both 26th and 27th June, there were performances of the Musical Pills, which meant Walter Bergmann performed in five concerts in two days! The two performances of the Pills were extremely successful. The programme of each performance ended with the audience joining in the singing of a rondelay, 'He who would happy be, here and eternally, let him learn to rejoice with instrument or voice in ear and heart'. An appropriate comment, the *Kentish Express* observed[40], to make on the Stour Festival, where music came first.

On the afternoon of Sunday June 28th Walter Bergmann played harpsichord and recorder in a concert of medieval and Tudor church music. It was given by the Deller Consort with the Bergmann Recorder Consort. Walter Bergmann played continuo and Don Smithers the crumhorn. The Bergmann Recorder Consort consisted of Elaine Kaye, Margaret Murray, Theo Wyatt and Walter Bergmann. The programme included consort music by Gabrieli, Gibbons, pieces attributed to Henry VIII, and a Byrd 5-part mass. On the Sunday evening, Walter Bergmann returned exhausted to London.

The following week found Walter Bergmann in Oxford, playing harpsichord in a concert conducted by Michael Tippett. Walter Bergmann had lunched with Tippett in early June to discuss the concert. Tippett was friendly and charming. The actual concert (on July 3rd), Walter Bergmann found depressing, although he was flattered to be asked to perform. The music consisted of works by Tippett, Bach and Stravinsky, including Tippett's *Songs for Ariel* from incidental music for *The Tempest* (1962) for contralto, harpsichord, flute, clarinet and horn, and Bach's *Sixth Brandenburg Concerto*. In the rehearsal it seemed to him that the concerto was played without any feeling for the right tempo or spirit of the music. Neil Black, the oboist, whose playing was much admired by Walter Bergmann, tried to cheer him up by saying that rehearsals commonly were like that with professional orchestral players. At the actual concert Walter Bergmann felt he played all right, but he did not like the overall performance. Following the concert Walter Bergmann picked up the threads of his friendship with Michael Tippett for the first time for several years.

During 1964 Walter Bergmann was also involved in a number of recorder concerts linked to his recorder classes, the SRP and school performances. His teaching and adjudicating activities continued as ever. He was always on the look out for musical talent in children and eager to encourage them. In particular in 1964 he tried to support and help Evelyn Nallen, then twelve, and her teacher Eileen Downer.

The summer saw the usual summer courses at Matlock and Roehampton. He travelled to Salzburg at the end of August to visit the Orff Institute and enjoyed attending some of the Salzburg Festival. Returning via Germany he visited Fritz and Hans Bergmann, the latter in hospital. He spent some time with Dietrich Gerhardt.

Walter Bergmann then travelled to Amsterdam by TEE (fast train). The journey brought back memories of his departure from Germany twenty-five years previously, particularly when his passport was inspected. The objective of the 1964 journey was to discuss with Frans Brüggen the joint editing of Schickhardt sonatas and the possibility of giving a concert together. As in 1939, Walter Bergmann visited the Rijksmuseum, a place he always enjoyed.

In October 1964 Walter Bergmann was delighted to have lunch with Michael Tippett. The lunch was not a particular success as Tippett told him that his (WB's) German translation of *A Child of our Time* had been much criticized. In spite of this, Walter Bergmann visited Michael Tippett at home a couple of weeks later and enjoyed spending a day there discussing Tippett's music and various musical acquaintances.

At the end of 1964, an even more shortened version of the Musical Pills was performed at the annual ISM Conference. Walter Bergmann was not sure how well the Pills went down with such an august audience, but he received a pleasant letter from the Secretary, thanking him for 'his delightful contribution' to the party[41].

In family matters Walter Bergmann was content. There was concern about his brother Hans' health, but he was enjoying watching his grandson David, now three, growing up.

Several significant events for Walter Bergmann happened in 1965. He gave recitals with Frans Brüggen. He was involved in the celebrations for Michael Tippett's sixtieth birthday. He began teaching at the Orff summer courses in Salzburg and was asked to contribute to Encyclopaedia Britannica. He was of course editing music throughout the year. Works edited in 1964 included the Purcell *Ode* of 1683 for Eulenburg.

Michael Tippett was sixty on January 2nd 1965. A birthday presentation was made to him on January 1st at the ISM Conference. On his actual birthday, a concert was given in his honour at Morley College. The programme consisted of his *First String Quartet*, the cantata *Boyhood's End* for tenor and piano, the *Songs for Ariel* and the cantata *Crown of the Year*. After the concert the Hartogs gave a party to which many people, including Walter Bergmann were invited. At the party, Peter Pears pleased Walter Bergmann by telling him that he wanted to put on a performance the following year of the Jeremiah Clarke Ode *On the Death of Henry Purcell*, edited by Walter Bergmann. On January 5th 1965, Faber published a tribute to Michael Tippett entitled *Michael Tippett, A Symposium on his Sixtieth Birthday*, edited by Ian Kemp. It consisted of contributions from many of Tippett's friends, many of whom were musicians he had worked with, including Walter Bergmann. In spite of his differences with Tippett, Walter Bergmann was fully aware of how Tippett had helped him in his early years in Britain and he had always valued Tippett's friendship. His contribution concluded[42]

'I owe to Tippett my enthusiasm for the English madrigalists, for Gibbons, Purcell and others. At a time when I was supposed to be an enemy alien, he let me take my modest part in English music-making and, in spite of great linguistic difficulties on my side, offered me friendship: nor do I forget the help he gave me and many others.

'Tippett and I have edited together a number of works of the basso continuo period. I have often been asked how we actually work together. In my opinion it would be a crime to keep him away from composing, so I saw and see it as my duty to do the work of writing the notes while he points his finger at the weak spots. He is mostly right: if I do not think so, we argue until we are both satisfied. There is, however, never a compromise, for there is no compromise in art.' (In his obituary of Walter Bergmann, Michael Tippett (1988) acknowledged Walter Bergmann's capable and skilled solutions to realising Purcell's basses[43].)

A presentation party for the book to be given to Tippett was arranged by Faber and Faber for the evening of January 5th. Unfortunately T S Eliot died during the previous night, so none of the Company's directors came to the party. The composer Arthur Bliss made the actual presentation to Michael Tippett in the absence of the directors.

A birthday concert was held in Michael Tippett's honour in Tunbridge Wells on January 31st under the auspices of the East Sussex and West Kent Choral Festival, of whom Tippett was President. Michael Tippett conducted the concert himself. The combined choral societies of East Sussex and Kent were trained for the concert by Dr Thornton Lofthouse. The programme consisted of *Five Mystical Songs* by Vaughan Williams, Tippett's *Crown of the Year* and *The Ode for St Cecilia's Day, 1692* by Purcell (edited by Tippett and Bergmann). The soloists were members of the Deller Consort, including Alfred Deller and Maurice Bevan, Sir William McKie (piano) and Walter Bergmann (piano and harpsichord). As well as the Festival Choirs and an orchestra, choirs and a percussion group from local grammar schools participated.

The Crown of the Year was a cantata written by Tippett in 1958 for the centenary of Badminton School; the text was by Christopher Fry. In the performance in Tunbridge Wells, Walter Bergmann played the piano. Theo Wyatt and Margaret Murray played the recorder parts. Walter Bergmann was not happy with his performance in

The Crown of the Year, but felt he played the continuo part well for the Purcell. However the report in the Sussex Express was uncritical. Of the *Crown of the Year* it said[44] that Dr Tippett 'electrified the Hall with his brilliant work *Crown of the Year*, assisted by an instrumental ensemble which included Dr Walter Bergmann, who delighted with his performance on piano and harpsichord'.

In March 1965 Walter Bergmann's performing career received a boost when Frans Brüggen came to London. They spent a hectic week together. At the beginning of the week, they recorded three sonatas together, - a Barsanti *Sonata in D minor*, the Handel *Recorder Sonata in C* and the Telemann *Recorder Sonata in F* (the last unrehearsed). In the evening of the same day, Walter Bergmann's evening classes at the City Literary Institute gave a concert. The Tuesday and Wednesday were spent in rehearsing for a concert held on Saturday March 6th. On the Thursday, the curator of the Chester Museum brought the Chester recorders to London to be played on the Friday at the BBC. Unfortunately it snowed and the train was delayed by five hours. Frans Brüggen had arranged to meet friends and telephoned to Walter Bergmann to say he could not make a rehearsal; Jeanette van Wingerden, the third performer was taken ill at the Bergmann's. In the middle of all the confusion, Edgar Hunt arrived - the only calm in all the storm![45] On the Friday Jeanette van Wingerden was still ill and Beverly Smith took her place to play the Chester Recorders with Walter Bergmann, Frans Brüggen and Edgar Hunt for the BBC recording. It went better than Walter Bergmann expected. A variety of music for one to four instruments was played.

To finish the week on the Saturday, Frans Brüggen gave a recital in the Wigmore Hall, with Walter Bergmann at the harpsichord and piano, and vocal items contributed by Clare Walmesley, Laura Sarti and Norman Platt. The programme included the first public performance of Walter Bergmann's *Sonata* for descant recorder and piano, dedicated to Frans Brüggen, a *Sonata in A flat* by Schickhardt, edited jointly by Frans Brüggen and Walter Bergmann, and *Chloe found Amintas lying all in tears*, for three voices, by John Blow. The concert was well reviewed, especially for Frans Brüggen. Anthony Payne, the critic for *Music and Musicians* observed that Walter Bergmann sounded happier playing the harpsichord than the piano[46]. Walter Bergmann was however delighted with how his *Sonata* for descant was received. He noted in his diary[47] that he was astounded at how well it had gone in performance. The *Daily Telegraph*[48] found it to be imaginative and well written. The *Theme and Variations* were ingenious and full of variety. Both *The Financial Times* and *Music and Musicians* commented on the 'Hindemithean' likeness of the sonata. It was a satisfactory climax to an enjoyable but exhausting week.

In June 1965 Walter Bergmann once again participated in the Stour Music Festival at the invitation of Alfred Deller. Alfred Deller directed two performances of Orazio Vecchi's *L'Amfiparnasso*, a work consisting of madrigals, which linked together by a narrative, told a story. (Groves' Dictionary describes[49] the work as a madrigal-comedy, written for five voices.) The singers were members of the Deller Consort, and the instrumentalists came from Germany and included Ferdinand Conrad and Hans Martin Linde playing recorders. Walter Bergmann played harpsichord continuo. The two performances went well and the BBC made a recording of one performance. Walter Bergmann also played in an afternoon concert of music by Handel and Purcell. He had been disappointed earlier in the year that there had not been an opportunity for him to direct a concert at the 1965 St Pancras Festival, but he had hopes of a concert in 1966. Performances of 'The Pills' were steadily continuing.

In the summer he taught as usual on summer schools at Matlock, Roehampton, Belstead House, and for the first time on the English-speaking course at the Salzburg Orff summer school. His visits to Salzburg to teach recorder became an annual event until 1973. Each summer Walter Bergmann travelled there by car with Margaret Murray. Margaret Murray wrote[50],

'He always called on (and stayed for a few days) his brother Fritz in Neckargemünd. Before this visit we often called on famous recorder players, usually to discuss business of some kind, perhaps a forthcoming concert or an edition that they were preparing together. Among these were Conrad, Scheck and Frans Brüggen. Or we would visit a place of cultural interest of some kind'. On this occasion (summer '65) they visited Wilhelm Twittenhof, living in Remscheid in the Bergisches Land. The visit brought back memories for Walter Bergmann - both of the time in the early 1930s when he had been involved with Twittenhof in early music performances in Halle, and of Fritz Bergmann's wedding in Witten in the Bergisches Land in 1926. In Salzburg he took a beginner's class, an intermediate class and an advanced ensemble class. Carl Orff's seventieth birthday was celebrated during the course. Walter Bergmann had time to also see a little of the surrounding Austrian countryside and to meet Daisy and Hans Bergmann in Basel. Having moved from East to West Germany and left all their possessions behind, lack of income was a problem for Hans and Daisy Bergmann. Walter Bergmann gave Daisy the text of Tippett's *Oratorium* to translate into German. The deadline was the end of August. The translation arrived promptly in London and both Walter Bergmann and Hilde Volhard felt the words had been well translated. Walter Bergmann then had to edit the German text and adjust it to fit Tippett's music. Walter Bergmann's other translation work in 1965 included the German translation of Richard Rodney Bennett's one act opera *The Ledge* premiered in Krefeld in May.

The 1965 summer school at Roehampton was an enjoyable week, as all the tutors worked well together. Walter Bergmann had a free half-day and his class was 'very nice'[51]. At one of his sessions, he conducted a Buxtehude motet, which was a resounding success.

Walter Bergmann returned to Schott on August 6th, where everything was not working well. Throughout 1965, he had been having arguments with Makings, and despairing over the number of meetings he had to attend. There was discussion about the publication of his *Sonata* for descant recorder, but Walter Bergmann felt that he had not been consulted on certain musical matters and he had understood that music was his particular domain. Makings was apparently 'impossible'[52] and Walter Bergmann worried about his future at Schott. On August 7th Grete and he attended Mark Deller's wedding in Salisbury Cathedral. Grete Bergmann then went on holiday to Scotland with friends.

Attending an optician's appointment in mid-August, Walter Bergmann was delighted to hear that his eyesight was still good and that he had been very fortunate in the eye-surgery he had received in 1954. His hearing was also in good order. However, much to his disgust, in September Walter Bergmann caught shingles, from which it took nearly a month to recover. Being invited to write five hundred words on Telemann for *Encyclopaedia Britannica* cheered him up a little. Back at Schott, after almost a month's absence, the atmosphere and general working situation worried him and kept him awake at night.

In November Walter Bergmann had a rare opportunity to meet Arnold Matz in England and to hear him playing in the Leipzig Gewandhaus Orchestra when it performed in London. Walter Bergmann found the concert outstanding. In the same month, he composed *Matilda*, a musical version, for children, of Hilaire Belloc's humorous poem about a girl who told dreadful lies.

In spite of setbacks at Schott, 1965 was overall a good year for Walter Bergmann. He had renewed contact with Michael Tippett and maintained his friendship and working relationship with Alfred Deller. He had spent time with old friends such as Dietrich Gerhardt, Arnold Matz and Norman Platt. He had several good professional engagements and the teaching side of his career was going well.

1966 was a busy year following the pattern of previous years. At the beginning of the year, things seemed to be running more smoothly at Schott. Walter Bergmann wondered how long it would last. In March 1966 Frans Brüggen returned to London to give a concert in the Wigmore Hall with Ilse Wolf and Walter Bergmann. The programme consisted of music by Telemann, Purcell, Barsanti and Dieupart, most of it edited by Walter Bergmann.

Frans Brüggen enjoyed working with Walter Bergmann, respecting particularly his theoretical knowledge of continuo playing and enjoying his wit[53]. *A Sonata in A minor* by Dieupart received its first modern performance at the concert. The concert finished with Telemann's cantata *In gering und rauhen Schalen* for soprano, treble recorder and harpsichord. The concert was well received, though *The Times* still cast doubts on Telemann's worthiness as a composer; the reviewer admired Frans Brüggen's technique and phrasing in the performance of two unaccompanied Fantasias by Telemann, but considered that this expertise covered up the mundane nature of the music![54] However *Music and Musicians*[55] described the two Fantasias as 'fascinating'. 'Their inventiveness and range of feeling were remarkable, and Brüggen's control of nuance must have been a revelation to many who have only thought of the instrument' (recorder) 'as a rather impoverished ancestor of the flute. Brüggen demonstrated beyond argument that true recorder music, properly performed, has a timbre and style of its own.' Walter Bergmann must have been delighted with the reviews, *The Times* describing him as 'the authoritative harpsichordist', and *Music and Musicians* as Brüggen's 'gifted' harpsichord accompanist. He continued to promote the music of Telemann with a concert at the Goethe-Institute in London three days later, with Sylvia Cleaver (violin) and Jennifer Ryan (cello).

In May 1966, Schott celebrated the 80th birthday of the previous Managing Director, Max Steffens. As Edgar Hunt wrote in his book *The Recorder and its Music*, recorder players owed 'much to his benign influence'[56] in encouraging and supporting the publication of recorder music. Also in May like many others, Walter Bergmann was shocked and saddened by the death of Richard Dolmetsch at the age of twenty one, 'the most gifted of the Dolmetsch family'[57]. It was a year of sad deaths. Edgar Hunt's wife Elizabeth died in August and in September 1966, Stanley Godman, the editor of *The Bird Fancyer's Delight* and translator into English of Hildemarie Peter's *The Recorder: its traditions and its tasks*. Walter Bergmann wrote of Stanley Godman that he was 'an intelligent man and loyal to me'[58].

In June 1966 Walter Bergmann was invited to

lunch with Peter Makings. He was very suspicious of Making's motives, but much to his surprise found him very pleasant. June also found Walter Bergmann back at the Stour Festival, when he accompanied Alfred Deller, and, at another concert, Sally le Sage and Maurice Bevan, when he had the opportunity to play a square piano.

On his way to Salzburg in the summer, Walter Bergmann visited his old friend Jan Versteeg, now 83 and unable to walk. He also visited Helene Novak, widow of the cellist friend who had founded a string quartet with Fritz Bergmann in 1924 and had played regularly with Walter Bergmann, who was also very elderly. He found these two visits a sad and salutary experience. He made happy and enjoyable visits to Hans and Daisy Bergmann, and Prunella and Wilhem Flatz, during his Salzburg trip.

At the 1966 Roehampton Summer School, Walter Bergmann shared an evening with Brian Bonsor, who 'conducted (brilliantly) Britten's 150th Psalm'[59]. Walter Bergmann conducted the first performance of his *Drummer Boy*, with which he was very pleased. He also intended to direct a performance of the revised version of *Matilda* in the final concert. But he did not allow enough time for rehearsal. He was furious with the performers and cancelled the performance, but in his diary noted that it was all the fault of his own mismanagement. Except for the year of his illness, it was the first time he had not conducted an item in the concert. At the annual Matlock course Walter Bergmann shared the recorder teaching with Erika Seelig and Hilda Hunter.

At the end of September Walter Bergmann had a memorable trip to the Leipzig Music Conference. The train journey from Berlin to Leipzig brought back memories of his father as he travelled through the stations. He remembered all the names of the stations from childhood. During his visit he renewed old acquaintances, and spent time with Arnold Matz. He spoke to Rudi Matz on the phone - Issi, his sister, had told him Walter Bergmann was dead! He stayed in the Hotel Astoria, where the food was 'astoundingly good' for East Germany. He managed to visit the Musical Instrument Collection where he saw some interesting recorders and was taken to the University Archives where he was shown, at his request, the registration of Telemann's matriculation. In his diary he noted the lack of cars, and the number of uniforms on the street, including Russian ones. Money was difficult - he was allowed only 15 Marks a day. The hotel room was cold with no hot water. He tried to take the opportunity to get to know Arnold Matz's wife and children but found it very difficult.

As usual Walter Bergmann adjudicated during 1966 and continued teaching. His recorder classes at the City Literary Institute came to an end, but those at Marylebone continued, as did his SRP activities, including the annual concert. His *Sonata for Descant Recorder and Piano* was published by Schott in October 1966. It was reviewed in *Music and Letters* by John Caldwell[60], who liked the first movement, but felt the second two movements were unbalanced.

Performances of the 'Musical Pills' continued, and in November 1966, Norman Platt's plans to found a chamber opera company came to fruition. Calling itself 'The Regional Opera' the new company gave four performances of Purcell's *Dido and Aeneas* and Telemann's *Pimpinone* at the Swan Theatre, Worcester. In the programme, Regional Opera was described as 'a new society formed to provide short seasons of professional opera at small theatres in towns and cities to which opera does not normally penetrate. Its repertoire will include works of all periods, excluding only the large-scale works which would be financially and physically impracticable in small theatres'. *Dido and Aeneas* was conducted by Roger Norrington and *Pimpinone* by Walter Bergmann; Norman Platt produced both operas. There were also two performances of the 'Musical Pills'.

The soloists for the operas included Laura Sarti and Clare Walmesley, and Norman Platt sang the role of Pimpinone. The orchestra was led by Sylvia Cleaver and Walter Bergmann played continuo for *Dido and Aeneas*.

Pimpinone was composed by Telemann in 1725, and had initially been in the form of three 'Intermezzi', or light scenes to be performed between the acts of serious operatic productions at the Hamburg Opera. The story relates the tale of an elderly man who unwisely enters into marriage with a maidservant. It formed the first part of the Worcester presentation.

The production of the two operas was supported by the Arts Council of Great Britain and merited reporting in *The Times* on November 8th 1966. Initially the performances were badly attended, but the final performance on November 12th was sold out. There was an excellent revue of *Dido and Aeneas* in the *Worcester Evening News* on November 9th. It reported 'The opera is effectively mounted: the costumes are appropriate and effective, the conductor knows exactly what he wants, and gets it'. The critic also wrote 'The Performance of *Pimpinone* was conducted from the harpsichord in authentic style by Walter Bergmann; under him the Midland Sinfonia revealed the humour latent in Telemann's simple ingenuities of orchestration.' *The Times* was not so complimentary[61]; the critic considered that Walter Bergmann's direction lacked pace.

Walter Bergmann was very pleased with Norman Platt's interpretation of the role of Pimpinone. Grete Bergmann came to see the final performances of the two operas.

During 1966, Grete Bergmann's health was beginning to give concern. In May 1966, she broke a finger in a car accident. In the summer she had a regular smear test for cancer, which proved positive. Walter Bergmann was devastated when she told him in November. They went twice to hospital together for further tests. He felt that his world was collapsing[62]. Grete had become the foundation of his life. She was always there. They had been married for twenty-seven years.

Walter Bergmann's sense of insecurity in the winter of 1966 was heightened by anxiety about his position at Schott. The atmosphere and situation had deteriorated again, and he started to look for another job. He approached John Thomson to see if there might be any post open to him at the publishers Faber. At sixty-four it did not seem to occur to Walter Bergmann that he perhaps ought to be thinking about retirement!

Grete Bergmann's tests were confirmed as positive, but the prognosis was good. The cancer was treatable and curable. The year ended more optimistically. They celebrated the New Year first with Hilde Volhard and Erika Seelig, and then with Erica and Peter Bendix, though the celebrations were tempered with some apprehension over the immediate future. But Walter Bergmann tried to look forward - to recovery for Grete and a rewarding year professionally. At the end of 1966 he was very pleased to receive an invitation from Alfred Deller to play for a recording in August 1967.

The first months of 1967 were overshadowed by Grete Bergmann's illness. At the very beginning of the year Walter Bergmann attended the annual ISM Conference held in Newcastle upon Tyne. As he tried often to do when he was travelling, he visited a cathedral on the way there (Lincoln) and on the way home (Southwell Minster). In Lincoln he had a few happy moments as 'the sun shone and Schott was forgotten for a while'.[63] Once home, he spent more time with Grete and they were both grateful for the support of their friends - to whom they have given so much over the years. Their home had always had an open door to anyone needing hospitality. At the end of January Grete went into hospital for further tests. The results showed that she would need radiotherapy and an operation. She went into hospital again on February 19th. This was 'a difficult day'[64] at the beginning of an expected three to six months of illness. But Water Bergmann noted in his diary that they must be optimistic through the coming months, as hopefully Grete would make a complete recovery. The disease had been caught in the early stages. He wrote 'in six months we can laugh again'.

It was a sobering time for Walter Bergmann, but not without its brighter spots. The Dutch recorder player, Elly Baghuis, gave her first concert in the Wigmore Hall, accompanied by Walter Bergmann, on January 28th 1967, sharing the platform with a pianist, Miranda Stronghill. The concert was well supported - by an audience which had primarily come to hear the recorder. The critic of *The Times*[65] wondered why the recital had not been solely devoted to recorder music, pointing out that Elly Baghuis, a pupil of Frans Brüggen, could have ably given a concert on her own. The programme included Beethoven's *Appassionata* sonata, which did not balance the recorder items and was apparently beyond the technique of the pianist. *The Times* noted that Walter Bergmann's accompanying was both discreet and sympathetic. A second concert was organised at the King Edward VI School at Bury St Edmunds by Choveaux Management, solely for recorder and harpsichord. Walter Bergmann accompanied Hans-Martin Linde in the Purcell Room on London's South Bank on March 18th, in a concert of music for recorder and Baroque flute. This concert also received very favourable criticism in *The Times* and *Daily Telegraph*. During March 1967, Walter Bergmann tried to continue working as usual, although concern for Grete was never far away. His activities included adjudicating in Coulsdon, Farnham and Tunbridge Wells, and a visit to Ripon for a week to tutor on the second Northern Recorder Course, which was run by Dennis Bamforth and Colin Martin. They had met Walter Bergmann at the Roehampton Summer School in 1964, when they attended his recorder class. Both men came from the northwest of England, where they had worked hard to promote the recorder and to establish a regular recorder course.

Grete Bergmann's radiation treatment was completed by the end of March. The operation she needed was performed in April, and by May she had recovered sufficiently to travel to Bognor to convalesce. Walter Bergmann stayed with his daughter Erica, while Grete was in hospital. She finally returned home on May 21st. Her doctor was pleased with her progress at her check-up on June 15th.

By June 18th Grete Bergmann was well enough to fly with Walter Bergmann to Berlin and then travel by train to Leipzig, where Arnold Matz met them. Walter Bergmann had been invited to lecture at the 1967 Leipzig Music Conference. The Bergmanns divided their time between Leipzig and Halle, initially staying in Leipzig. Grete Bergmann visited family and friends in Halle, while Walter Bergmann worked on his lectures and met old friends. In Leipzig, he lectured on Purcell and afterwards had an enjoyable supper with Grete, Arnold Matz and other friends. The following day both Bergmanns travelled to Halle, where they stayed in the Interhotel.

Like all the hotels they stayed in East Germany, it was comfortable and a 'luxury' hotel only for foreigners. In Halle Walter Bergmann lectured on 'The Recorder Movement in England' to a small audience in Handel's birthplace. During the day he had walked through Halle and knocked on the door of his old friend, the cellist Otto Neumann who had been such a supportive friend when Erica was born, only to find the door opened by a stranger who said Herr Neumann had been dead for a year. 'It is another piece from the middle of my life gone', he wrote sadly in his diary.[66] The Music Conference officially opened in Magdeburg on June 22nd, where there was also a special exhibition to commemorate the two hundredth anniversary of Telemann's death. In the evening Walter Bergmann enjoyed a performance of Handel's *Scipio* and was impressed by the recorder playing of Eva and Harald Grossmann. He gave his thirty-minute lecture on Telemann's continuo parts on June 24th, and was delighted with how well it was received. His talk concluded with two Telemann songs. He was quite overcome with the comments he received.[67] He was also approached by a representative of the publishing firm Peters, who asked if he would edit recorder music for Peters.

On his return to England Walter Bergmann agonised over his future. Peter Makings was determined he should retire on October 1st, just after his sixty-fifth birthday. Makings had presented three possibilities to Walter Bergmann. These were (i) to have a new contract with reduced and limited responsibilities; (ii) to retire, receive a pension and a retainer fee for first refusal of his arrangements and compositions; or (iii) to retire completely and receive his pension from the pension scheme plus an extra pension from Schott (as had some other ex- employees).

Before travelling to Germany and Salzburg in July, Walter Bergmann had a meeting with John Thomson from Faber who offered him a yearly retainer fee of £500. On July 6th he spoke to Donald Mitchell, who said Faber were keen to employ him and confirmed an annual fee of £520 plus 10% royalties from October 1st. He travelled as usual to Salzburg, making his regular visit to family and friends. On July 20th Grete Bergmann telephoned her husband to say that Faber had officially confirmed their offer. Deciding that the working situation at Schott had become intolerable, Walter Bergmann sadly wrote his letter of resignation to Peter Makings and wrote to Eulenburg as well. He met with Makings on August 17th. It was not an easy meeting. Walter Bergmann had hoped that after retirement he would be kept on at Schott with as many or more responsibilities, including that of Editor of Eulenburg. Makings on the other hand had made major changes at Schott London, having moved the warehouse, printing and trade sales to Ashford in Kent and reorganised Schott's offices at 48 Great Marlborough Street. He only wanted to continue employing Walter Bergmann if he accepted having less responsibility, and was therefore quite prepared to accept his resignation. On previous occasions when Walter Bergmann had threatened to resign, Edgar Hunt had intervened and helped to resolve the situation. This time things had gone too far and Walter Bergmann was practically sixty-five. 'It was a sad day when Walter left'[68] wrote Edgar Hunt. Makings offered Walter Bergmann £1500 per annum (three times the Faber offer) for first refusal of his future compositions and editions, but Walter Bergmann turned down the offer. He felt that he would have greater freedom and appreciation from Faber. It was agreed that on his retirement from Schott he would receive a single payment of £500, his pension and an additional pension of £400 to be paid in monthly instalments and reviewed annually.

The autumn saw him depressed and miserable, although delighted at Grete's good recovery. He joined Alfred Deller for a recording session at the beginning of September, although he had not been invited to the Stour Festival in 1967. Walter Bergmann prepared 16 items for the session, and found it very tiring particularly as he had to conduct some items for Deller. In October he went to Holland to lecture on a music course, which he did not enjoy. Sitting looking in his hotel mirror he saw an old man. He had been unwell again, and had received injections for varicose veins. Even new projects planned for after he had left Schott, which included the editing of twenty-four recorder sonatas by Schickhardt with Frans Brüggen, failed to raise his spirits. He did feel more cheerful after the success of a thirty-minute broadcast he gave for the BBC, in which he talked about Telemann. It was transmitted on the Third programme on October 24th. Although the programme was broadcast late evening, he received a number of complimentary letters. One from Michael Muskett began 'Congratulations on last night's clear and forthright talk. I had been very disappointed that Telemann had hardly received a mention this year. I hope your talk will herald a new era of recognition for G.P.T.'[69]

October 25th was Walter Bergmann's final day at Schott after he had worked there for almost twenty-six years. He was now 65 and past retirement age. John Thomson kindly asked him out to lunch the following day. Life continued with editing, private teaching, adjudicating etc. There was his work with teachers and children - during 1967 he had lectured to teachers, for example in Poole, and conducted the first performance of *The Drummer Boy* by children in Southend. At the Easter of 1967, he had taught for the first time at the Northern Recorder Course held at Ripon.

In November 1967, Walter and Grete Bergmann were shaken when Erica Bendix was rushed to hospital with appendicitis, but fortunately she made a full recovery. They celebrated Erica's birthday on December 26th together as a family, thankful that Grete and she had both recovered from serious illness. With the exception of his leaving Schott, an enormous upheaval, 1968 and 1969 followed the pattern of preceding years. In January 1968, Walter Bergmann enjoyed working with Gustav Scheck, an eminent German flautist and recorder player. They gave two concerts together in the Purcell Room on January 10th and 13th, and Walter Bergmann accompanied Gustav Scheck at the two master classes he gave at Fenton House, Hampstead on January 12th. Gustav Scheck's background bore remarkable similarities to that of Walter Bergmann. He was of a similar age (Scheck was born in 1901 in Munich) and as a young man he could not decide whether to study medicine or music. He initially studied medicine, but changed to music. He studied the flute, and started playing the recorder in 1929. During the 1930s Scheck formed a chamber trio, with a cellist and gamba player, August Wenzinger and a harpsichordist. Fritz Neumayer. He also founded a chamber orchestra that played on original low-pitch instruments, and taught the flute and introduced recorder teaching at the Berlin Staatliche Hochschule für Musik. He played a key role in establishing the recorder during the 1930s. Edgar Hunt[70] remembered hearing Gustav Scheck playing the recorder at the 1934 Kasseler Musiktage, and the esteem in which he was already held as a player, scholar and writer.

Gustav Scheck was strongly opposed to the Nazis, which led to the disbanding, during the war, of what had been a highly successful trio. By 1945, Scheck was penniless, his only possessions a flute and copies of the Mozart flute concertos. Undaunted, the following year (1946), Scheck founded the Staatliche Hochschule für Musik in Freiburg (in Breisgau). Among his pupils at the Hochschule were Ferdinand Conrad, Hans Martin Linde and Hildemarie Peter. He retired in 1964, having made an invaluable contribution to establishing the recorder as a solo instrument. He was one of the first modern performers to use the recorder in its rightful place in Bach's *Brandenburg Concerto No.4*. He helped to establish a new approach to the performance of early music within mainstream music in Germany.

Walter Bergmann and Gustav Scheck had much in common. Scheck stayed with the Bergmanns for ten days. In his first recital, he was a little uncertain during the initial part of the programme, but the problems resolved themselves. According to *Music and Musicians*, Walter Bergmann gave 'perceptive support on the harpsichord' [71]. The concert was well received. *The Daily Telegraph*[72] commented that with such a distinguished performer as Scheck there was no need to question the scholarship behind his playing and approach to ornamentation. It recorded his involvement in the performance of Baroque music since the 1930s and admired his use of ornamentation, describing it as discreet and unobtrusive, but affective. The programmes for the two concerts were different. Both included music by J S Bach, Handel and Telemann. The first included works by Loeillet and Vinci and concluded with the Handel *Sonata for Treble Recorder in A minor Op. 1 no. 4*. The second concert contained works by Hasse and Barsanti and concluded with Bach's *Flute Sonata in E minor*, BVW 1034. Scheck played flute and treble recorder in both concerts. It was a memorable start to 1968 for Walter Bergmann, and the concert audiences must have felt they were hearing two aspects of twentieth century recorder history coming together.

In March, Walter Bergmann accompanied Katharine Jeans at two recitals for recorder and harpsichord, the first at Loughborough University of Technology, the second at the University of Surrey. The first concert included Walter Bergmann's *Theme and Variations* from his Sonata for descant recorder. Walter Bergmann played solo harpsichord items in both concerts. In Loughborough he played two Telemann Fantasias and at Surrey University, a Telemann *Partita* from *Der getreue Music-Meister*. The two concerts fell on succeeding days, Thursday and Friday and on the following day, the Saturday, the London SRP gave its annual concert, at which Katharine Jeans played accompanied by Walter Bergmann. Other performers included a young recorder player called Ross Winters, the Northampton Recorder Consort, conducted by Richard Coles, and Michael Arno, who played descant recorder solo in the first modern performance of Robert Woodcock's *Concerto No. 2*. Faber agreed to publish Walter Bergmann's edition of the concerto.

At the end of March 1968 Walter Bergmann went to Germany with Margaret Murray. In Stuttgart, they attended a performance of Carol Orff's *Prometheus*, and met Dietrich Gerhardt and Fritz and Anneliese Bergmann. The beginning of April found Walter Bergmann in Ripon, tutoring on the Northern Recorder Course. He also accompanied Joannes Collette in a recital given to the course students.

During the beginning of 1968, Walter Bergmann's eyes were giving him some problems again. This was initially resolved with new glasses, but in April, the retina detached in his left eye, necessitating surgery in Moorfields Eye Hospital. The first operation in April was not successful. The second on May 18th was successfully completed and Walter Bergmann left hospital on June 7th. He sadly turned down the offer of a year's visiting professorship from September 1968 at Louisville University in the USA, as it was impossible to even consider it with his eye problems. The day after his operation on May 19th, BBC Television broadcast a programme on Alfred Deller in conjunction with the launching of a biography of Deller by Michael Hardwick. The programme included Alfred Deller singing songs by Dowland, Purcell and Wilbye, with Walter Bergmann among the artists accompanying him. The recordings Walter Bergmann had made with Alfred Deller the previous September were also released in 1968 as two volumes entitled 'Homage to Purcell'. (The other performers included April Cantelo, George Mallern, Maurice Bevan and Neville Marriner.)

In July, Walter Bergmann was well enough to travel again through Germany to Salzburg with Margaret Murray. They made a detour via Maastricht to meet the Collettes and then travelled to Marburg to visit Hans Bergmann. Walter Bergmann also visited the Versteegs and enjoyed the journey through the Eifel and Odenwald to Fritz and Anneliese. On arrival in Salzburg, he was worried about his eyes again and visited an optician who reassured him there was no need to return to London. He travelled home via Amsterdam where he met Frans Brüggen to discuss their joint edition of the Schickhardt sonatas. The Roehampton Summer School followed in the first week of August. In the middle of August Walter Bergmann began to drive again.

At the end of August he took the opportunity for a real holiday with Grete and Erica, Peter and David Bendix in Italy. Grete and he looked after David during the second week, while his parents had a week away on their own. He enjoyed 'Gelegen, gelesen, gesessen' (resting, reading and sitting)[73]. It was a time for thinking and reflection. He realised that both Grete and he had been very fortunate in both recovering from serious illness.

In September life settled back to normal. On October 5th, the BBC broadcast Blow's *Ode on the Death of Purcell*, a recording made by Alfred and Mark Deller (countertenors), Anna Shuttleworth (cello) and Walter Bergmann (harpsichord). From October 7th – 12th, the Regional Opera Company performed its 1966 programme in Exeter at the Northcott Theatre. Roger Norrington once again conducted *Dido and Aeneas* and Walter Bergmann directed *Pimpinone*. 'The Musical Pills' were also performed. The result was extremely disappointing. It became apparent that the publicity for the week had been practically non-existent. There were less than one hundred in the first night audience in spite of the calibre of the singers and players, who came from Covent Garden, Sadlers Wells, Glyndebourne, the English Opera Group and the English Sinfonia. Aeneas was sung by Benjamin Luxon and Dido by Maureen Lehane. Other singers included Clare Walmesley and Gloria Jennings in *Dido and Aeneas*, and Norman Platt once again in the title role of *Pimpinone*. Norman Platt was also artistic director. One indignant member of the audience wrote to the local paper to complain. The Theatre's pre-tour publicity had made 'no mention of the operas to be performed, no names of singers, no references to orchestra or conductor. Yet the facts are astounding. Performing to rows of empty seats are London singers of national reputation: Maureen Lehane the distinguished mezzo-soprano; Clare Walmesley, well known in the concert and broadcasting world; Benjamin Luxon, one of the most admired of the new generation of baritones and several other fine artistes. An excellent chamber orchestra is conducted by Roger Norrington, the conductor who is so widely admired for his direction of 17th and 18th century music. These are Royal Festival Hall names yet the Northcott do not think them worth a mention.'[74] Another commentator observed 'if this is the sort of reception that opera is going to get in the west, it is not surprising that it is rarely staged there professionally'[75].

Walter Bergmann must have felt again, as he did after visiting Sadler's Wells in January 1968 to see Richard Rodney Bennett's opera *Penny for a Song*, when he wrote 'The English don't understand anything about opera'[76]. It was not a happy week. The Theatre demanded £350 from Norman Platt for compensation for its losses in spite of its lack of publicity. It was the last time Regional Opera performed as a company.

At the end of October, Walter Bergmann's eyes were checked at Moorfields. Everything was fine. He discussed future work possibilities with Dennis Bamforth and Colin Martin, worked at editing music and lectured on Telemann at Trinity College of Music. Grete helped with playing the recorded musical illustrations. Life was becoming normally busy again, with a weekend course in Scarborough at the beginning of November. In November he bought a new Broadwood piano.

He was however disappointed in the apparent slowness at which Faber were accepting work from him. By December, John Thomson was also depressed by the lack of a significant list of Faber recorder publications. It transpired that Faber wanted to pay Walter Bergmann for any works such as continuo parts after their publication. He agreed to this.

The year ended with engagements at St Mary-le-Bow, Cheapside, where he played the harpsichord for a Christmas concert by The Collegium Sagittarii, and at the German Institute, where he gave a recital of German Baroque Music with Jane Ryan, Michael Arno and Herbert Hersom. Christoph Gerhardt (Dietrich Gerhardt's son) came to stay over Christmas. The Bergmanns enjoyed having him as they found him an easy guest. They spent Christmas Day at the Bendixes, where they were joined by Margaret Murray. On December 30th Walter Bergmann enjoyed going to see *La Boheme*.

1969 began with wrangles with Schott over his pension and discussions with Martin Kingsbury over the Faber catalogue. Neither seemed to be going very smoothly. More positive and exciting was Frans Brüggen's visit to London in January to give a concert with Neville Marriner in the Queen Elizabeth Hall, playing concertos by Naudot and Vivaldi, and to plan, with Walter Bergmann and Edgar Hunt, a visit in March where he would undertake several engagements, including master classes. Walter Bergmann would accompany him. Walter Bergmann went to the January concert, and described Brüggen's performance as being of 'unbelievable virtuosity'[77]. It was however the slow movement of the Vivaldi concerto he enjoyed the most during the performance. Another exciting prospect for Walter Bergmann was a letter inviting him to Seattle to participate in a recorder workshop in 1970.

Frans Brüggen's week of engagements in March included a concert in the Wigmore Hall, recitals in Manchester and Norwich and two very successful master classes. Brüggen played Walter Bergmann's *Sonata for Descant Recorder* at the Manchester recital. It was the first time Frans Brüggen had undertaken so many consecutive engagements in England. Brüggen was well aware that as well as acting as accompanist for his concerts, Walter Bergmann was a link with many recorder players.

Apparently on one visit to London, Walter Bergmann persuaded Frans Brüggen to visit an SRP meeting. Brüggen was somewhat reluctant to do so, but at his recital the next day he realised where a large proportion of his audience came from as he recognised them from the day before.

Walter Bergmann was very unhappy with his performance at the beginning of the week of his engagements with Frans Brüggen. He was sure he had played very badly in the Wigmore Hall concert. By the final concert in Norwich he felt he was playing much better. The concerts were well supported, particularly the one in Manchester. At the end of the week, the day after the Norwich concert, Walter Bergmann travelled to Northampton to rehearse a new work (*Chaconietta* for cello and 6 recorders) he had written for Richard Cole's recorder consort to be played at the SRP Annual Concert. He returned to London exhausted - he was after all sixty-seven. Ten days later, Walter Bergmann accompanied a pupil of Brüggen's, Hans Linnartz, in a recital in Leicester.

He enjoyed the Easter Northern Recorder Course at Ripon, working with Colin Martin, Dennis Bamforth, Dom Gregory Murray and Ferdinand Conrad. It gave him great pleasure to play with Conrad again.

In May Walter Bergmann was engaged to play in a concert with Celia Bizony in the Purcell Room. They were to play together in W F Bach's *Concerto in F major* for two harpsichords. Unfortunately the two performers found it impossible to work together and Walter Bergmann withdrew from the performance, though he did contribute to other items in the programme. Colin Tilney replaced him in the Bach, which according to Walter Bergmann was played 'too slowly and boringly'.[78] His anxiety about the concert was heightened by the fact he had lost his playing glasses a week before the concert, but luckily found them on the day.

Other engagements in May 1969 included adjudicating in Darlington and Leigh on Sea and performances of *Matilda* and the *Drummer Boy* by 340 children in Stockport. He was disappointed by the performances as he felt the children were not well enough prepared. At the end of May Fritz Bergmann had a prostate operation, causing some concern for the family.

In June Walter Bergmann bought a new car to replace the old one, which was becoming unreliable. Grete and Erica went to Germany together. Walter Bergmann enjoyed playing in a concert in the Box Hill Festival given by Alfred Deller. Katharine Jeans and he played treble recorder in two songs by David and Henry Purcell. It was hard for him however to hear someone else accompany Alfred Deller in *Music for a While*, especially as he did not like the performance. His evening classes at the Marylebone Institute finished for the year. He was very pleased with the progress of the Intermediate Class over the preceding year. At the end of June, Edgar Hunt celebrated his sixtieth birthday. Walter Bergmann gave up an opportunity to play continuo in a performance of *Jephta* at the Stour Festival to be at the party.

He travelled as usual to Salzburg in the summer, visiting Fritz and Anneliese Bergmann. Fritz was very depressed since his operation. This worried Walter Bergmann, but he still enjoyed a visit to Augsburg. In Salzburg, his new recorder work *Accent on Rhythm* was well received. It consisted of trios for descant, treble and tenor recorders which were based on Czech and Yugoslav folksongs and was published by Faber. While in Austria he visited the Grossglockner with Hilda Hunter. Back in London, the 1969 Roehampton course was a great success. At Walter Bergmann's evening presentation, twenty-six players played his *Chaconietta* with Janet Coles (Richard

Coles' daughter) playing the cello part. This was followed by his arrangement of Vivaldi's *Concerto for 4 violins*, with Brian Bonsor, Paul Clark, Carl Dolmetsch and Edgar Hunt playing solo recorders parts. Much to his delight, the whole of the Vivaldi was encored.

In August rehearsals began again for the 'Musical Pills'. In October, the revue was performed in Horsham and Bradford, the performers being Clare Walmesley, Norman Platt, Gloria Jennings and Walter Bergmann; Douglas Craig was the producer. The productions still continued to be a success, with an audience of two hundred and fifty at the Bradford Music Club. Afterwards Walter Bergmann travelled to Scotland via the Lake District. He was impressed by both the Lakes and Yorkshire. He stayed with Brian and Mary Bonsor and conducted recorder meetings in Kelso and Edinburgh. November found him adjudicating and teaching. He was flattered to be told that the students at Trent Park College liked him as a teacher because 'he played music rather than notes'[79] In December the Bergmanns and Erica Bendix went to see a performance of *L'incoronazione di Poppea* by the newly formed Kent Opera Group. The production was conducted by Roger Norrington and produced by Norman Platt. Walter Bergmann was impressed by the production, though he felt Roger Norrington did not fully understand Monteverdi. Also in December, it pleased him that his *Pastorale* for flute and countertenor was broadcast in the Midlands by Radio 4.

By the end of 1969, Walter Bergmann had completed two years of 'retirement'. It was no retirement. In 1967 he had written in a letter to Max Steffens (from whom he had asked for advice on his pension), 'I hope you and Mrs Steffens are keeping well. I myself have not yet started enjoying retirement and I am sure I never will.'[80] The arrangement at Faber had not developed as he had hoped - although Faber had published *Accent on Rhythm, Accent on Melody*, arrangements of *60 Daily Hymns*, which Walter Bergmann made with Leslie White and a Purcell *In Nomine*. During 1969, the wrangling with Schott over his retirement had continued. In a meeting at the end of January 1969, Peter Makings had accused Walter Bergmann of setting up through Faber in direct competition to Schott. In a subsequent letter he informed Walter Bergmann that unless he gave Schott first refusal of all his new work, the voluntary pension from Schott would be withdrawn! Walter Bergmann was furious; he felt he had given a significant part of his life to Schott. He wrote to Makings, 'For the uncertain (annually renewable) pension of £400 you claim suddenly the first refusal of my works and practically a unilateral control of my artistic output. This contradicts everything we have discussed. A pension is granted for services rendered in the past and must not deprive the receiver of his livelihood nor interfere with his creative vocation. It will rest with your conscience if you want to cancel my pension as from October 1969.'[81]

The doubt over his pension caused Walter Bergmann great anxiety during the whole of 1969. Thus by the end of year, he had significantly increased his number of private pupils and continued to accept every opportunity he was offered to adjudicate at music festivals. Fees from music courses also provided a significant contribution to his income - they had become part of the regular pattern of his life. He had also been fortunate at the continuation of his performing career during the late sixties, particularly through Frans Brüggen and Alfred Deller, and of course through the 'Musical Pills', but performing did not make a large contribution to his income, and some concerts made a loss.

Although Walter Bergmann had financial worries

at the end of 1969, from a professional point of view, he was now internationally recognised as an authority on continuo playing and Telemann, and well known as a recorder teacher and editor and arranger of recorder music. His work with children had increased over the years and he delighted in receiving letters from children who had enjoyed playing in his compositions, such as *Matilda* and *The Drummer Boy*, and being conducted by him personally. Giving children an understanding of the joy and pleasure of music making was of great importance to him. There were occasions when performances were not pleasurable, as he mentioned in his diary after a visit to Stockport, where he was faced with 340 under-rehearsed children and only 35 minutes to rehearse! But it was not always like that.

One developing interest for Walter Bergmann was photography, in which he took great delight. Life was full and busy. Friends were still always welcome at Belsize Square and these included close friends of many years standing, Erika Seelig, Hilde Volhard, Margaret Murray, Norman Platt; his German friends, whose children, such as Christoph Gerhardt, now came to visit, and many others. Family ties were also close and he made regular visits to Germany. His life was firmly based in Britain, but he had both professional contact with and recognition in Germany, including in his own hometown, Halle. By the end of 1969 his diary changed back and forth from German to English. Although people sometimes found him difficult, his genuine concern for music and musicians, including amateurs, meant he was much loved and respected. He was grateful he had managed to retain his friendships with both Alfred Deller and Michael Tippett both of whom he found charming and at times, impossible. He did not see himself in the same light! One of his greatest talents was managing to bridge the gap between professional and amateur musicians. By the end of the sixties Walter Bergmann still had a healthy, if overworked, musical life.

1   'Es war mein bestes Amateurs-dirigen das ich gemacht habe.' ; Diary 14, 16.02.60
2   'Conducting a Recorder Class' in *Recorder News*, New Series 31, Nov/Dec 1960, p.6
3   *Recorder News*, New Series 31, p.7
4   'Mein bestes Konzert.'; Diary 14, 18.03.60
5   'Das schönste Stuck, das ich kenne.'; Diary 15, 17.04. 60
6   Diary 15, 14.11.60
7   Diary 15, 05.01.61
8   *Times Educational Supplement*, 20.01.61
9   Diary 15, 01.61
10 *The Scotsman*, 25.03.61
11 The *Yorkshire Post*, 27.03.61
12 Diary 15, 01.05.61
13 Walter Bergmann to William Glock, 05.04.61
14 Eric Warr to Walter Bergmann, 16.05.61
15 Diary 15, 28.06.61
16 *Times Educational Supplement*, 09.06.61
17 Diary 15, 17.07.61
18 Diary 15, 11.08.61
19 Jennifer Vyvyan to Walter Bergmann, 14.12.61
20 Diary 15, 25.08.61
21 Diary 15, 11.12.61
22 *The Times*, 03.03.62
23 *Hampstead News*, 09.03.62
24 Diary 15, 04.03.62
25 'Ich bin 60, aber sehe nur vorwärts und nicht zurück.', Diary 16, 23.01.63
26 Diary 16, 16.10.62
27 *Musical Times*, January 1963
28 Diary 16, 23.10.63
29 'den Walter Bergmann recht geschickt übertragen hat'; Frankfurt Allegemeine Zeitung, 29.01.63
30 *Financial Time*, 11.03.63
31 *The Guardian*, 26.06.63
32 'Es war furchtbar.' Diary 16, 23.09.63
33 'Ich bin sehr traurig.' Diary 16, 29.09.63

34 *The Times*, 02.03.64
35 *Financial Times*, 02.03.64
36 *Musical Times*, April 1964, p. 280
37 *Music and Musicians*, May 1964, p.34
38 Diary 17, 30.05.64
39 'Er findet meines Cembalo besser als alle andern.' Diary 17, 27.05.64
40 *Kentish Express*, 03.05.64
41 Denis Brearly to WB, 07.01.65
42 Walter Bergmann in Ian Kemp (ed.), *Michael Tippett, A Symposium on his 60th Birthday*
43 Michael Tippett, 'Walter Bergmann' in *Early Music*, May 1988
44 *Sussex Express*, 05.02.65
45 Diary 17, 07.03.65
46 *Music and Musicians*, May 1965
47 'Ich bin sehr erstaunt, dass meine Sonata gut gefallen ist.' Diary 17, 04.03.65
48 *Daily Telegraph*, D.A.W.M., 08.03.65
49 William R. Martin 'Orazio Vecchi' in S. Sadie (ed.), The New Grove Dictionary of Music and Musicians, vol. 19, (London: Macmillan 1980), p. 585
50 Margaret Murray to Anne Martin, 08.03.95
51 Diary 18, 07.08.65
52 Diary 18, 07.08.65
53 Letter from Frans Brüggen to Anne Martin, 09.06.94
54 *The Times*, 07.03.66
55 *Music and Musicians*, May 1966
56 Edgar Hunt, The Recorder and its Music, (London: 1977 Eulenburg), p.140
57 'Er war sehr begabt musikalische der einige wirklich Begabte der Familie.' Diary 18, 19.05.66
58 'Er war ein Kluger und mir treuer Mensch.' Diary 18, 20.09.66
59 Diary 18, 08.08.66
60 *Music and Letters*, October 1966, p. 379
61 *The Times*, 07.11.66
62 Diary 19, 01.12.66
63 'Die Sonne schien, u. Schott war vergessen (für eine Weile).' Diary 19, 21.01.67
64 Diary 19, 19.02.67
65 *The Times*, 30.01.67
66 'für mich ist wieder ein Stück meiner mittleren Lebensperiode vergangen.' Diary 19, 21.06.67
67 'Ich bin heute noch überrascht, dass mein Vortrag so e rfolg war. Viele sprechen mich darauf an.' Diary 19, 24.06.67
68 Letter from Edgar Hunt to Anne Martin, 09.03.94
69 Letter from Michael Muskett to Walter Bergmann, 24.10.67
70 Edgar Hunt, The Recorder and its Music, (London; 1977 Eulenburg), p. 135
71 *Music and Musicians*, March 1968
72 *Daily Telegraph*, R.L.H., 11.01.68
73 Diary 19, 31.08.68
74 Letter from Vivian Summers in The Echo
75 *Western Evening News*, 12.10.68
76 'Die Engländer verstehen nichts von Oper.' Diary 20, 04.01.69
77 'Unglaubliche Virtuosität.' Diary 20, 24.01.69
78 Diary 20, 25.05.69
79 Diary 20, 13.11.69
80 Letter from Walter Bergmann from Max Steffens, 18.11.67
81 Letter from Walter Bergmann to Peter Makings, 16.02.69

Miller's Music Shop, Cambridge, January 1961 reproduced by permission of Cambridge Newspapers

Walter Bergmann at Schott

Walter and Grete Bergmann and Erica Bendix in the 1970s

8. The Seventies

In spite of his increasing age, there were new experiences and achievements for Walter Bergmann during the 1970s. These included his first trip to the U.S.A., publishing his own poems, the commissioning of his *Sonata* for treble recorder and piano, lecturing at Cambridge University and the establishing of his own summer school. He could not of course avoid the effects of developing old age, and the unfortunate accompanying ill health affecting both Grete and himself.

Walter Bergmann's diaries for the 1970s are written in an interesting mixture of English and German. Whenever he wrote, he used the most convenient word from either language, so that sentences constructed in English include the odd German word and vice-versa.

1970 was a busy and successful year, although he worried as to how his age would affect and limit his still very active working life. The year began with the ISM Conference, which Walter Bergmann found extremely enjoyable, in spite of the meeting being blighted by illness. Benjamin Britten and Imogen Holst were both absent through illness. Peter Pears was the new ISM President, and he impressed Walter Bergmann with how well he fulfilled his role. The high point of the Conference was an outstanding lecture-recital given by David Munrow, accompanied by his wife Gillian Reid. A concert by Benjamin Britten and Peter Pears had to be cancelled.

During January 1970, Walter Bergmann made plans for the rest of the year. He discussed with Norman Platt a new project, a children's Christmas opera, planning the first performance for December 1970, in spite of the fact he had not yet written a note. At the end of January Paul Esswood came to Belsize Square to plan with Walter Bergmann the contribution he would make to a concert to be given with Frans Brüggen in March. Walter Bergmann's growing number of private pupils, such as Sarah English and Susan Gosling, took up a significant amount of his time, and he enjoyed being with his grandson, David, who was now aged nine. He was also completing his work for children *King Cole*, scored for unison voices, recorder, strings, percussion and piano.

In February, Walter and Grete Bergmann were both delighted to be invited by their local Chinese Restaurant to join its celebration of the Chinese New Year. The following day a new pupil said to Walter Bergmann 'It must be marvellous to be famous.' Perplexed by this, he replied ' Are you talking about Brüggen?' Receiving the answer that the pupil was actually talking about him, Walter Bergmann responded ' I am not famous, nor do I want to be. I am not gifted for it.'[1]

Towards the end of February Walter Bergmann went to Birmingham to participate in a schools' music day entitled 'Walter Bergmann's Day', which had been organised by Paul Clark. Unfortunately a strike by teachers significantly reduced the choir and audience, but Walter Bergmann was appreciative of how well the recorder players had been taught and prepared by Paul Clark. He found it a delightful and successful day.

Back in London, he began to be apprehensive about the approaching concert with Frans Brüggen and Paul Esswood, now only approximately three weeks away, for which he had agreed to compose a new work, a second *Pastorale* for descant recorder and countertenor. He initially found it hard to settle down and compose, but then managed to complete the work in five days. (Walter Bergmann revised the second *Pastorale* in 1971, re-scoring it for soprano voice and sopranino, and it was published in 1972 under the title *Pastorella*.)

He received a letter from the BBC asking if the second recital to be given by Frans Brüggen and himself in Liverpool, following the London concert, could be recorded. Walter Bergmann was uncertain as to whether he should accept the offer. He was spending a great deal of time preparing for the two concerts, and becoming anxious about his own standard of performance. At the keyboard he practised finger patterns and exercises to strengthen the movement of his fourth and fifth fingers so that he felt he could be absolutely secure playing in the two concerts. By the beginning of March he had also lost a significant amount of weight. This however returned very quickly. He finally decided to agree to the recording.

A more relaxing experience was his participation with Dick and Janet Coles and the Nene Recorder Consort, which Dick Coles directed, in a concert given at the Leicester College of Education on March 11th. The concert included Walter Bergmann's *Chaconietta*, with Janet Coles again playing the cello part, and Dick Coles' arrangement of Purcell's *Chacony in G minor*, for which he had asked, and received, advice from Walter Bergmann. Dick Coles wrote to Walter Bergmann after the concert, saying how much the student audience, particularly those studying the recorder, had enjoyed both the programme and the performance. 'They were enormously thrilled with the music, and the *Chaconietta* came in for particular praise. This clearly created fascination and enjoyment among the audience and they loved those harpsichord solos. I am particularly grateful to you because I always learn from you in the rehearsals we have. This helps me to improve the music making when you are not here. You have a vicarious influence Walter.'[2] Walter Bergmann was touched by Coles' letter, and he put into his scrapbook collection of programmes and reviews. Dick and Janet Coles came to London three days later to play in the London SRP's annual concert, along with Ross and Leslie Winters, Michale Arno and Walter Bergmann's recorder classes from the Marylebone Institute.

Dick Coles, a doctor specialising in skin complaints and an active recorder player, teacher and conductor, was extremely fond of Walter Bergmann, in spite of the latter's idiosyncrasies. Prior to any concert in which he was collaborating with Dick Coles, Walter Bergmann would stay with the Coles family in order to plan the programme. Together they would spend around five hours discussing, planning and agreeing the content. Walter Bergmann would then return home and produce a completely different programme! Dr Coles was, however, extremely aware of the support and encouragement Walter Bergmann gave to promising young musicians, including his own children.

The day before the first concert Frans Brüggen was to give in London at St John's, Smith Square, Walter Bergmann heard from the Chouveaux Concert Agency that none of the London music critics were interested in covering the concert. He was very disappointed at the lack of interest. The concert itself was successful. Both Walter Bergmann's *Pastorales* were sung by Paul Esswood, and the programme included a Schickhardt *Sonata in C sharp minor*, edited by Frans Brüggen and Walter Bergmann. Margaret Murray also participated in the concerts, joining Walter Bergmann in Elizabethan keyboard duets.

The Daily Telegraph did send a critic to the concert held in Liverpool the following day, March 19th. The concert included music from the London concert programme, plus the addition of Berio's *Gesti*, which had been specially composed for Brüggen, and Telemann's *Sonata in D minor* from *Essercizii musici*.

Walter Bergmann performed six early English keyboard pieces. Neil Tierney wrote in his complimentary review[3] of Frans Brüggen's outstanding artistry and that his recorder playing had 'dazzled' the audience. Tierney enjoyed the performance of *Gesti*, which he saw as an opportunity for Brüggen to demonstrate his superb virtuosity and he found Brüggen's performance of *Engels Nachtegaeltje* 'spellbinding'. Walter Bergmann must have been delighted with Tierney's comments which were complimentary about his harpsichord playing, making particular reference to the performance of Telemann works with Frans Brüggen and in the 'gloriously authentic' performance of early English virginal pieces. The critic[4] from the *Liverpool Post* was just as complimentary of the concert, writing that 'Frans Brüggen is to the recorder as Casals to the cello, Segovia to the guitar, Goossens to the oboe, and I have seldom seen more musicians in the audience than there were at his recital.' The *Liverpool Echo* also published a complimentary review with the exception of its reference to Berio's *Gesti*, of which the reviewer wrote[5] 'as far as I am concerned, need never be heard again!' Overall, the evening must been one of the most exciting and satisfying of Walter Bergmann's life, with a performance in front of a large and appreciative audience.

Walter Bergmann and Frans Brüggen parted company in London the following day at Euston Station. The exchange between them was as follows; [6]
'Thank you for putting up with me.'(WB)
'Thank you for playing with me.' (FB)

The success of the Liverpool concert was followed by a disappointing meeting with John Thomson and Rod Biss to discuss publication by Faber of music edited and written by Walter Bergmann. Faber were only currently interested in publishing two items, these being the *First Trios* for recorders and *Initial Duets Book 2*. Thomson and Biss suggested that Walter Bergmann really ought to consider setting up his own company solely to publish educational recorder music. It seemed unlikely that Faber would publish a significant amount of Walter Bergmann's work. March ended for Walter Bergmann with adjudicating work in Portsmouth. He had also adjudicated in Brighton and Bedford during March. It had been a hectic few weeks.

April proved to be just as busy and rewarding a time for him. The Northern Recorder Course was held in Dunfermline College, north of Edinburgh. Grete Bergmann accompanied her husband. They travelled by car, taking Walter Bergmann's harpsichord with them. They broke the journey in Northumberland, where they stayed overnight with Layton Ring. Two days after returning home, Walter Bergmann accompanied Ferdinand Conrad in a concert held in the Wigmore Hall. The concert was organised and promoted through the concert agency Chouveaux and consisted of Baroque music for recorder, harpsichord and viola da gamba. Jane Ryan played viola da gamba, and the programme included works by Telemann, Quantz and Boismortier. Both the *Times* and the *Daily Telegraph* carried reviews of the concert. The critic in the *Telegraph*[7] commented on the close teamwork between the three players. Commenting on the authoritative knowledge Walter Bergmann brought to Baroque music, the reviewer also acknowledged the innate musicality apparent in his performance. Walter Bergmann was exhausted after the concert. He had one day in which to recover before accompanying Ferdinand Conrad in a lecture recital entitled 'Improvised Embellishments on the Recorder'. The following weeks found Walter Bergmann busy with his regular activities of teaching, arranging, writing and adjudicating. Adjudicating was proving to be a very welcome reliable source of income, which considerably helped his general financial situation.

The Brüggen recital recorded in Liverpool was broadcast on May 13th, omitting Walter Bergmann's harpsichord solo. He was not disappointed at the omission. He wrote in his diary 'I'm not a soloist'[8] He was beginning to worry about his next concert, which was to be held at the Marylebone Institute at the end of May. In spite of his anxieties, the concert went well. He wrote 'It went better than I had reason to hope'[9]. The programme included songs by Blow and Purcell, Telemann's *Cantata No 33 Ergeuss Dich*, from *Harmonischer Gottesdienst*, and *Concerto a 4 in A minor* for treble recorder, oboe, cello and continuo. The participants were Clare Walmesley and Laura Sarti, Michale Arno (recorder), Roy Goodman and Sidde Shirman (violins), Felicity Leslie (oboe and recorder) and Janet Coles. The performers participated without a fee and a silver collection at the door just covered the financial costs. However Walter Bergmann quietly gave some money to the two young professional players, partly out of his own pocket. 'Why should they play for nothing?'[10] he asked.

The day after the concert, Norman Platt visited Belsize Square to discuss the planned children's opera. In spite of the fact Walter Bergmann had not written any of the music, the Marlowe Theatre in Cambridge was booked for two performances in December. He was depressed by his inability to get started on the project and by Faber's apparent reluctance to publish music he had written and arranged for them. His finances were also not in particularly good shape, although they were helped slightly by adjudicating work in Watford and the Isle of Wight. During May he went as a guest conductor to the Stockport Primary Schools Festival of Music. He conducted his arrangement of *Men of Harlech*, which was scored for massed choirs, recorder and percussion. Other recorder works were conducted by Dennis Bamforth and Colin Martin.

Walter Bergmann had received an invitation from Alfred Deller to play the recorder in two concerts on June 19th and 20th at the Stour Festival. Lunching with Deller at the beginning of June, he realised that this was probably the last time he would be invited as a professional to the Festival. He played with Katharine Jeans in two performances of John Eccles *The Judgement of Paris*. He stayed in Canterbury, where he was impressed by the cathedral, but he disliked having to drive the ten miles to and from festival venues. Walter Bergmann also enjoyed the opportunity to spend time with Antony Hopkins, and to reminisce about the 1940s. On June 20th he noted in his diary that it was farewell to Stour, as he was not needed any more[11]. His next concert on June 23rd was a complete contrast. The Telemann Ensemble Group, directed by Walter Bergmann, gave a concert with the Ionian singers in Streatham in aid of the N.S.P.C.C.. Michael Arno, Felicity Leslie, Katharine Jeans and Susan Gosling were soloists in Vivaldi's *Concerto Grosso Op. 3 no. 5*, which Walter Bergmann transcribed for recorders. He was pleased with the concert, which 'for amateurs'[12] went well.

At the beginning of July Walter Bergman at last received £200 from Faber in royalties. He also had received work from the publishers Peters, and Schott published his edition of Telemann's *Partita no. 4* for descant recorder and keyboard. As usual he set out for Salzburg with Margaret Murray, visiting Hans and Daisy Bergmann and Fritz and Anneliese Bergmann en route. He also met Christoph Gerhardt, and spent an enjoyable evening with the Versteegs. Jan Versteeg was now 87, but still active and lively. At the Orff course in Salzburg it was satisfying to find that there were three full recorder classes. He enjoyed teaching the advanced class and conducting a successful performance of *The Little Drummer Boy*. The weather in Austria was glorious, and Walter Bergmann took the opportunity to relax, meet old friends, think about work and catch up with correspondence. The latter included a letter to Frans Brüggen in which he said that he would not accompany the Dutch player again because Brüggen was now far too good a professional recorder player for him to play with. Walter Bergmann's pleasure in Salzburg was partly marred by trouble with his hearing. He was aware both on the Orff course and at the Roehampton Summer School that his hearing had noticeably deteriorated. Sometimes he could only understand half or even less of what was said to him. He still enjoyed parts of the Roehampton course, in particular conducting a group playing Byrd's *The Leaves be Green*. 'What a piece of music!'[13] he wrote in his diary. As usual he found Brian Bonsor's evening outstanding, and he took great pleasure in playing Arnold Matz's *Sonata for recorder and keyboard* with Paul Clark in the course concert.

In spite of reservations about how his hearing would affect him, Walter Bergmann was excited about his first trip to the U.S.A. in August 1970 to teach at the Seattle Summer School. He had received the invitation through Dennis Bamforth and Colin Martin, organisers of the English Northern Recorder Course, in which he had participated since 1967. The Seattle course had been started by Donald and Jenny Winters, who had lived in Britian in 1967, and played regularly with Dennis Bamforth and Colin Martin, who had helped the Winters set up the American course, based on English courses, in 1968.

It was extremely successful in its first year, and able to expand from the original group of three tutors, Bamforth, Martin and Paul Seibert.

Walter Bergmann was to remain in the States for a month. Staying for four weeks meant he could purchase a cheaper air ticket. It enabled him to travel, contact American publishers and visit friends and acquaintances. The journey out to Seattle was exceptionally clear, and he was able to see Scotland, Iceland and Greenland from the air. The Winters family welcomed him on his arrival. On the course Walter Bergmann taught technique classes, conducted ensemble classes, coached smaller groups and played in a tutors' concert. He found the workshop demanding but rewarding and friendly. He was pleased to be invited back for the following year.

Following the course, Walter Bergmann went to New York, where he enjoyed the Metropolitan Museum and the Rockefeller Building. He called at the New York offices of Peters and visited a number of friends including Susi Frankl, the daughter of the family he had known so well in Halle in the 1920s and 30s. He also conducted a meeting of the American Recorder Society, which was attended by a hundred members, which pleased him greatly. Walter Bergmann recorded all his experiences in detail in his diary, which for once, he had plenty of time to write. He finally flew thankfully home on September 19th, where the lights of London were a delightful picture from the air.

His immediate task was to consider the proposed children's opera, and face the fact that there was no way he could compose such a work in time for Christmas 1970. The existing libretto was unsuitable, and the project would have to be postponed. Reluctantly he acknowledged that this was the only course to take. On a more positive note, Faber had agreed to allow his Study Duets to be published in the States, and he was extremely pleased with his new recorder evening classes at the Marylebone Institute. The beginners' class was full.

October 1970 saw a pleasant visit from Fritz and Anneliese Bergmann and performances of the Musical Pills in Teignmouth, Bristol, Freshwater and the Cotswolds. November found him conducting a one-day recorder workshop in Huddersfield. At the annual meeting to discuss the 1971 Recorder in Education Summer School, Edgar Hunt, Freda Dinn and Walter Bergmann took the sad decision to cancel the course. A new venue had been found in Chichester to replace Roehampton. However the Chichester college wanted to increase the cost by £2 per student, which was considered to be an unacceptable increase. Shortly after the meeting, Walter and Grete Bergmann flew to Germany for five days in connection with war reparations. They initially stayed in Neckargemünd with Fritz and Anneliese, and then travelled to Heidelberg to attend court proceedings. The hearing was without any problems, and they were awarded 10,000 DM in reparation money in addition to money they had previously received. Following the hearing, Walter Bergmann visited the family grave, and then for light relief, Grete and he visited the casino. He lost 64 DM and Grete won 107!

On returning home. Walter Bergmann determined to start planning the Christmas opera for a year hence in December 1971 to be performed by schools in Southend. He had a depressing meeting with Donald Mitchell from Faber. His contract would expire on March 21st 1971, and Faber had no plans to accept any more work from him or publish any recorder music in 1971. Two Telemann works (a *Partita* and *Four Fugues*) would be published in 1972. Walter Bergmann felt he needed to find new challenges and goals. While teaching next day at Trent Park College, he decided on a new objective; to re-examine and re-edit the Handel recorder sonatas.

On December 9th, Walter Bergmann took his recorder evening class students and three young private pupils to a concert given by Elly Baghuis and her trio in the Purcell Room. He reviewed it for *The Recorder and Music* magazine. A few days later Grete and he went to the premiere of Michael Tippett's third opera, *The Knot Garden*, at Covent Garden. The opera explores human relationships. Walter Bergmann's reaction to it was to write 'Brilliant score, ridiculous libretto. The title should be 'Mignon kennst du das Land wo die Neurosen blühen' oder 'The war of the neuroses.''[14] December was a busy month. December 20th found him performing in a concert of music and poetry held in aid of the East Pakistan Disaster Fund. Laura Sarti, Clare Walmesley and Michael Arno took part, and Jeremy Brett read the poems. Christmas itself was a quiet family affair with the Bendixes. Walter Bergmann was also pleased to hear of his Christmas carol arrangements being played at the Harvard Club in Boston.

January 1971 was a low-key month after December. He completed his *Solo Album for Bass Recorder* for the American publisher Magna Music and conducted an enjoyable meeting of the Exeter SRP. He ran a weekend recorder course with Dick Coles at Knuston Hall. As usual he enjoyed working with Dr Coles, but his hearing problems were becoming more pronounced and his frustration was apparent when he became impatient with amateur players. Walter Bergmann was not unaware of his shortcomings. He confided in Dick Coles that he knew he was sometimes too sharp with those he was conducting. Dick Coles told him that it did not matter — and mostly it did not, as most of the players he conducted knew, respected and admired all that he had given to recorder players over many years.

Back in London the Dellers came to lunch and Walter Bergmann had a friendly meeting with Makings at Schott to discuss music and royalties. There were three performances of the Musical Pills at the end of January and beginning of February in Yorkshire, Henley on Thames and in Poole, Dorset. The production was still proving to have a successful formula, the performing group continuing to be Clare Walmesley, Laura Sarti, Norman Platt and Walter Bergmann, with Douglas Craig producing. He completed another work for children, *Casey Jones*, and lunched with Edgar Hunt to discuss the possibility of them working together to produce a new edition of the Handel recorder sonatas. In March the Bergmanns moved flats within the same building in Belsize Square. On discovering that 28 Belsize Square was for sale, Peter Bendix bought it, converted the two lower floors into one flat, installed central heating and rented it at a nominal rent to his parents in law. It was much more suitable than the top flat for an elderly couple. The extra restitution money helped pay for the move. There was less storage space in the new flat, and Walter Bergmann had to make difficult decisions about how much of his vast amount of music he could keep and what he would have to give or throw away. He knew that he would no longer conduct orchestras or choirs, which meant that he could dispose of a significant amount of music, but he found this difficult to accept. He wrote 'I have today thrown away cupboards full of Bach cantatas – hand-copied parts; chorus parts – heaps of orchestral music, chamber music, mountains of choral music. The clock has struck. Conducting is over. Those dreams are now finished'.[15] He felt more cheerful the next day, when he taught Catherine Marwood, a talented twelve year old and pupil of Lorna Burroughs. He did have plenty of musical events to look forward to. He had arranged to carry out three more concerts with Frans Brüggen in spite of the fact he had protested that he was no longer good enough to play with Brüggen, and had received an invitation to lecture at the Dartington Summer School. The Bergmanns held a flat warming party on April 10th, to which they were glad to welcome Ilse Wolf whom they had not seen for some while.

May 1971 found Walter Bergmann at the age of sixty-eight travelling to and fro across Britain. He went to Northampton for a concert with Dick Coles and the Nene Consort. He adjudicated in Tamworth and Lewisham and conducted the first performance of *Casey Jones* in Stockport. He was gratified that the children participating enjoyed the music From Stockport he travelled to Aberdeen to conduct an SRP meeting and enjoyed being taken round old Aberdeen by Ian Kemp (who edited the 60th Birthday published tribute to Michael Tippett). He then travelled south to Edinburgh, where he accompanied the winner of the 1970 Concerto Class at the Edinburgh Competitive Festival, a recorder player Donald Holloway, in a recital and adjudicated at the 1971 Festival the following day. He returned to London by sleeper. Two days later he was in Liverpool with Frans Brüggen. They gave two concerts; an afternoon lecture-recital for schoolchildren in the Bluecoat Hall, which was well supported, and an evening concert which was only half full. The programme spanned from music by van Eyck through Quantz to modern compositions by Makoto Shinohara and Walter Bergmann. The Liverpool papers were not enthusiastic about the choice of programme, and the *Daily Post* described it as 'dull in the extreme' in spite of Brüggen's 'beauty of phrasing and tone'.[16] *The Liverpool Echo* was complimentary about Walter Bergmann's *Sonata for descant recorder and piano*, reporting that its performance was' the most rewarding of a rather unexciting evening's experiences. Its delicate, fine-drawn textures and skilful adaptability of piano sonorities to those of the recorder were a constant delight.'[17] While he was in Liverpool, Walter Bergmann learnt of Felix Wolfes' death at the age of seventy-eight. He had been the most gifted of his teachers. 'Britten is now the best accompanist' he wrote in his diary.[18]

In contrast to the Liverpool concert, the recital at the Wigmore Hall in London the following day was sold out. Four major newspapers, *The Times*, *The Financial Times*, *The Daily Telegraph* and *The Guardian*, covered the concert with sympathetic reviews, although the reviewer from *The Guardian* had nothing positive to say about Brüggen's performance of the modern work by Shinohara. The papers were kind to Walter Bergmann. *The Times* observed that his playing was 'punctual and safe'[19] and *The Financial Times* astutely observed 'Mr Brüggen's ideal recital partner is probably the distinguished Belgian harpsichordist Gustav Leonhardt with whom he has made a number of records. Last night he played with his friend Walter Bergmann, perhaps better known as a musicologist (these pieces were edited by him). In technical terms he was not really a match for Mr Brüggen: but this is typical of Brüggen's attitude towards giving concerts that he should prefer to work with a sympathetic colleague like Bergmann than to pick up a more showy pair of fingers for the occasion.'[20] After the concert the Bergmanns entertained thirty-eight guests at a wine and cheese party. The following day Walter Bergmann accompanied Frans Brüggen in three master classes arranged by The Society of Women Musicians. He then had a day's enforced rest, while Brüggen taught in his music room at Belsize Square. In her usual generous manner, Grete Bergmann fed anyone who arrived at the flat. Finally they gave two concerts together in Manchester similar to the Liverpool concerts. As in Liverpool, the evening concert was not full, but was better supported. At the end, Walter Bergmann was firmly convinced that he should not accompany Brüggen in public again.

He went straight from Manchester by train to Carlisle to adjudicate in Galashiels in the Scottish Borders on May 26th. He stayed with the Bonsors, who met him at Carlisle. Brian Bonsor took him to lunch with Marie Dolmetsch, but Walter Bergmann felt that it was not a success as he really no longer had contact with the Dolmetsch family or interest in what they were doing. He returned to London very tired. Waiting for him was a letter from Hargail Press in New York accepting *Casey Jones* for publication. He had very mixed feelings about accepting agreements with American publishers. There were never any royalties, as they always bought copyright outright, but American sales had helped finance his trip to the States in 1970 and would support in his 1971 journey, and helped to get his name known. In June he completed an album *For the Tenor Recorder Player* for the American firm Magnamusic. The next few weeks found him catching up on outstanding work including translating and accepting new private pupils. On a visit to Birmingham to conduct the SRP he met Dennis Bamforth and Colin Martin to discuss future recorder courses and had dinner with Hilda Hunter to discuss the recorder classes at the forthcoming Salzburg Orff course. Much to his relief, and those around him, Walter Bergmann had managed to start writing his children's opera by the beginning of July with the help of his daughter Erica. He also met with Harold Newman from Hargail in New York to discuss publications and sign a contract.

He set out as usual with Margaret Murray for Salzburg. En route they visited the Dutch recorder player

Elly Baghuis, Hans and Daisy Bergmann, both his nephews, now married with children, the Versteegs and Fritz and Anneliese Bergmann. He was pleased to find Fritz and Anneliese in good health. While staying with them, Walter Bergmann spoke to Issi Matz for the first time in forty years. It was strange experience remembering back to a different life when he had been engaged to her. The Orff course went well. As he often did, he contacted Helene Novak, widow of his friend Hermann Novak. He was shocked to find her in an old people's home because she had tried to commit suicide. Visiting her was a depressing experience. She was extremely lonely and her daughter lived in the USA. Walter Bergmann tried to see whether it could be arranged for someone to visit her regularly.

Back home from Salzburg, Walter Bergmann caught up with correspondence. He was pleased to hear that a new venue had been found for the Roehampton Summer School for the following year. He also worked on the Christmas opera with Erica. He enjoyed giving two lectures at the Dartington Summer School, one of which was entitled 'Telemann the 'In' Composer'. He lunched with John Amis and attended a recital by Szymon Goldberg and Radu Lupu, at which he particularly appreciated pieces by Bartok and Hindemith. Once his lectures were over he relaxed, enjoying the atmosphere at Dartington and shopping for a birthday present for Grete. He found two rugs for her, which he gave to her with what remained of the restitution money from Germany.

Ten days later Walter Bergmann was in Provence for Alfred Deller's summer school, accompanied by Erika Seelig. They both stayed at the Deller's French home, as there was no other accommodation available. As usual, Walter Bergmann appreciated his surroundings. 'The evening in the open air was incredibly beautiful — peace and nature and stars, nice company and — after the awful heat in Avignon — ideal temperature.'[21] He enjoyed the good food and wine. He found the town of Avignon very beautiful, in spite of its apparent decay. He taught recorder and keyboard realisation, and accompanied singers in Alfred Deller's classes. He also played the keyboard in the course concert. He thought it was unlikely that he would be invited back.

As ever, Walter Bergmann methodically kept a diary, recording all the events of the summer. Until visiting Provence, he was writing predominantly in English. On August 18th he suddenly wrote 'Warum soll ich eigentlich in Englisch schreibe, wo ich mich doch besser in Deutsch ausdrücken kann?'[22] (Why should I write in English, when I can express myself better in German?)

He had no time to return home between his visit to France and travelling to the USA. He flew from Marseilles to London, where he was met at Heathrow by Hilde Volhard and Grete. Together they repacked his suitcases with clean clothes, had lunch and then Walter Bergmann boarded the plane for Seattle and Grete returned home with anything he did not require in the States. As in the previous year, Walter Bergmann spent his time in the USA teaching, conducting, seeing publishers and visiting places and friends. He went to visit the eminent recorder maker Friedrich von Huene and rang Helene Novak's daughter. He was relieved to hear that Helene Novak had been moved into pleasanter surroundings.

In New York Walter Bergmann once again conducted a meeting of the American Recorder Society. He was horrified at the low standard of playing. However this may have been at least partly due to the fact that the players were not organised and there were 70 players crammed into a small room. A reviewer of the evening wrote[23] 'there were sopranos, altos, tenors and basses scattered throughout the room. I wondered if the overall effect was changed by this arrangement. I felt as if I were playing a soprano solo (which might have sounded better had it been played by someone else). Dr Bergmann is a charming and personable man who radiated a warmth which had nothing to do with the very warm basement room in which we were playing. The evening was made even more enjoyable because of Dr Bergmann's sense of humour.' In the interval between the playing sessions Walter Bergmann showed his unique collection of photographic slides. This had been built up over many years and consisted of pictures of the recorder in many guises - paintings, woodcuts, sculptures and photographs. The collection included paintings by Goya and Rembrandt and photographs of Marlon Brando, Diana Dors and Twiggy playing the recorder. Later in his visit Walter Bergmann conducted a meeting of 30 members of the North Jersey Chapter of the American Recorder Society, where the standard of recorder playing was much better.

As in the previous year, he met with Susi Frankl, who showed him three recent photographs of his first wife, Marthel Kolb. He found it a strange experience. They discussed common friends and acquaintances. Travelling around, Walter Bergmann enjoyed chatting to American taxi drivers, who were often very well travelled.

On returning home at the end of September, as expected he received a letter from Alfred Deller stating that he would not engage him again for the French summer school. He did however have the prospect of a concert with Deller, for which he would compose a new work. At the beginning of October he gave up the plan to perform his children's opera in 1971, realising that he could not complete it in time and that it would have to be postponed for yet another year. Walter Bergmann was also dismayed to learn that Brian Bonsor was proposing to resign from the Recorder Summer School. He started writing *The Passionate Shepherd*, based on a poem by Marlowe, for two countertenors, two treble recorders and harpsichord on October 15th for the Deller concert on October 31st! In the first performance given under the auspices of the Wye College Music Society, the voice parts were sung by Alfred and Mark Deller, Ruth Dyson played the harpsichord, and Walter Bergmann and his pupil Susan Gosling played the recorder parts. The work was well received by the audience and encored at the end of the concert. Walter Bergmann was pleased with the performance.

November 1971 found him in Stratford on Avon to give a weekend recorder course. Back at home the Bergmanns had acquired a new dog, although Erica and Peter Bendix did not think this was a good idea. He lunched with John Thomson and discussed founding a new music-publishing firm. December was a month of mixed emotions. The new dog was run over and killed – they had become very fond of it in a short time. The Bergmanns also received news of the death of Jan Versteeg at the age of 89. A much happier prospect was the realisation of a very personal project, the private publication of a number of poems he had written over the years. Entitled Krystall der Sprache (Crystals of Speech), it consisted of eleven individual poems and six linked poems written in German.

The eleven individual poems were entitled
Das Gedicht (Poem)
Bitte (Please)
Musik
Altes Bild (Old Picture)
Die Hexe (I and II) (The Witch)
Der Goldene Gott (The Golden God)
Abend (Evening)
Nacht (Night)
Sommeraufgang am Meer (Sunrise by the Sea)
Gebet (Prayer)

The six linked poems had the overall title *Oper* (Opera), and were individually entitled

Ouverture
Arie
Duett
Quartett
Erstes Finale (First Finale)
Schluss Finale (Final Finale)

The earliest poems dated back to the 1930s. Walter Bergmann wrote *Bitte* during his imprisonment in 1938 and *Sonnenaufgang* was written in internment on the Isle of Man. The poems all had special associations for him. When he wrote the six 'Opera' poems, he had particular pieces of music in mind. In *Arie* he was thinking about Hindemith's opera *Cardillac*; *Duett* had associations with Mozart's *Die Entführung aus dem Serail* and *Quartett* with Verdi's Rigoletto. The poem *Musik* reflected the importance music had played in Walter Bergmann's life and how it had sustained and supported him through difficult times.

The first 50 copies of the poems arrived at Belsize Square on December 23rd. They celebrated with sekt and a special lunch. Walter Bergmann sent out 43 copies straight away. He had hoped that all the copies would arrive in sufficient time to be sent as Christmas presents. The initial recipients of the poems were close family and friends, such as Hilde Volhard, Dietrich Gerhardt and Margaret Murray, and musical friends like Michael Tippett, Frans Brüggen, Carl Orff, Norman Platt and John Thomson. Over the following three years Walter Bergmann sent out around 200 copies to friends and acquaintances, including extra copies requested by Dietrich Gerhardt. He kept a list of all the recipients, which reveals how many people he had kept in touch with over the years. This included his old secretary Charlotte Zimmermann, Arnold Matz, Prunella Flatz, Helene Novak and Issi von Arps-Aubert (Matz) and included the children of some of his closest friends, such as Christoph Gerhardt. The reaction of the recipients was surprise and delight.

Musik
Während eure Herzen beben
Heiss vom tönenden Erleben
Rinnt die Zeit aus euren Venen
In die Dinge, die da tönen,
Und wo ihr zu nehmen glaubt,
Werdet tödlich ihr beraubt.

Unter diesem Opfernmüssen
Blüht das ewige Geniessen:
Die musikgewordne Zeit
Schwebet durch der Ewigkeit
Räume wie ein goldnes Boot,
Ein Kristall gewordner Tod

Music
While your heart throbs
Churning from exuberant life
Time flows out of your veins
Through the demands that clamour there,
And where you have faith to accept,
Death will deprive you of it.

Beneath the inevitable sacrifice
Flourishes the eternal nourishment:
Time will music
Suspend in eternal space
Like a golden boat,
Where death turns to crystal.

Michael Tippett was one of the first to acknowledge the poems, writing 'I like the verses a lot, as one whose job is to invent 'Die musikgewordene Zeit''.[24] Prunella Flatz also replied immediately, commenting 'Well, well! How little one knows about one's friends', and that her husband thought the poems to be 'bloody good'![25] Walter Bergmann received compliments from many friends. Hans Gal was appreciative of his command of language and the effectiveness of the spoken sound of the poems. Frans Brüggen wrote how much he had enjoyed the poems saying of the collection 'It is really you'[26]. Heinz Schneider-Schott of Schott, Mainz wrote that Walter Bergmann was both a first-rate musician and a gifted poet. Ludwig Strecker, also from Schott, expressed his amazement at Walter Bergmann's command of German in spite of the fact he had lived in England for so many years. Peter Pears was delighted to receive the poems, and particularly liked *Nacht*. Dietrich Gerhardt distributed several copies of the poems in Germany and sent a copy to the University of Hamburg's department of literature by German exiles. It was acknowledged by Professor Dr H. Wolffheim, who described the poems as having a very personal voice, and that although he did not know Walter Bergmann, it was obvious that the poems were written by a musician[27].

The success of the poems made a happy start to 1972. The year followed the pattern of previous years with a small number of special high lights, such as the lecture-recital in the Purcell Room he gave in June, the first SRP Festival, also in June and held in Birmingham, the Dartington Summer School, the celebrations for his seventieth birthday in September and finally, in December, the realisation of his children's opera, staged in Southend. He taught on the usual courses, Knuston Hall in January, the Easter Northern Recorder Course, at Salzburg on the Orff course and at the Roehampton Summer School in its new venue. He did not visit the States in 1972. Walter Bergmann was becoming aware that his eyesight was beginning to fail, and he began to reduce the distances he drove, but that did not restrict the amount of travelling he did. He adjudicated in Edinburgh, Hull, Southend, East Grinstead and Worthing, conducted at a number of SRP branches, and lectured and taught on a number of short courses including a teachers' course in Huddersfield. In April he gave a lecture to the Viola da Gamba Society on the role of the gamba and cello in the music of Telemann. He was accompanied by four players, including Janet Coles.

On June 14th Walter Bergmann gave a lecture-recital in the Purcell Room, at London's South Bank complex, entitled 'The Continuo Accompaniment of Songs'. It was promoted by the Nicholas Choveaux Concert Agency. Ilse Wolf, Clare Walmesley, Laura Sarti, Norman Platt and Anthony Brown (baritone) sang during the evening, which was a memorable occasion. The following day found Walter Bergmann in Northampton to give a concert with the Coles family and the Nene Consort, and then he travelled to Birmingham to participate in the first SRP Festival, which became an annual event. This first festival involved massed recorder playing with three conductors, Edgar Hunt, Walter Bergmann and Paul Clark, contributed branch items and a solo competition adjudicated by John Joubert. Ross Winters won the solo competition, with Catherine Marwood whom Walter Bergmann was now teaching being placed second. Walter Bergmann agreed with the adjudication. Back in London his three recorder evening classes combined for an evening party, and showed their appreciation, which still surprised him, with the gift of a bottle of brandy.

On the way to Salzburg and the Orff course, Margaret Murray and he spent an enjoyable few days with Fritz and Anneliese Bergmann. Arnold Matz came to join them for 2 days. As he was now over sixty, there were no restrictions on him travelling in and out of East Germany, but there were of course financial restrictions. In Salzburg Walter Bergmann enjoyed going to concerts, in particular two given by the Bartok String Quartet playing Bartok, Beethoven, Mozart and Schubert, and a lecture-recital at the Orff Institute, which involved a Gamelan orchestra. As in the previous year, he visited Helene Novak and was pleased to find her in much better health and a pleasanter environment. He flew directly home to London from Salzburg, and after re-packing, drove with Erika Seelig to Keyworth, just outside Nottingham, to the college that was to be the new venue for the Recorder Summer School. He went to bed exhausted, only to wake next morning to discover that his car had been stolen. The police found it burnt out around ten miles away. Fortunately he had completely unpacked it. He had to spend a considerable amount of time during the week with the police.

1972 was to be the last year that Carl Dolmetsch tutored and played a full role in the summer school. During 1971 he had run a small scale 'Dolmetsch' summer school, which he had plans to establish as a regular summer school. He therefore wanted to significantly reduce his role in the course at Keyworth. He wished to come the following year for only a concert or lecture. It was agreed that the course directors would meet in the autumn to discuss the 1973 course. At the end of the week, Herbert Hersom drove Walter Bergmann home.

The atmosphere at Dartington was much more relaxed. He drove there in a new car. His lecture on 'The Continuo' was full, and a second class he gave was well supported, which pleased him greatly. He lectured on Frederick the Great and played organ continuo in a performance of Bach's *motet Jesu meine Freude* and in D. Scarlatti's *Stabat Mater*. He had to write out a part for himself for the Scarlatti, as it was impossible to play from the score. He had a pleasant return journey home, well pleased with the new car. Unfortunately at home there was a tax bill for £650 waiting for him. The new car had taken all his savings and he did not know where the money would come from to pay the demand. The arrival of a cheque for £520 from the insurance company paid out for the old car helped ease the situation.

Walter Bergmann's seventieth birthday on September 24th 1972 arrived with telegrams, presents, flowers and a small celebratory party. Dietrich and Suzanne Gerhardt came to stay and Don Winters visited. The rest of the year passed mainly in routine activities. He was becoming acutely aware of his failing eyesight. He had an unpleasant experience trying to negotiate the notorious spaghetti junction on the M1 outside Birmingham on his way to the Music Festivals Annual Conference, and after a performance of the Musical Pills in Kensington in November he was extremely depressed about his keyboard playing. He felt he was playing too many wrong notes due to failing eyesight, lack of practice and a fear of going wrong. The usual 'Pills' performing team were joined by Ilse Wolf for the performance, but it was unfortunately not a success. Walter Bergmann wrote in his diary 'I think this was the end of the 'Pills''[28] He was saddened by the end of something he had enjoyed so much and depressed that his keyboard playing might have contributed to this. On a more cheerful note he received a contract from the publishers Peters to act as their editor of recorder music, and from Schott for the publication of his editions of four recorder sonatas by Telemann from *Der Getreue Musik-Meister*. He corrected proofs of *18 American Folksongs* for Hargail. The evening classes for 1972/3 were also going well, particularly the beginner's class. 'After 30 years I can now teach recorder beginners'.[29]

At the beginning of December the Bergmanns were shocked and saddened to learn that Hilde Volhard required immediate surgery for bowel cancer. Both the Bergmann lives had been irrevocably bound up with those of Hilde Volhard and her sister Erika Seelig for so many years. At the same time, Walter Bergmann's children's Christmas opera was finally staged. Called *The Rehearsal* and described as a 'Christmas Venture' jointly written by Erica and Walter Bergmann, it was performed at the Southend College of Technology by students from the college, three primary schools and six secondary schools, produced by Hilary Clulow and conducted by Maurice Bailey. The work was dedicated to Margaret Murray. The opera meant a great deal to Walter Bergmann. He spent three days from December 4th to 6th rehearsing with the children. Hilde Volhard came with him, presumably to keep herself distracted from the forthcoming operation. The first audience came for the dress rehearsal on the afternoon of December 6th. Walter Bergmann paid close attention to the reaction of the children who had been invited to watch. The children listened attentively and quietly, but he felt that they did not respond enthusiastically. Unfortunately this was the only performance that Margaret Murray could attend, which disappointed Walter Bergmann.

Hans, Fritz, Anneliese and Rolf* Bergmann all came from Germany to attend the first performance on the evening of December 7th. Hans came to stay for just two days. Walter Bergmann felt that the standard improved during this and the second performance the following night, but it was not as high as he would have liked. The parental audiences were enthusiastic. Overall he concluded that both the libretto and music were good, but parts of the opera were too difficult and needed revision. He was profiled in the local Southend paper in conjunction with the two performances, which received rather a mixed review afterwards. One of the two reviewers wrote 'I found Dr Walter Bergmann's music rather mixed – with sophisticated Stravinsky-style themes jostling against the genuine operetta style. Frankly I thought the operetta tunes came off best. The lively opening chorus was just one example of the sort of tune children could really sing with conviction, While the Gloria was an example of the sort of tune they could not sing with conviction.

The pastorale and the Christmas Music interludes were delightful. To sum up, the music was at its best when at its most traditional.' A second reviewer wrote[30] 'Musically it was a fascinating experience, with plenty of choral work from a massed children's choir of angels, descant recorders, tambourines and triangles providing the constant tinkle of Christmas bells.

The libretto, by Dr Bergmann's daughter Erica, was suited to children without being childish, and illustrated effectively that the Christmas message applies all the year round.'

Two days after the production, Walter Bergmann succumbed to flu, followed soon after by Grete. He recovered just before Christmas, and was well enough to visit Hilde Volhard shortly after her operation. She made a steady recovery over 1973, helped and supported by both Walter and Grete.

1973 was to prove a rewarding year musically for Walter Bergmann, and he was delighted when Britain joined the European Community at the beginning of the year. He was also very pleased when he received a

---

* Fritz's son

commission to compose a sonata for treble recorder for the young Italian, Amico Dolci, a talented fifteen year old, who had started playing the recorder at the age of eleven when he was given a recorder by an English visitor. Following lessons with Edwin Alton, he went to study the recorder with Ferdinand Conrad. He had enjoyed playing Walter Bergmann's *Sonata* for descant recorder, which prompted his father to commission a work for him.

Over 1973 Walter Bergmann's main activities continued with some occasional variants. In January he was asked by the BBC to prepare a talk on Telemann's *St Matthew Passion*, to be completed by February 1st. He did a considerable amount of work for the talk, but found it difficult to complete with the commission for the recorder sonata and a 10,000-word article he was writing on German music. He was relieved when he made the decision to give up the BBC commission, and recommended Percy Young to them to complete the work and give the talk. Later he heard that the talk had been cancelled. He was subsequently surprised to discover the following month that Charles Cudworth, who he met at a lecture, had been engaged to give the talk. Cudworth had no idea that the BBC had initially employed Walter Bergmann for the work, and a few days later he sent a letter to him enclosing half the fee he had received. 'There are still wonderful people'[31] Walter Bergmann wrote in his diary. He would of course, he noted, return the money. Later in the year, he was delighted to be asked again by the BBC to talk on Telemann, this time on the*Tafelmusik*. The talk was to last for 12 minutes, and to include 5 minutes of musical examples. It was recorded on October 4th and broadcast on October 7th.

He taught on the same regular courses as in previous years. He thought a great deal about teaching and what could be achieved with amateur players. Working on the Knuston Hall course, he noted, 'It is better to sacrifice one bar for a whole piece, then one piece for a whole bar'.[32] He found the players enthusiastic and exhausting. The Northern Recorder Course held in York at Easter was a rewarding experience, in particular one of the two concerts in which he played continuo and had to improvise a continuo part for a recorder concerto by Telemann that he did not know. He was among old friends on the course, Denis Bamforth, Colin Martin, Ferdinand Conrad, Hilda Hunter, Paul Clark and Theo Wyatt. It was the last time he was to participate on the course, though he did not realise it at the time.

Following the London SRP's annual concert held in May in which pupils and evening class students of Walter Bergmann played a significant role, was a belated 70th birthday celebration for him. This was a concert, held in the Purcell Room on June 4th, devoted to Walter Bergmann's compositions, which he conducted himself. The performers were Michael Arno, Adrian Bush, Janet Coles, Alfred and Mark Deller, Desmond Dupré, Susan Gosling, Catherine Marwood and Margaret Murray, with members of the London SRP and children from Southend schools. The programme include the premiere of two new works, the *Sonata for Treble Recorder and Piano*, played by Catherine Marwood and Walter Bergmann, and *Three Songs* with lute accompaniment (*Mater cantans filio, Plaudite caeli* and *To Musick*) sung by Alfred Deller with Desmond Dupré. The rest of the programme consisted of

The Passionate Shepherd to his love and *The Nymph's reply* (1971) for 2 countertenors, 2 recorders and keyboard
The Sonata for Descant Recorder and Piano (1965)
Chaconietta on a Ground by Purcell (1969) for cello and recorder consort

The Drummer Boy (1967)
Casey Jones (1972)
The Old Brass Wagon (1972)
all for unison voices, recorders, percussion and piano.

The concert was sold out and the whole evening was well received by the audience. A short, complimentary review appeared in the Daily Telegraph on June 5th. Entitled *The music is for players*, the paper's critic wrote[33] that although at the end of the concert Walter Bergmann had modestly described his music as being for players rather than listeners, the audience had still enjoyed listening to the imaginative use of musical ideas in his compositions. The review went on to acknowledge that, although Walter Bergmann's music had not often been heard in concerts, his work had been known by singers for many years through his 'scholarly editions'.

His compositional style in the *Sonata for Descant Recorder and Piano* was likened to that of Hindemith's and as being fresh and inventive. The first performance of the *Sonata for Treble recorder* by Catherine Marwood was enthusiastically greeted. The work was described as sectional in its construction and as having a concise sequence of ideas.

The review in *Recorder and Music*[34] pointed out that it was fitting that the concert should start 'with the sound of solo treble recorder and finish with the small stage crowded with singers, recorder players and percussionists.' The reviewer was particularly complimentary to the new treble sonata. Its first performance was 'the high spot of the evening' and the writer considered that it was a work 'which will undoubtedly become part of the recorder's standard repertoire. Miss Marwood combined an impressive technique with sensitive musicianship to convey both the contemplative beauty of the slow movement and the rhythmic vigour of the *Rondo Danzante*, an extending movement of alternating fast and slow sections which explores the possibilities of its folk-like themes with great economy of notes, indeed one suspects that the piano part has been carefully written so as to minimise the chances of over-enthusiastic pianists dominating their less powerful partners.'

The latter comment was an astute observation; anyone who had participated in Walter Bergmann's classes on continuo accompaniment knew of his fanatical concern that the keyboard should not be too loud!

He was interviewed by the local Hampstead paper[35], which remarked on his comment at the end of the concert that, as he wrote his music for players, 'any credit reflects only on the performers'. This deferential announcement 'reflected much of the man who for 33 years has worked from his home in Belsize Square, Hampstead, escorting thousands of children through their first steps in music, obligingly arranging early music for pupils, composing for friends who have achieved greater fame in the music world and playing a quiet but important part in England's musical renaissance.' The paper noted his scholarly and academic work 'drawn on frequently by renowned performers of early music' and summed him up as 'a man with special love for children and music-making'. Walter Bergmann cited Hindemith as his main inspiration and Mozart as his favourite composer.

He was especially touched after the concert by a letter from Catherine Marwood saying that rather than being thanked to play in the concert she felt that it is 'I who should be thanking you for asking me to play at your concert!' It had been a wonderful experience for her to give the first performance of the treble sonata. Overall he was quite overwhelmed by the reaction to the concert and to his compositions. He could be difficult, irascible and sometimes unrealistic in what he expected and demanded from people, but he always had a genuine desire for those he taught to experience the joy of successful music-making. All through his life he found it difficult to believe in himself, and to positively and objectively assess all that he did. In some areas he underestimated his abilities and in others he overestimated them. As the years went by, it was difficult for people to explain to him, and for him to accept, that old age was beginning to restrict his competence

For the first time ever, the car broke down on the way to Salzburg. Margaret Murray and he eventually reached the home of Fritz and Anneliese Bergmann, and spent an enjoyable few days with them and with Rolf Bergmann and his wife. He took the opportunity to put flowers on his parents' grave in Wiesbaden. He wondered who would look after it when Fritz was no longer alive, and if his and Grete's ashes could be interred there after their deaths. They all went to visit two König cousins, which proved to be a difficult occasion. He had friendly, successful recorder classes at Salzburg. He enjoyed the company of Hilda Hunter, finding her easy to talk to in spite of the fact that her mother died during the week. He noted in his diary how expensive he found Austria. He visited Helene Novak, who although in pleasant surroundings was desperately unhappy and still wished to end her life. Walter Bergmann agonised over whether he should help her, but decided that it would be impossible to do so, even if it was the right thing to do.

The Recorder Summer School at Keyworth marked the end of an era. Carl Dolmetsch attended to give two master classes and to play in the concert. His visit was not a great success and it was the last time he participated in the course. Freda Dinn also left. Walter Bergmann wrote[36] 'The 'Roehampton School is unravelled. Dinn and Dolmetsch have separated: Hunt, Bonsor and I travel forward'. Two days after returning home he was off to Dartington with Grete. Hilde Volhard went with them. His two lectures, 'Wit and Music' and 'Purcell as seen by a foreigner', were well received. Attendance at his classes was low due to the fact that they clashed with the master class. He had twenty-four hours at home before leaving on August 18th for Seattle and the Northwest Recorder Course – a punishing schedule for a man of seventy. Due to the success of the course in previous years, the University of Washington was providing sponsorship. String players also joined the course. As well as his regular recorder classes, Walter Bergmann gave a continuo master class and played the continuo for two items, trio sonatas by Antonio Lotti and Telemann, in which Ferdinand Conrad played the recorder.

He was pleased with his earnings for the week ($625) and he agreed to come back for the 1974 summer school. Added to cheques from his American publishers, it was a profitable summer for him. As in previous years, he visited friends and publishers. He visited Don Winter one evening and found him very depressed. He did his best to cheer him up, and told him about his unhappiest period of his life when he was imprisoned in 1938, and he had wanted to commit suicide, but decided to see what the future held 'and here I am'[37]. In his diary, he debated about human existence. Asking the question 'why' he believed separated humans and animals.[38] He lunched with the American player Martha Bixler, and invited her to tutor at the 1974 Recorder Summer School. He once again conducted a meeting of the New York Guild of the American Recorder Society. As in 1971, he did not consider it a success. He took new music direct from the publishers to the meeting, including his own arrangement of a Purcell *In Nomine* and Dennis Bamforth's edition of Froberger's *Ricercare*. Very few people were prepared to buy music and there was in consequence insufficient music to go round the players. The players all sat in formal straight rows, which made conducting and listening difficult.

On his return home he was straight into the new autumn term. After his first new advanced recorder class at Marylebone, he went to an enjoyable recital given by Frans Brüggen in the crypt of St Martin's in the Fields. In spite of his protestations about no longer being competent enough to play with Brüggen, he accompanied the recorder player in a concert in Norwich on September 29th, and played a harpsichord solo. In October he travelled north to conduct the Edinburgh and Aberdeen SRP branches, and enjoyed spending time with Hans Gal, with whom of course he been interned on the Isle of Man. Walter Bergmann also received a letter from Peter Pears inviting Catherine Marwood and him to play the new recorder sonata in Aldeburgh in June 1974. In contrast he was saddened to receive a letter at the end of the year from Dennis Bamforth saying that his elementary/intermediate recorder class would not be included in the 1974 Easter Northern Recorder Course. After discussing it with Grete, he decided to resign from the course completely. He had an apologetic phone call from Colin Martin a few days later, who found the situation very difficult, caught between the dilemma of Dennis Bamforth wanting changes on the course and Walter Bergmann's hurt at not being able to continue. Dom Gregory Murray had also resigned.

Overall, 1973 had been a good year. As well as the successful concerts and courses, Schott had accepted the *Sonata* for treble recorder for publication as well as his new editions of Telemann recorder sonatas and a Quantz trio. Faber published his *Descant Recorder Lessons*, a project close to his heart. It included 124 pieces of music and exercises with piano accompaniment, which Walter Bergmann had aimed to set out in an interesting progressive scheme. It was dedicated to Hilde Volhard and he wrote in the preface to the recorder part that the aim was for young players 'To make music from the very beginning'.

Walter Bergmann found it very strange not to attend the 1974 Easter Recorder Course at York. Otherwise the year took its usual shape, with the addition of weekend courses in March at Charney Manor, with Dick Coles, and at the end of the year at Wansfell College. He found that he had an increasing number of musicians visiting him at Belsize Square. They came to consult him on a variety of musical issues. For example, Ross Winters, the recorder player who had won the first SRP solo competition, came and they played Walter Bergmann's new sonata together. Walter Bergmann was impressed by his playing. David Munrow came to visit in March and borrowed pictures, music and instruments. Another visitor was a young Cambridge music student called Judith Weir.

On March 16th the Bergmanns went with Margaret Murray to see the Kent Opera's production of Telemann's *The Patience of Socrates* at the Marlowe Theatre, Canterbury. It was produced by Norman Platt and conducted by Roger Norrington. Walter Bergmann provided the programme notes. He was impressed by the production and by the continuo playing of Jonathan Hinden. He felt that the audience responded very positively. In April Grete and he spent two weeks together in Germany, the first in Hamburg and the second with Fritz and Anneliese Bergmann in Neckargemünd. On his return home, Walter Bergmann concentrated on the commission he had received to write a piece of music for the London SRP to play at the 1974 SRP Festival to be held in Northampton. Activities in May included SRP meetings in Cambridge and Birmingham and a trip to Stockport for a schools' performance of his arrangement of *When the Saints* come marching in. It was not a success. The piece was played again in June at a schools' meeting in Southend, but Walter Bergmann was not happy with this performance either, although he thought the rehearsals had gone well. At the end of May he was invited to dinner at the German Embassy. The dinner was preceded by a concert of music by Beethoven, Britten and Schumann. During May he also had a minor operation for the removal of a small growth on his hand. It proved to be non-malignant, but he was worried that it might re-occur.

One of the most important events of 1974 for Walter Bergmann was the performance of his new *Sonata for treble recorder and piano* at the Aldeburgh Festival. It was played by Catherine Marwood and himself at the opening concert held in the Maltings, Snape on Friday June 7th. The other performers in the concert were Wilbye Consort of Voices, directed by Peter Pears and the organist Ralph Downes. The concert made use of a new chamber organ installed at the Maltings. As well as the treble sonata, Catherine Marwood played two descant sonatas by Cima and Bigaglia. The rest of the programme consisted of fifteenth and sixteenth century organ music, played by Ralph Downes, folksongs arranged by Gustav and Imogen Holst and rounds, canons, catches and glees by Byrd, Purcell and Boyce. It was a happy and enjoyable occasion. Benjamin Britten, was well enough to attend the second part of the concert, so that he heard Walter Bergmann's sonata. It was Catherine Marwood's 16th birthday, and Walter Bergmann presented her with a bunch of flowers at the end of the concert. She wrote to him afterwards[39] 'I will always remember the occasion as being one of the happiest of my life and am very grateful to you for giving me the opportunity to play in that wonderful hall'. The occasion was the last time Walter Bergmann saw Benjamin Britten. In 1973 Britten had had a stroke following a heart operation, which partly paralysed his right side. Britten came and shook Walter Bergmann's hand after the concert, and he realised that in spite of his friendly smile, Britten was a very sick man. Grete, Erica, Margaret Murray, Hilde Volhard and Erika Seelig all came to the concert. At the party afterwards Walter Bergmann embarrassed himself when he asked the Chairman of the Aldeburgh Festival Council, the Countess of Cranbrook, who she was.

In the programme notes for the concert, Walter Bergmann set out his objectives while writing the *Sonata for Treble Recorder and Piano*. 'This sonata aims at the liberation of the recorder from its imaginary bondage to a harpsichord or a fortepiano – how many people own such instruments? – and confronts half a pound of wood (the weight of the treble recorder) with some centiweights of the same material (a grand piano), in the hope that the underdog will win.

The first movement is quasi an improvisation *a due*. The second movement is an extended dance rondo with two enclaves: another, written down improvisation, and a kind of minuet looks back with nostalgia to the eighteenth century – the hey-day of the recorder.' The reviewer for *Recorder and Music* wrote[40] of the sonata 'This modern work has great quality, and shows a fine and discriminating partnership between recorder and piano. ....It is not avant-garde music but it belongs to our time'. The review also praised the performance by Catherine Marwood and Walter Bergmann of the two descant works, in which Walter Bergmann played the chamber organ. 'The instruments blended exquisitely in softness and intonation.' *The Yorkshire Post* commented[41] on 'the brilliant recorder playing of a very young artist, Catherine Marwood, in a new *Sonata* for that instrument by Walter Bergmann, who accompanied her'.

The excitement of the Aldeburgh concert was followed by the 1974 SRP Festival held in Northampton on June 22nd As in the previous year, SRP branches contributed items to the programme. In his work for the London SRP, entitled *Variations and Theme*, Walter Bergmann tried to address the problem found frequently in amateur recorder groups of a discrepancy between the really competent players and the average players. He wrote for the festival programme 'Variations and Theme — not vice versa. The audience can work a bit by extracting the theme from the variations before it is played (twice) at the end. My friends say that the theme is second rate... that is not true, it is third rate, but by me. The piece is scored for two groups of players with different technical standards: experienced players and more experienced ones.

The SRP should cultivate such music because it keeps the best players interested in Branch meetings; music which is too easy drives them away.'

Walter Bergmann had arranged for Antony Hopkins to adjudicate the solo competition at the SRP Festival. It was won by Evelyn Nallen, with Catherine Marwood sharing the 3rd prize.

Back in London, Walter Bergmann went to see Peter Makings at Schott. In collaboration with Frans Brüggen, he had begun to edit twenty-four sonatas by Schickhardt. These sonatas had been originally written to be played by flute or violin or recorder. They could be transposed, as the composer himself did, for the appropriate instrument providing a sonata for each of the twelve major and minor keys. In Schickhart's day the players were expected to decide themselves to which key a particular sonata should be transposed. By using a different clef, actual transposition could be avoided. Preparing all twenty-four sonatas for publication was an attractive challenge for Walter Bergmann and Frans Brüggen. Makings threatened to cancel Walter Bergmann's pension of £400 per annum if Schott were not given the right to publish the sonatas. Walter Bergmann felt like cancelling the project. He contacted Brüggen and they decided that they would work out what they should do when they met later in the year. At the end of June Walter Bergmann enjoyed returning to the Stour Music Festival to give a concert with Clare Walmesley, Ann-Frances Ellis (clarinet and recorder) and members of his Marylebone recorder evening classes for 'Children and their Parents'. The programme was wide ranging, and concluded with his arrangement *The Old Brass Wagon*. Much to his delight it was well attended. He was invited to lunch with the Dellers, which he found a difficult occasion.

In July Margaret Murray and he travelled to Salzburg via Calais. They visited his brother Hans, now 78 and living on his own in Bad Berleburg, south east of Dortmund. They stayed in a hotel near to his home. Hans Bergmann had placed flowers, fruit juice and chocolates in their rooms and, much to Walter Bergmann's dismay, he had paid the hotel bill. Hans was ill and Walter Bergmann was very worried about him as he obviously could not continue living on his own, and Bad Berleburg was a significant distance from Fritz Bergmann in Neckargemünd (near Heidelberg). He would have to move, but the problems was where to. They travelled on to Neckargemünd, where Arnold Matz came to spend a day with Walter Bergmann.

In Salzburg Walter Bergmann managed to sell all the recorders he took with him (12 descants, 4 trebles and 1 tenor) and reasonable amount of music. Simple music and ensemble music sold best. Students on the course were unacquainted with English ensemble music. On his free afternoon Prunella Flatz collected him and took him to her home in St Jakob. Back in England, the first summer school without Carl Dolmetsch went well. Martha Bixler was a great success as a friendly and considerate contributor to the course. She proved to be an excellent teacher and easy to work with. Ross Winters came for the first time as a tutor and Walter Bergmann was delighted with his contribution. Walter Bergmann's class sent him a poem at the end of the week.

'Off Keyworth
Please don't go yet for we've something to say
There is a big thank you a-coming your way.
We know it must irk you to hear our wrong notes
You don't lose your temper, you just tell us jokes.

We don't tongue portata we tongue tongued legato
How long is a crotchet when we play staccato
Don't worry if you have wrong intonation
It turns out all right with articulation.

Read from a stave if you don't like the system
But always remember those four rules of wisdom
Fingers down quickly and always together
Then notes that are sharp can be blamed on the weather.'

He flew to Seattle on August 15th. He told Don Winters at the beginning of the American course that it would be the last time he participated. He made his decision partly on grounds of age and also because of the slightly strained relations with Dennis Bamforth and Colin Martin. He wrote in his diary[42] 'At night I lie awake for hours and know that from this year I am old'. Both Grete and he found it difficult to be apart for so long a time and so far from each other. As they got older he felt that they both worried more about each other and being apart. They had been married for 35 years and together for over 40 years. He also felt that his hearing and sight were getting significantly worse, which made him more insecure. The Northwest Recorder Course went better than Walter Bergmann had expected. Relations with Dennis Bamforth and Colin Martin proved to be less stressful than he had anticipated, and he particularly enjoyed the evening conducted by Dennis Bamforth. Walter Bergmann specialised in Elizabethan music during the course. Ferdinand Conrad and he played his treble sonata in the course concert. 'The audience awarded it the warmest, most sustained applause of the evening.'[43] In the following weeks Walter Bergmann travelled to San Francisco, Vancouver, New York, Pittsburgh and Boston. On September 14th he gave a workshop at Amherst and on the 16th he lectured at the University of Pittsburgh on 'The enjoyment of rhythm with special reference to English Elizabethan rhythm'. The following day he worked with recorder players at Wellesley College and gave an evening lecture entitled 'What soloist and accompanist should know about basso-continuo'. Friedrich von Huene came to the lecture. Visits to friends and publishers continued throughout his visit. He tried without success to interest a publisher in the Christmas opera. One of the most pleasurable activities during his time in the USA was a visit to the Metropolitan Museum in New York. Don Winters told him that the Seattle course would not be the same without him, but he knew that this was the last time he would work over the summer in America. He returned home after a month away, utterly exhausted.

Confirmation of Walter Bergmann's success in writing music for schools came with reviews of *The Old Brass Wagon* in the summer 1974. George Odam wrote in *The Music Teacher*[44] that it was 'A practical enjoyable piece of American woolly-west-music, non-taxing, ready for instant performance. Just add children of 9-11 and rehearse lightly.

Ingredients; descant and treble recorders, pitch and non-pitch percussion, piano, open strings pizzicato, 'cello (ad lib.) and voices.'

Edward Price in *Music in Education*[45] was equally complimentary. 'When I say that this piece consists of variations on a corny tune, I use the adjective in its best affectionate sense. For unison voices, it epitomises the Wild West, and is dedicated to Brian Bonsor, who was in the vanguard of the hoe-down school. Both the tune and the words of the six verses are simple and repetitive, but the wagon is kept rolling by interesting but fairly easy parts for recorders and percussion.......For top juniors and over, and would make an excellent piece for an older group with limited vocal range and the help of a few reasonably competent instrumentalists.' *The American Recorder* gave the music a very positive review. Around the same time as these reviews, Walter Bergmann received the extract of his entry on Telemann for the 1974 edition of *Encyclopaedia Britannica*, which pleased him greatly.

In the autumn of 1974 he was still trying to sort out who could publish the 24 Schickhardt sonatas without upsetting Schott. He met with Martin Kingsley (of Faber) and a representative of the Japanese firm Zen-On, who were interested in the Schickhardt works and a recorder sonata by Finger. At the beginning of November 1974, in spite of his resolution in 1971 not to accompany Brüggen again, Walter Bergmann went to Amsterdam to rehearse with him for three recitals to be given at the Royal College of Music in Manchester, Winchester College and Nottingham University starting on November 16th. He took the opportunity to revisit the Rijksmuseum, where he found the Van Gogh exhibition enthralling. Brüggen and he took the decision to accept Zen-On's offer to publish the Schickhardt sonatas. Walter Bergmann noted in his diary how considerate Frans Brüggen was for the four days they were together for the actual concerts. He felt that the recitals went well, although he made 'unnecessary slight mistakes — fear of the mighty Frans'[46]. The programme for all three concerts included Walter Bergmann's *Sonata for Treble Recorder and Piano*, a Telemann recorder *Sonata in f minor*, music by Van Eyck and *Fragmente* by Makato Shinohara. There were contrasting reviews for the recitals.

J. C. Potts, writing in *The Recorder and Music Magazine*,[47] remarked how enjoyable it was to hear Frans Brüggen and Walter Bergmann play together again in the Manchester concert. The programme, including Walter Bergmann's sonata, was well received with the exception of *Fragmente*. In contrast, the report for the Winchester College magazine[48] described this piece 'as the most fascinating piece of avant-garde music' the writer had heard for some while. The venue for the concert at Winchester had not been ideal for a concert of small-scale chamber music, which the reviewer pointed out in his article. The harpsichord had also not been ideal for accompanying the recorder, and Walter Bergmann had to close the lid to try to reduce the volume of sound. This led to the stand for music falling down during the performance of the Telemann sonata. He was extremely irritated to read in the review that the writer believed that the stand had fallen down because he was hitting the keyboard much too hard.

At the end of November Catherine Marwood and he made a recording of the content of his *Descant Recorder Lessons* to accompany the music books. He always enjoyed working with her. Martin Kingsbury was pleased with the recording. Other pupils included a mature student, Ursula Groke, who became a personal friend and involved in Walter Bergmann's teaching. In December he taught at Wansfell College on a Schumann weekend, lecturing on German romantic poets in relation to Schumann. It must have brought back memories of his pre-war life in Germany. Hans Bergmann arrived to stay two weeks before Christmas, and the Bergmanns had a family photograph taken. By the end of the year Walter Bergmann had completed the continuo part of eight of the Schickhardt sonatas. He felt they were the best realisations he had completed. 1974 had been a good year for reinforcing his capabilities as a composer and editor. He felt confident enough to send a copy of his treble sonata to Michael Tippett as a birthday present in January 1975.

1975 was a quieter year. In January he was a little perturbed to read in *The Gramophone* that he was the 'late' Walter Bergmann. He received a number of telephone calls during which he was able to reassure people that he was very much alive! He wrote a tribute for Tippett's seventieth birthday, which was published in the March edition of *Recorder and Music*. In it he reminded recorder players how much they owed to Tippett. 'As conductor, he was the first to employ recorders in a (modern) performance of Purcell's big *Ode for St Cecilia's Day*, thus making recorders presentable with a professional orchestra.' At Morley College 'he created recorder classes (up to four) and sponsored recorder meetings even in the darkest hour of the war'. He described Tippett as 'one of the strongest, deeply human personalities I have met in my whole life. Though his music aims to go beyond art, it is art and for me art of the highest quality. Apart from this great aesthetic pleasure it gives me it gives me strength (as opposed to Weltschmerz), joy (not miserable self-indulgence) and a positive vision in this world full of cruel realities.'[49] Later in 1975 Ian Kemp came to interview him about his experiences of working with Michael Tippett for a book he was writing. Both Grete and he liked Kemp and found him a sympathetic interviewer.

After the Knuston Hall and Charney Manor courses with Dick Coles in January and February, Walter Bergmann went in March with Erika Seelig to Hamburg to attend a meeting about restitution money for the Hüth-Seelig Firm. The lawyer handling the matters impressed him. The actual legal documents establishing the status of the firm appeared to be in a legal muddle, but once this had been sorted, prospects seemed hopeful for a satisfactory settlement for the Seelig family. During the visit Walter Bergmann managed to spend some time with Dietrich Gerhardt.

The year passed with teaching, conducting, arranging, editing and writing. He saw new friends such as Ursula Groke, and old friends visited Belsize Square, for example Norman Platt and his second family, and on another occasion Platt's older son came to see Walter Bergmann to ask for advice. Although Walter Bergmann still had a number of private pupils, he had begun to recommend Ross Winter as a teacher rather than taking some new pupils himself. He was still having no success in finding a publisher for the Christmas opera, but continued to work on the Schickhardt sonatas with Frans Brüggen, and a Babell recorder concerto with David Lasocki. His fluctuating income was causing some problems in balancing his income with tax demands.

He was very relieved to receive royalties of £450 from Faber and eventually £1100 from Schott.

In June Walter Bergmann enjoyed the SRP Festival, which was held in Galashiels in the Scottish borders. Brian Bonsor had invited him to adjudicate the solo competition. The weather was good, the weekend well run and he enjoyed the journey home via the Lake District. The summer brought his regular trips to Salzburg and Keyworth. He was disappointed at the standard of recorder playing in Salzburg and the presence of many German-fingered recorders. At Keyworth he was worried and depressed about his hearing. However Walter Bergmann's conducting evening on the course still went well and he enjoyed the company of Friedrich von Huene and his wife, who were guests on the course.

In September 1975 Walter Bergmann offered Belsize Square as the venue for a new teacher's examination for the SRP. Both he and Dick Coles had worked hard to persuade the society to replace their old teacher's test with a new certificate. Doubts were expressed as to whether the SRP should take it upon itself to award a certificate. It was eventually agrees that a certificate would be awarded to those considered competent enough to direct groups and teach the recorder, and that it should be emphasized that the award was quite distinct from and not a music diploma. There were two examiners at this first examination, Walter Bergmann and Dick Coles, and two observers, the recorder teacher Eileen Cobb and Dr Sam Taylor, a college of education music lecturer, who was closely involved in recorder teaching. Ross Winters accompanied the candidate during the performance part of the exam. With the exception of Eileen Cobb, the candidate was asked to conduct her examination arrangement played by those present. She was asked to treat them as complete beginners. This was difficult, as they made no mistakes at all! (The author was the candidate.) In the usual Bergmann tradition, all those present were offered superb hospitality by Grete Bergmann in the form of a buffet lunch after a successful conclusion to the examination.

There were no significant concerts for Walter Bergmann in 1975 until the end of the year. In the London SRP annual concert held in May, Catherine Marwood had played the treble sonata, and Ross Winters played the Vivaldi *C minor Recorder Concerto* with Walter Bergmann leading the continuo group from the harpsichord. He was invited as a guest to attend the gala concert to celebrate the 10th anniversary in July of the Southend Children's Music Day and to hear his arrangement of a Purcell song and *John Brown's Body*. In October Walter Bergmann accompanied the Nene Consort in a concert for the Northampton Festival. The programme concluded with his transcription of Vivaldi's *Concerto Grosso in G minor*, written for 4 violins and string orchestra and adapted for 4 recorders and continuo. At the beginning of December Walter Bergmann accompanied Ross Winters in a recital in Wolverhampton. (The programme again included the treble sonata.) Two days later on December 11th, there occurred the most significant event of the year for Walter Bergmann, a 'Musical Soiree' in the Purcell Room supported by Choveaux Management. The programme consisted almost exclusively of Baroque music; the only exceptions were Walter Bergmann's two songs, *Pastorale* and *Pastorella*, for voice and recorder. The soloists were Catherine Marwood (recorder and viola), Ross Winters (recorder) and Anne Richards (soprano). Janet Coles and Margaret Murray also played with a number of Walter Bergmann's other pupils. One unusual item in the programme was C.P.E. Bach's *Trio Sonata* for bass recorder. This Walter Bergmann accompanied on the piano, as the composer had preferred the piano to the harpsichord. The review[50] in *Recorder and Music*, which was accompanied by an appropriate cartoon, wrote 'it did seem incongruous to see Walter Bergmann playing a gargantuan concert grand piano sempre pp....... The result was a beautifully balanced performance.' Walter Bergmann explained to the audience that he had refrained from calling the evening a concert for several reasons; not everybody had a white tie, he had no baton and he wanted to include works not originally written for recorder, which he felt he could not do in a formal concert. The concert was sold out and the audience obviously enjoyed the evening. The young soloists appreciated the opportunities and help Walter Bergmann gave them.

The year finished with a mixture of emotion for Walter Bergmann. There was the enormous success of his concert and an invitation to lecture at Dartington the following summer, but at the end of December they heard that Hans Bergmann was in great pain and also had cataract. Walter Bergmann also found himself caught up in a row between two American publishers about his opinion of recorder prices. He was most upset as what he saw as a questioning of his integrity.

Walter Bergmann was still finding it difficult to come to terms with his life as it had now evolved, and with growing old. His life was full and busy for a man of seventy-three, yet he was not happy. He was worried about his deteriorating eyesight and hearing, and at the beginning of January he had a car accident, which upset him greatly. This was followed by an unexpected visit from Alfred Deller, who took him out to lunch, which he did enjoy.

He had no big professional engagements in 1976, but he did have the annual SRP Festival to look forward to. It was to be held in May at Morley College in London, and the young Danish recorder player, Michaela Petri, would give a recital accompanied by Walter Bergmann. At seventeen she was already becoming internationally recognised, having played in ten European countries, and broadcast in several. In March, Walter Bergmann met Michaela Petri and her brother, after she had given a recital for the BBC. He took them both out to lunch, with one of his pupils Irene Llewellyn. Afterwards they returned to Belsize Square so that Michaela Petri could hear his treble Sonata and with him plan the programme for May. Walter Bergmann was impressed by Michaela Petri's astonishing technical fluency, but felt she still had to develop and communicate deeper emotional feelings in her performances.

Walter and Grete Bergmann continued to be generous with hospitality, in spite of their uncertain finances. Frans Brüggen offered to buy Walter Bergmann's Stanesby tenor recorder for £3000, and he finally decided to accept the offer to ease their financial situation. Brüggen collected the recorder when he came to dinner with the Bergmanns in May to discuss the final details for the publication of the Schickhardt sonatas. April and May were relatively busy months. At the end of April Walter Bergmann conducted a weekend course in Dublin for the Irish SRP branch and in May he had a concert with Dick Coles and adjudicated in Cheltenham. It was also a worrying time family-wise. Fritz and Anneliese Bergmann were to celebrate their fiftieth wedding anniversary in April, but Fritz had to spend a month in hospital following an operation for prostate cancer, postponing the celebrations, and Hans Bergmann was also ill. He was sad to hear of the death of Rudi Matz, brother of Arnold, who had been a good friend. Like the rest of the musical world, Walter Bergmann was shocked at the death of David Munrow at the age of thirty-three. An enthusiastic and gifted musician, Munrow did much to increase the popularity of early music, particularly through his BBC Radio series 'The Pied Piper'. His performances tried to establish a balance between authenticity, musicality and vigour. No-one knew why he had taken his own life, though it was known he had been depressed by his father's death. Walter Bergmann considered that Munrow had overworked and driven himself to undertake to do more than he realistically could hope to do. In the end everything was too much for him.[51]

Michaela Petri arrived to stay on May 15th. The Bergmanns found her a strange mixture of adult and child. Walter Bergmann described her as 'recorder possessed'[52] and self-centred, but she was enchanted by a visit to the Tate Gallery and appreciative of the excellent meals Grete Bergmann cooked. At home she apparently never had time to eat properly. Her upbringing as a gifted performer appeared to have made her unquestionably accept being looked after and entertained. Walter Bergmann interviewed Michaela Petri for *Recorder and Music*. She had left school at the age of ten to follow a solo career, studying with Ferdinand Conrad and privately at home. She was already teaching advanced recorder players. She said that she practised eight hours a day, including rehearsal periods with her mother and brother. At the SRP Festival on May 22nd she performed a varied programme in her recital, including works by Handel, van Eyck, Vivaldi, Berio and Walter Bergmann's *Sonata for Treble and Piano*. Walter Bergmann noted that she played 'technically perfect: there was not one wrong note.'[53]

The SRP Festival was extremely successful, being on a bigger scale with greater variety than in previous years. There were two competitions, one solo and one for recorder consort. There were twenty-nine entries for the solo competition, which, much to Walter Bergmann's delight, Catherine Marwood won. Her group, the Tabor Consort, also won the consort competition. Michaela Petri flew home the following day. The Bergmanns were pleased to receive a thank you letter from her, which included a recent recording as a gift, saying how much she had enjoyed her visit to London.

In June 1976, Walter Bergmann began planning for a new venture to be held at Easter 1977. He wrote to Sylvia Cleaver to ask if she would be interested in joining him set up a course for recorder and strings in Oxford. He was horrified to hear from her husband that she had died of stomach cancer in March. Hans Bergmann was eighty on June 18th. Walter Bergmann spoke to him by telephone, and then went to visit him in Bad Berleburg, on his way to Salzburg at the beginning of July, with Fritz Bergmann to belatedly celebrate his birthday. Hans Bergmann was extremely ill and in the last stages of cancer. He was being looked after by two former patients. His Doctor told Walter Bergmann that he believed Hans was hanging to life until his two brothers has visited him, and that he would probably collapse afterwards. Hans was in great pain, as cancer had spread to his spine. Walter Bergmann hoped that the doctors would not prolong his life. He wrote[54] 'I hope they will help him departing from this world without more pain.' 'Dying is a full-time job.' He was very worried about Hans and felt guilty about wondering how the next few weeks' work would be affected by Hans' death. He spent a few days with Fritz and Anneliese, during which time

Arnold Matz came to visit. Walter Bergmann gave him some money, as he was of course unable to bring any money out of East Germany. He had brought with him a composition, a *Sonata* for viola and piano, which Walter Bergmann took to investigate the possibility of it being published in London. Walter Bergmann also met Eva Zilling in Neckargemünd, the supportive friend who had looked after Grete when Erica was born. He gave her a copy of his poems.

The week at the Orff Institute went better than expected. Originally only 47 English-speaking students had registered for the English-speaking course, putting its future in jeopardy, but a further ten people joined for the week. The students were the most pleasant Walter Bergmann had experienced during the years he had taught on the Orff course. From Salzburg he went directly to the Italian recorder course held in Urbino, where he joined a number of well-known recorder teachers, including Ferdinand Conrad and Edgar Hunt. Walter Bergmann was asked in the capacity of a continuo player and musicologist. He accompanied Amico Dolci in a concert, which included both of his recorder sonatas, the treble sonata having been commissioned for Dolci. Walter Bergmann invited Dolci to come to his new recorder and strings course the following Easter.

Back at home, Walter Bergmann had three days in which to recover and organise himself before setting off to the Recorder Summer School at Keyworth. Jeanette van Wingerden was the guest tutor for 1976. He led a seminar on continuo playing at the Dartington summer school, which he found very enjoyable and gave two lectures on Bach, Handel and Telemann. He also found time to edit a volume containing music for descant recorder and piano by Baroque composers for Hargail in the States. He had completed a volume for the treble recorder the previous year. On August 16th he returned to Germany for a few days to visit Hans and, with Fritz and Rolf Bergmann, help him sort out his legal and financial affairs.

He returned home on August 22nd, and Hans died eight days later on August 30th. Walter and Grete Bergmann flew to Frankfurt the following day, where they were met by Fritz, who drove them to Bad Berleburg. At the funeral on September 3rd, Walter Bergmann played the recorder and Fritz Bergmann the viola. Walter Bergmann was saddened by the distance between Hans' children and the rest of the family, which he felt would become even greater with Hans' death. The following day Walter and Grete Bergmann played through all of Hans Bergmann's record collection, including some discs belonging to Walter Bergmann. In particular recordings of music by Loewe, Schumann and Schubert reminded him of the past and re-awakened his love of Schumann. There was a recording of Casals playing Schumann's cello concerto, which particularly moved him. One of the two friends, who had looked after Hans, insisted that he took the recording home with him.

In spite of the sadness of Hans' death, Walter Bergmann enjoyed celebrating his birthday on September 24th with Grete, the Bendixes, Margaret Murray, Erika Seelig and a pupil of Dietrich Gerhardt who was visiting them. They listened to the recording of the Schumann cello concerto and looked at slides. He was also very pleased that the publishers Oxford University Press had accepted for publication a violin tutor he was co-writing with Faith Whiteley. In October he was once again worrying about his own health, convinced that he had bowel cancer. His doctor thought that he did not. He attended the 1976 annual conference of the Federation of Music Festivals held in Edinburgh. Walter Bergmann was not impressed by the adjudicators' meeting, during which there was a long discussion about the educational role of competitive music festivals and bringing the music of the great composers to a wide audience. 'I think this is all nonsense. The c(ompetitive) f(estivals) furthers amateurs in making music' he wrote[55] in his diary. Overall he founded it a dreary conference except for the dinner and the after-dinner speeches, especially that given by Lord Birsay. He enjoyed a visit to the 'magnificant' National Gallery of Scotland and conducted the Edinburgh SRP. On arriving home, he at found a cheque for over £800 from Zen On in Japan as payment for the work he had done on the Schickhardt sonatas. October ended with two of his recorder pupils achieving high marks in the Hounslow Music Festival, which greatly pleased him.

The rest of 1976 passed with the usual round of teaching, adjudicating and one or two concerts. He was disappointed he could not get tickets for a concert given by Frans Brüggen in the Queen Elizabeth Hall. He was saddened by the news of Benjamin Britten's death at the age of 63 on December 4th. He had been ill for some while following a heart operation in 1973. Walter Bergmann wrote Britten's obituary for the March (1977) edition of *The Recorder Magazine*[56]. He wrote of his personal recollections of Britten, telling readers that they could read elsewhere of Britten's life and achievements. On December 6th he joined with Frank Dawes (baritone and keyboard), Catherine Marwood and Jane Sung (piano) to give a concert of British music in Ilford. Walter Bergmann realised that yet another of his colleagues, Frank Dawes, was gravely ill with cancer. The programme included music by Tomkins, Blow, Purcell, Stanford, Vaughan Williams, Warlock and Walter Bergmann's *Sonata* for treble recorder. Frank Dawes was admitted to hospital during the week following the concert, and Walter Bergmann took over an accompanying engagement for Dawes and the regular December weekend course held at Wansfell College from December 16th – 17th. Frank Dawes actually managed to attend to lecture, but he was back in hospital by Christmas. Walter Bergmann visited him regularly and was full of admiration for Dawes' continual enthusiasm and energy for life, in spite of being very ill.

On January 23rd 1977 Walter Bergmann went to visit Michael Tippett. The main purpose of the visit was to show Tippett two songs by the late seventeenth century English composer, Philip Hart, which had been discovered by Frank Dawes, who was an expert on Hart. Walter Bergmann found Tippett visibly older, but content and happy. He had completed his opera *The Ice Break* the previous year, which was to be premiered at Covent Garden in July 1977, and was working on his fourth symphony. Walter Bergmann brought a gift of homemade bread from Grete, German sausage and a bottle of good red wine. He enjoyed the lunch provided by Tippett's housekeeper. Tippett liked the Hart songs and was in agreement that they should be published by Schott in the series of music for voice and keyboard edited by himself and Walter Bergmann. They also agreed that all the royalties should go to Frank Dawes – Walter Bergmann had cleared this with Peter Makings at Schott, with the proviso that Tippett agreed.

During January Walter Bergmann worked on arrangements of the *Symphony* and *Song Tune* from Purcell's 1683 *Ode for St Cecilia's Day* and completed the violin tutor he was writing with Faith Whiteley – who did not find him easy to collaborate with. He lunched with Martin Kingsbury of Faber to discuss publishing a book entitled *The Solo Treble Recorder Book*, rather than a tutor for treble recorder. Other activities included chairing the SRP's examination syllabus to discuss revising the syllabus and teaching on the regular Knuston Hall course with his old friend Dick Coles. He also attended a course in Devon on Renaissance and Baroque tunings and temperaments. Unfortunately his deteriorating hearing made it difficult for him to understand what was said.

In February he flew to Berlin with the Galpin Society to view old instruments. While in Berlin he met Issi von Arps-Aubert (Matz), Arnold Matz's sister, to whom he had been engaged. It was the first time he had met her for thirty-four years. On returning home he learnt off Frank Dawes' death. Walter Bergmann had visited him at the beginning of the month and realised he had little time to live. He taught on the weekend recorder course at Charney Manor, and returned home to find Grete quite ill. They were both worried, thinking it was heart trouble, but it proved to be a bad attack of bronchitis.

March 1977 was a busy time for Walter Bergmann. It included the annual London SRP concert. His advanced evening class from the Marylebone Institute played, as did two recorder-playing families, the Wyatts and the Winkelmanns. Edgar Gordon also played in the concert, and Ross Winters was the soloist in the final item of the concert, Telemann's *Concerto in C* for recorder, strings and continuo. The following few weeks found Walter Bergmann adjudicating in Portsmouth, Brighton and Bristol. On April 3rd the Bergmanns flew to Frankfurt for the belated celebration (by a year) of Fritz and Anneliese Bergmann's fiftieth wedding anniversary. They stayed two nights in Frankfurt and collected 9000DM of restitution money from the bank, which they divided between them. Annerose von Mayenburg, who had helped look after Hans Bergmann, stayed with them. Walter Bergmann took the opportunity to visit Schott Mainz. The German company now owned 60% of Schott London. The Bergmanns travelled by train to Heidelberg, where they were met by Fritz Bergmann, who drove them to Neckargemünd for the celebrations.

The first Baroque Chamber Music Week was held at Wycliffe Hall, Oxford in April. The course was directed by Walter Bergmann and Jurgen Hess. The aim of the week was to bring together string, recorder and woodwind players. The course secretary was Ursula Groke, who was also a tutor on the course. About half the students were string players. Erica and David Bendix, now sixteen, looked after the course library, which contained around 350 pieces of music. The course guest performer was Amico Dolci, who delighted and charmed the audience with his recorder playing at the tutors' concert on the final evening. The only big problem on the course was the self-organisation of consort groups, which did not always go smoothly. Plans were made to run the course in August the following year.

Directly after the course on Sunday April 24th, Amico Dolci joined Catherine Marwood (recorders), Christabel Mulvey (soprano), Antony Brahms (baritone), Janet Coles (cello) and Walter Bergmann (keyboard) for a 'Matinee Musicale' in the Wigmore Hall. The programme consisted of trio sonatas by Haym and Telemann, songs by Purcell and Loewe, two ricercari composed by Amico Dolci, Arnold Matz's *Sonata* for treble recorder and piano, a revised version of Walter Bergmann's *The Passionate Shepherd to his love and the Nymph's Reply* for soprano and baritone voices and a performance of Henry Hall's *Music upon the Death of Henry Purcell* for soprano and bass voices, two treble recorders and continuo, which Walter Bergmann had revived in 1959. He was fortunate enough to be lent an original Andries Ruckers harpsichord from 1635 by Michael Thomas to use in the concert. The first part of the concert did not go as well as Walter Bergmann has hoped, as there were problems of ensemble and communication. The second half of the concert was much more successful, in particular Amico Dolci's performance of his own ricercari, in the second of which he was joined by Catherine Marwood, and Walter Bergmann's setting of the *Passionate Shepherd* setting texts by Christopher Marlowe and Sir Walter Raleigh. The review in *Recorder and Music* stated 'Walter Bergmann's programmes can be relied upon to include some unexpected delights and this was no exception........We can remember many of Walter Bergmann's recitals (or whatever else he likes to call them) but this afternoon seemed to us the best devised programme and choice of artists'[57] After the concert, Walter Bergmann received a postcard from John Amis[58] saying 'Walter, that piece of yours is of very great beauty, it was a tremendous pleasure to hear it.' In spite of the apparent success of the concert, Walter Bergmann was very unhappy with his own performance, He felt he had not played competently in either the last movement of Arnold Matz's *Sonata* or the Loewe songs. It spoilt the concert for him, in spite of the celebratory party held afterwards at Belsize Square. His was happier with the recital that Amico Dolci and he gave two days later in Wolverhampton. This included two of Dolci's solo *Ricercare* and the *Variations* from Walter Bergmann's Sonata for descant recorder. In the evening after the concert Amico Dolci accompanied Walter Bergmann to his evening class. They also played through the twelve Schickhardt *Sonatas* together.

At the beginning of May Catherine Marwood and Walter Bergmann gave a concert together in memory of Frank Dawes. It included a *Sonata da Camera* by Thornowitz for treble recorder and continuo, edited by Frank Dawes, and *Peruvian Tunes* for piano, which Walter Bergmann had written on the afternoon before the concert. He was content with his performance in this concert.

From May 14th - 16th 1977 an 'Early Music Conference' was held in the Festival Hall, London. The aim of the conference was to bring together anyone involved in 'Early Music' – performers, instrument makers, musicologists, teachers, concert promoters and publishers. It was organised by Anthony Rooley, lutenist and director of the Consort of Musicke, with John Thomson and financed by the Gulbenkian Foundation. The first whole day of the conference was devoted to looking at each specialised area of Medieval, Renaissance and Baroque music and the split between looking at financial and educational considerations. It was very well supported. A few days later a schools' conference entitled 'The Recorder – A Musical Instrument for Life' was held at Philippa Fawcett College, Streatham. Organised by the SRP, the Conference Chairman was Pamela Turner, a recorder player and lecturer at the college. This event was also well supported by over 120 participants from all round Britain. The conference examined all aspects of recorder teaching in primary and secondary schools and of problems that arose. It also looked at adult education and topics such as composing and arranging for recorders. Walter Bergmann led a seminar on adult education.

May and June marked sad events for two of Walter Bergmann's close friends. Norman Platt's first wife, Diana, died in May, having accidentally electrocuted herself. Norman Platt stayed with the Bergmanns the night before the funeral. Norman Platt himself was not well, having developed glaucoma. In June, they were disturbed to hear that Dietrich Gerhardt's wife, Suzanne, had tried to commit suicide. Walter Bergmann tried to contact Dietrich Gerhardt, but without success. The problems of their friends troubled the Bergmanns greatly.

The annual SRP Festival was held in Bradford, Walter Bergmann being among those who conducted massed playing. There was a new innovation of two Renaissance Band sessions, attracting non-recorder players. The solo and consort competitions, adjudicated by Paul Clark and Carl Dolmetsch, were well supported, but the overall standard was disappointing compared with previous years. The concluding concert was given by three previous prizewinners, Catherine Marwood, Evelyn Nallen and Ross Winters. Walter Bergmann was impressed by their playing of the Hindemith *Trio* and particularly by Evelyn Nallen's descant playing.

At the end of June 1977 Walter Bergmann was relieved to receive £2500 in royalties from Schott and a further year's contract for his evening classes at the Marylebone Institute. As ever his income was unevenly spread and erratic. As usual he provided a new arrangement, *Marching through Georgia*, for the annual schools' concert in Southend. Alfred Deller came to rehearse with him for an afternoon concert to be held on July 3rd at the Stour Festival. They were to perform together Walter Bergmann's *Pastorale* for countertenor and recorder, which he had written for Deller and himself. It would be the first time they had performed it in public together. The concert also included two songs for countertenor and lute composed by Walter Bergmann in 1973. After the concert Walter and Grete Bergmann drove to Maidstone where he conducted Faith Whiteley's string pupils in music by Purcell and Dowland. It was an extremely hot day and he arrived home exhausted and depressed. He was also worried about Grete, whose hands were painful and she had difficulty moving them.

Walter Bergmann once again became involved with other people's family problems. Ursula Grokes's mother was in hospital in Solingen in Germany. On her return home from visiting, he collected Ursula from Liverpool Street Station and drove her home to Grove near Wantage in Oxfordshire. In London, he attended a performance of Tippett's new opera *The Ice Break*, which he found short and violent. He returned to Grove to plan the 1978 Baroque Chamber Week.

Walter Bergmann made his annual trip to Salzburg, this time with Hilda Hunter. It was hot and tiring, especially when the car broke down. They broke the journey in Bad Berleberg, meeting up with Fritz and Anneliese Bergmann. Walter Bergmann noticed that Fritz, now 78, was slowing down. The family was troubled by the possible break-up of Rolf Bergmann's marriage, and there was a great deal of discussion concerning the matter. Arnold Matz came to visit for a day and surprised and irritated Walter Bergmann by only talking about himself and his own problems. It was not a restful visit, and Walter Bergmann was concerned about the extra work it made for Anneliese Bergmann.

In Salzburg Shimpei Matsuoka from Zen On greeted him. When he came into the evening meal, his arrival was applauded. A course for Japanese speakers had been introduced, and it ran each day from 2 – 5 p.m.. None of the Japanese spoke English except for the translator and Matsuoka. Walter Bergmann's lectures were translated into Japanese sentence by sentence. He had made an arrangement especially for the course entitled *Yu-Yaki-Koyake Variations*, which Matsuoka took for Zen On to publish. On returning to London by plane on August 3rd, he had less than 24 hours to prepare before travelling to the Recorder Summer School, this time in Doncaster, with an adult pupil, Irene Llewellyn. His pace of life did not slow done. On August 21st he took the night train and boat to Amsterdam and spent six hours with Frans Brüggen writing the foreword for the forthcoming edition of the Schickhardt sonatas. He returned to the London the same day on the night boat. He visited Ursula Groke in Grove to discuss the Baroque Chamber Course, but it was difficult to achieve a great deal, as Ursula was now looking after her elderly and difficult mother.

Shortly after starting to teach his evening classes for the new academic year at the Marylebone Institute, Walter Bergmann was troubled to receive a letter from ILEA (the Inner London Education Authority) informing him that all adult education lecturers over the age of 65 would be given notice. This shook him greatly; 'what will my life be? Should I also resign from the summer school?'[59] In spite of the approach of his 75th birthday, he had not even contemplated such a move. Shortly after his birthday he felt very unwell. The Doctor put him on a strict diet. Both were worried that he might have cancer. Although unwell, Walter Bergmann enjoyed seeing Hellmuth Wolff for the first time for many years. Wolff stayed with the Bergmanns for three days. He was well enough to attend the annual Musical Festivals Conference in Llandudno with Hilda Hunter. He decided it would be the last time he attended, as he did not wish to appear at the adjudicators' conference wearing a hearing aid and he found it very difficult to hear. He spoke once at the meeting, after a speaker had stated that the recorder was a very simple instrument to play. Walter Bergmann pointed out that the recorder was as difficult as any woodwind instrument to play well. On a visit to Ursula Groke he cooked a meal of plain rice for himself for the first time, as prescribed by his Doctor. His and Grete's increasing age and frailty was finally being brought home to them both by their ill health and a small car accident Grete Bergmann had.

Walter Bergmann's private pupils were still rewarding and delighting him. Some were very able and gifted. In particular he enjoyed teaching Karen Winkelmann, who at the age of eleven had taken the Grade 6 recorder examination, and a young boy aged eight, called Patrick Welche, who after an hour-long lesson, told his mother he wished he could have a lesson for two hours. Another gifted pupil was the 12 year-old Robert Ehrlich, who came from Belfast for a lesson. Walter Bergmann was impressed by his playing. In October he went to Northampton, staying overnight with the Coles family, to have tests that had been arranged with a specialist, Dr Peter Robertson, who was also a recorder player. The results were available the following day, and showed that he did not have cancer. Grete's ill health was more worrying. She was having some kind of minor attacks, and was eventually admitted to hospital but nothing definitely wrong could be found. A friend came to stay while Walter Bergmann returned to Northampton to conduct a recorder workshop. While he was there, Lyndon Hilling, a teacher and bassoonist approached him, and asked if he would edit a bassoon book with him. Faber agreed to publish the book and the earnings would be split equally between them.

Walter Bergmann's *Sonata* for treble recorder was performed by Catherine Marwood and himself at a concert in Richmond at the beginning of November. The other performers included Janet Coles and Catherine Marwood's sister Caroline (oboe and recorder). He was delighted to be described in the local paper as an 'eminent musicologist' and that Telemann's qualities as a composer were at last being recognised, the critic having written that the playing of a trio sonata in the concert by the Marwood sisters had thoroughly justified Telemann's 'superior reputation'.[60]. 'The arrangement bug' had bitten him again. 'I am an addict' he wrote in his diary[61]. He had promised a Handel album for Hargail and started working on it immediately when they rang to remind him. He tried out the new arrangements when he visited the Oxford SRP. He was also writing an introduction to numbers 7-12 of the Schickhardt sonatas.

1977 had been a busy year for Walter Bergmann. At the end of the year he lunched with John Thomson, and was sad to learn that he was leaving Britain to take up a post in his home country, New Zealand. He worked on the bassoon book and discussed editing projects with David Lasocki. He saw Dietrich Gerhardt, who was visiting London with a friend. Christmas was spent as usual, partly at home and partly with the Bendixes.

1978 finally saw the realisation of the Schickhardt project. At the beginning of the year Alfred Deller sang two of his songs in a concert at the Queen Elizabeth Hall, which was reviewed in *The Guardian*. He enjoyed teaching six Norwegians who joined his class at Knuston Hall. He received a letter of thanks from the British Council for the welcome he gave them. Work continued with Lyndon Hilling on the bassoon book. Following the February Charney Manor course, it gave him much pleasure when a course participant described[62] his 'scholarly analysis of Bach's Allegro for treble recorder'... as 'the highlight of the course'. He enjoyed a recital given by Carl Dolmetsch in the Wigmore Hall and a visit by Norman Platt and his family. He was relieved, when after all ILEA wrote him re-engaging him to teach his evening classes from the following September, in spite of his age. He celebrated with a glass of sekt with Grete and Erika Seelig.

To coincide with the publication of the first twelve Schickhardt sonatas (edited by Frans Brüggen and Walter Bergmann) in April 1978, Walter Bergmann was invited to lecture, on the twenty-four sonatas, at the annual conference of the Royal Music association held in Cambridge from April 7th – 9th. Edgar Hunt and Faith Whiteley helped illustrate the lecture with musical examples. The lecture was followed by dinner, then Christabel Bridge (soprano), Ursula Groke, Catherine and Caroline Marwood and Janet Coles joined Walter Bergmann, Edgar Hunt and Faith Whiteley in concert in the University's new concert hall (where the lecture had also been). The concert included three works by Schickhardt, the tenth sonata in the new publication, a trio sonata and one of Schickhart's concertos for four recorders. Grete Bergmann came to both the lecture and the concert.

Back at home, Suzanne Gerhardt came to visit for a few days, and the Bergmanns tried to listen sympathetically to her unhappiness over the break up of her marriage with Dietrich Gerhardt. Immediately afterwards Walter Bergmann travelled to Northampton for a concert with Dick Coles, which included a Purcell anthem which had been included in the programme of the Cambridge concert and Walter Bergmann's arrangements of two overtures to odes to St Cecilia, one by Purcell and the other by Handel. The performers included Janet Coles and Lyndon Hilling. On his return home, Walter Bergmann sent a copy of the newly published Schickhardt to the music section of the British Library. He received an enthusiastic and friendly thank you letter from the librarian, Tim Neighbour, who mentioned how much he had enjoyed Walter Bergmann's Cambridge lecture and concert.

By the end of April, he had finished the keyboard realisations for the Schickhardt sonatas numbers 12 –18, and starting working on the remaining twelve. May found him back adjudicating in Northampton, and participating in SRP activities including the 1978 Festival held in Bath. He acquired a new pupil, whose family connections were of great interest to him. He was the nephew of Claus von Stauffenberg, one of the German resistance killed for his central role in the plot to assassinate Hitler. He completed and dispatched to Japan the remainder of the Schickhardt sonatas at the beginning of June. With Ursula Groke, he ran a new weekend recorder course at Wansfell College. He was not happy with how it went, feeling that they had not made a good team, but there was a complimentary review in *Recorder and Music*. Working sessions on a new edition of the Handel recorder sonatas were going well with David Lasocki, and Walter Bergmann was pleased to receive significant royalties from Schott, who had accepted his realisations of sonatas by Dieupart. He started a new diary in July 1st 1978, and in his first entry wrote down what he believed was the status of the continuo and its relationship to a piece of music. He stated[63] 'Basso continuo is not subordinated to harmony and part-writing, on the contrary the latter are the former's slaves.'

It was the first summer for many years that Walter Bergmann did not teach on the Orff course at Salzburg. Grete and he spent three weeks in Germany visiting family and friends. During his stay he had an appointment with an ear specialist in Heidelberg, who informed him that he now only retained 35% of his hearing. This depressed him greatly, as did a visit to the dentist, on his return home, who advised the removal of two teeth and dentures. He attended the Recorder Summer School as usual and enjoyed a small class of ten pupils and lecturing on Schickhardt. Michaela Petri was to have given a concert at the course, but she had to withdraw, due to illness. Philip and Margaret Thorby, who were tutoring on the course, provided a replacement concert of Baroque music at short notice. Walter Bergmann enjoyed and appreciated their playing. The most memorable event on the course for him was Brian Bonsor's arrangement of Rachmaninov's *Vocalise* played at an evening session by 150 recorders and accompanied by Bonsor on the piano. He found it a magical sound. August continued to be busy with visitors from Germany and the Baroque Ensemble Week in Oxford. This did not run smoothly. 'The accommodation was tatty and inconvenient, the food dreadful.'[64] The organisation of ensemble groups also proved a headache. Walter Bergmann could not bring himself to write about it in his diary. Ferdinand Conrad's 'genial' presence helped the situation, as did the smooth running of the library of music by Erica and David Bendix. In spite of the problems, course participants were keen for the course to be repeated.

The 1978 June edition of *Recorder and Music* carried a large advertisement placed by Schott for the twenty-four Schickhardt sonatas edited by Paul J. Everett and published by Musica Rara in six volumes of which the first, containing four sonatas, was available for £6.50. The September edition carried a similar advertisement for the same sonatas, edited by Frans Brüggen and Walter Bergmann and published by Zen On in four volumes of which the first two volumes, each containing six sonatas and costing £8.50 per volume, were available. Edgar Hunt reviewed both editions at the same time and wryly wrote[65] 'It is extraordinary that two editions for recorder of these sonatas should be in the process of publication at the same time.' The sonatas were transposed into different keys in the two editions, the editors having approached decision-making about this in different ways. David Lasocki had contributed a life of Schickhardt to the Zen On edition, and also written articles about the composer for Recorder and Music. Hunt pointed to the fact that most of the biographical material for the preface to the Musica Rara edtition had come from these articles. He acknowledged the scholarly approach to key and well-tempered tuning in both editions, but felt that the Zen On edition showed 'a fuller understanding of the problems'. Much to Walter Bergmann's delight, Edgar Hunt preferred 'the generally lighter texture and more imaginative treatment of Walter Bergmann's continuo realisations'.

Walter Bergmann was still receiving a pension from Schott, even if they were not happy about the Zen On publication. They had agreed to publish five Dieupart recorder sonatas he had edited. (Forsyths were publishing a rival edtion which did not impress Walter Bergmann.) He had also nearly completed editing the new edition of the Handel sonatas for Faber with David Lasocki.

The rest of the year passed with the usual round of activities. He still had good numbers for his three recorder evening classes, including 20 students in the advanced class. The proofs of both the bassoon and violin books, on which he had worked in conjunction with Lyndon Hilling and Faith Whiteley, arrived in December. Grete Bergmann's arthritis was giving them both concern. She had undertaken a course of acupuncture, which although promising initially, did not help her significantly. They were both resigned to getting older, slow and less efficient. Walter Bergmann was finding social occasions more and more difficult because he could not follow conversations. At the beginning of 1979, Grete had her annual cancer check-up. In spite of this being clear, it was obvious that she was far from well, as she was having difficulty walking and swallowing. He continued with his regular activities, leaving her at home when he travelled to weekend courses. Grete saw a specialist in March, who said there was little he could do to help her. She bought herself a book entitled Arthritis and Commonsense, which included a diet for arthritic problems. They discussed together whether she should follow it, and Walter Bergmann said he would try to do it with her.

He had only a few concerts in 1979. The annual London SRP concert included one of the Schickhardt sonatas, and a performance of *The Passionate Shepherd to His Love* by Christabel Bridge and Michael Mulvey, which Walter Bergmann considered to be one of the best he had heard. He flew on his own to Germany to celebrate Fritz Bergmann's eightieth birthday. His old friend Dietrich Gerhardt collected him from the airport. While in Germany, he sorted out financial matters for Hilde Volhard and Erika Seelig. After the festivities, his nephew Rolf drove him back to the airport, and he was very touched when Rolf insisted in giving him some money towards Grete's medical treatment. On returning to London, he immediately drove to Wansfell College for the annual weekend course, which he taught with Ursula Groke. After a successful course, he drove her home, and went out with her and her mother for a meal to celebrate Ursula's birthday. – Walter Bergmann's friendship with Ursula Groke was beginning to raise a few questions, especially with Grete's ill health. However he cared greatly for Grete and both he and Erica Bendix were extremely worried about her. In the summer she was well enough to host an end of term wine and cheese party for Walter Bergmann's evening classes, with the help of Erica Bendix and Erika Seelig. It was to be the last such evening.

On July 17th 1979, yet another friend died, Alfred Deller, at the age of 67. The television announcement of his death showed him singing *Music for a while* accompanied by Walter Bergmann. He attended the funeral held in

Ashford, Kent. Grete Bergmann had been admitted to hospital for tests, but no diagnosis had been made. Her condition continued to deteriorate and she was losing any independence. She could no longer drive. He drove to the Recorder Summer School in a new car, accompanied by Erika Seelig. His general state of anxiety and increasing frailty was apparent. He asked Brian Bonsor to accompany the guest soloist, Kees Otten in the concert, with the exception of one work.

To the relief of all participants, the 1979 Baroque Chamber Week was much more successful than that held in the previous year. It was held in Newland Park College, which had excellent accommodation, and tennis courts and a swimming pool available. The guest was Fritz Spiegl and the tutors included Faith Whiteley (violin) and Katharine Jeans (recorder). The overall organisation functioned better and there were plenty of harpsichords available. Two days after Walter Bergmann's return, Grete Bergmann had a stroke. Her left side was badly affected.

'August 26th was a very sad day' he wrote[66] in his diary. He had sciatica for week, which he believed was his body's reaction to the shock of Grete's stroke. From now on, life would have to be very different. On Grete's return home, Erica Bendix helped look after her and to make arrangements for her long-term care. Fortunately Walter Bergmann still had income from a significant number of royalty payments, but finding sufficient money would not be easy. They were lucky in their close friends and relatives. Erika Seelig gave Walter Bergmann the gift of some money towards Grete's care. They found a neighbour, Betty Burke, who could help three mornings a week from nine until twelve. Grete Bergmann did not make good progress. By the time of Walter Bergmann's seventy-seventh birthday on September 24th, she was still unable to stand. They celebrated quietly at lunchtime with a cold meal and sekt and Erika Seelig, Erica Bendix and an old friend, Danya. Hilde Volhard did not join them because of strained relations between herself and Erica Bendix, which the Bergmanns found very difficult. They had a Chinese take-away meal in the evening with the Bendixes.

Inevitably Walter Bergmann's pre-occupation with Grete affected his work. John Thomson rang him to request an article he had been commissioned to write on Alfred Deller, due in a couple of days, which he had not even started. In twenty-four hours he managed to write the article and deliver it. Erica Bendix typed and corrected it for him. He attended a memorial service for Alfred Deller at St Paul's Cathedral, the music of which he enjoyed. At home, he still could not work. Faber were waiting for twelve studies for descant and treble recorder. There were family arguments at home. A substantial part of Grete's care was falling on her daughter, who also had her own home to look after. Both the Bendixes felt that Walter Bergmann had to take on more responsibility for mundane domestic matters. Erica wanted to be able to return home at night and sleep in her own bed. She was tired and exhausted from helping look after her mother and sleeping downstairs near to her. There needed to be some way in which Grete Bergmann could summon help if she needed it.

The Bergmanns' financial situation looked like easing a little as gradually more of Walter Bergmann's work continued to be published. Eulenburg published a miniature score of his edition of Purcell's Chacony and both the books for bassoon and violin were published. He also managed to complete an edition of six Telemann sonatas for two recorders for Schott. His recorder pupils continued to come for lessons and he managed to conduct an SRP meeting in Birmingham, but life was very different from previous years.

A bell was installed in Grete's room that rang if necessary in her husband's bedroom. It was a miserable Christmas. For the first time for many years they did not have a Christmas tree. Christmas Eve was spent at the Bendixes; Margaret Murray joined them. Walter Bergmann and Erica argued again about Grete's care and the running of everyday life, which affected the whole of the Christmas period. On New Year's Eve, Walter and Grete Bergmann spent the evening quietly on their own and went to bed early.

1. Diary 21, 18.02.70
2. Richard Coles to Walter Bergmann, 14.03.70
3. *Daily Telegraph*, (Manchester Edition), Neil Tierney, 20.03.70
4. *Liverpool Post*, 20.03.70
5. *Liverpool Echo*, 20.03.70
6. Diary 21, 20.03.70
7. *Daily Telegraph*, D.A.W.M., 13.04.70
8. Diary 21, 30.04.70
9. Diary 21, 24.05.70
10. Diary 21, 24.05.70
11. 'Für mich war das alles farewell, denn ich werde nicht wieder das Stour festival besuchen. Man braucht mich nicht.'; Diary 21, 20.06.70
12. Diary 21, 23.06.70
13. *'Was für ein Stück!'*; Diary 21, 02.08.70
14. Diary 21. 06.12.70
15. Diary 21, 25.03.71
16. *Liverpool Daily Post*, 21.05.71
17. *Liverpool Echo*, 21.05.71
18. Diary 21, 20.05.71
19. The Times, 22.05.71
20. *Financial Times,* Joan Chisshell, 22.05.71
21. Diary 22, 14.08.71
22. Diary 22, 18.08.01
23. *New York Recorder Guild News, Vol. XI,* October 1971
24. Michael Tippett to Walter Bergmann, 30.12.71
25. Prunella Flatz to Walter Bergmann, 01.01.72
26. Frans Brüggen to Walter Bergmann, 25.02.72
27. Professor Dr H. Wolffheim to Dietrich Gerhardt, 06.10.72
28. Diary 23, 15.11.72
29. Diary 23, 01.12.72
30. *Southend Standard,* December 1972
31. 'Es gibt doch noch wunderbare Menschen', Diary 23, 22.02.73
32. Diary 23, 22.01.73
33. *Daily Telegraph,* A.E.P., 05.06.73
34. Recorder and Music, Vol. 4, No. 7, September 1973
35. *Hampstead and Highbury,* 08.06.73
36. Diary 23, 31.07.73
37. 'Und hier bin ich.', Diary 24, 02.09.73
38. Diary 24, 02.09.73
39. Catherine Marwood to Walter Bergmann, 10.06.74
40. *Recorder and Music, Vol.4, No.11,* September 1974
41. *Yorkshire Post,* 10.06.074
42. 'Nachts bin ich stundenlang wach u. weiss seit 1974 bin ich alt.' Diary 25, 17.08.74
43. *Recorder and Music, Vol. 4, No. 12,* December 1974
44. *Music Teacher,* August 1974
45. *Music in Education,* July/August 1974
46. Diary 26, 19.11.74
47. *Recorder and Music, Vol.5, No.1,* January 1975
48. *The Wykehamist,* No. 1233, Dec. 10th 1974
49. *Recorder and Music, Vol.5, No. 1,* March 1975
50. *Recorder and Music, Vol. 5, No. 5,* March 1976
51. Diary 27, 29.05.76
52. Diary 27, 29.05.76
53. 'Sie spielte technisch perfekt, nicht eine Note ging fehl.' Diary 27, 29.05.76
54. Diary 27, 03.07.76
55. Diary 27, 18.10.76
56. *Recorder and Music, Volume 5, No 9,* March 1977
57. *Recorder and Music, Volume 5, No 10,* June 1977
58. Postcard from John Amis to Walter Bergmann, 24.04.77
59. Diary 27, 21.09.77
60. *Richmond and Twickenham Times,* 11.11.77
61. Diary 27, 09.11.77
62. *Recorder and Music, Volume 6. No 2,* June 1978
63. Diary 28, 01.07.78
64. *Recorder and Music, Volume 6, No 4,* December 1978
65. *Recorder and Music, Volume 6, No 4,* December 1978
66. 'Der 26 war ein trauriger Tag.' Diary 28, 08.09.79

John Amis and Walter Bergmann at W.B.s Birthday Concert, 13th November 1982

Photo: John Cuerden (reproduced by kind permission of Simon Cuerden)

9. The Final Years

Grete's illness marked the end of an era. Although Walter Bergmann continued to work during the 1980s, his life had changed irrevocably. He no longer performed regularly in concerts, and apart from individual private work, his teaching commitments began to diminish. His deafness was a major problem. At the beginning of 1980 he felt a little more optimistic about the immediate future. He was invited to a concert and reception for Michael Tippett's 75th birthday. The Lindsay Quartet played Tippett's fourth string quartet and a Beethoven quartet. Walter Bergmann met many old friends and acquaintances from his years at Schott. Tippett was pleased to see him and wanted to discuss the Purcell *Chacony*, which he was to conduct in the States. There had been major managerial changes at Schott. Peter Makings had left, selling his shares in Schott Mainz on his departure. John Harper was the new Managing Director, and Walter Bergmann wondered how Schott London would be affected. He went to a second enjoyable Tippett concert, in which Tippett conducted his *Concerto for Double String Orchestra*.

He was beginning to find it easier to work at home, recovering from a mental paralysis[1] that had overcome him. He had a great deal of preparation to do for the 1980 Baroque summer school. His tribute to Alfred Deller appeared in the January edition of *Early Music*. He recalled his first meeting with Deller and wrote of their musical collaboration. He wrote 'I became his accompanist for a number of years until the time when it became evident that my wings were too weak to follow him on his meteoric flight. We remained, however, very good friends to the end of his life.'[2] He described the problems that Deller had to overcome to succeed as a countertenor and the experience and confidence Deller had gained through working and performing at Morley College. One of Walter Bergmann's special memories was of Deller writing in his copy of Deller's biography, 'To dear Walter, old friend, who believed when I often doubted.'

He thought it would be the last year that he taught on the Knuston Hall course, but he was invited back for 1981, after a tiring but enjoyable week. He also was able to teach as usual on the Charney Manor course in March, where he lectured on Schickhardt and conducted. Walter Bergmann felt extremely guilty that he was managing to live a relatively normal life, while Grete suffered. There was little improvement in her condition, but she never complained. He tried hard to be patient with her, and was ashamed of himself when he did not succeed. Friends and acquaintances continued to be supportive of them both. John Amis asked him for a complete list of his publications, as he thought they ought to be brought to the attention of the BBC. Shimpey Matsuoka from Zen On visited him, partly to see him and also to report on the success of the Schickhardt edition. Michaela Petri contacted him to ask to use his realisations of two Telemann pieces and whether he would realise another sonata for her.

In March Walter Bergmann received from Faber the first copies of *The First Book of Descant Solos*. It looked as if it would be extremely successful; 2000 copies had been ordered in the U.S.A. before publication. He was also slightly bemused by a letter[3] from the Principal of the Marylebone Institute, J.P. Adams, informing him that he would retire at the end of the summer term having reached the retirement age of sixty-five! He was touched by Adam's comment: 'No words of mine are adequate to express my own personal regret that you will be leaving Marylebone. Your service and yourself will be sadly missed, and I, in particular, will feel the poorer without you in the team.' Through the late spring, visitors to Belsize Square included Martha Bixler and her husband and two

König cousins. Walter Bergmann continued to adjudicate at Northampton, Gillingham and the SRP Festival. He was not impressed at the standard of playing at the latter and found it impossible to hear at the Society's Annual General Meeting. Arguments with Erica over Grete's care continued at home.

At the end of May Grete went to stay in Carrick House, Harrow for respite care, so that Walter Bergmann could go to Germany for a week to visit Fritz and Anneliese Bergmann. He brought some asparagus home with him for a special meal with Grete, which they shared with the Bendixes. It was not a happy meal. The cost of Grete's week at Carrick house had been high. Erica and Peter Bendix felt that Walter Bergmann was continuing to be selfish in trying to continue to live as he had done before Grete's stroke, and that Erica was shouldering too much responsibility. The Bergmanns wanted to try and live their lives as normally as they could in the circumstances. Erica felt that it was wrong for Grete to have to be cared for away from home while Walter Bergmann enjoyed himself, especially as she would be returning to Carrick House in July. Walter Bergmann wrote[4] in his diary 'Peter and Erica attempt to run our (Grete and mine) lives'. Rolf Bergmann sent him 500 DM towards the cost of Grete's care. He was very touched, and rang Fritz Bergmann to see if his nephew could afford the gift. John Amis continued to be an encouraging and supportive friend. He suggested that Walter Bergmann should write a book on Telemann. Walter Bergmann was desperately trying to complete a musical tribute to Alfred Deller, which was to be performed at the Stour Festival on June 25th by the Deller Consort. He finished it on June 13th, leaving little time for rehearsal. It was entitled *Music on the Death of Alfred Deller*. He taught his last two evening classes, and they combined to give him a farewell party on June 24th. He had been working for the LCC/ILEA* for 38 years. Another new work of Walter Bergmann's was premiered on July 1st in France. Entitled *Musique sur le theme populaire 'Auprès de ma blonde'*, it was written for the L'Ensemble de flûtes à bec de Lyon and consisted of a ten minute work for female voices, recorders and instruments. The first performance was apparently a great success and the work was encored. The director of the ensemble wrote to Walter Bergmann expressing her regret that he had been unable to be present and informed him that her pupils were eager for a second composition from him. Another success, which pleased him, was a performance of his transcription for recorders of the Vivaldi *Concerto in G minor*, which was performed at the Haslemere Festival on July 19th.

The new edition of the Handel recorder sonatas, edited by David Lasocki and Walter Bergmann and published by Faber, was reviewed in the July edition of *Early Music*. It was the first time the four sonatas had been issued in one volume. The review[5] pointed out that 'this new edition must count as the first true critical edition, not merely of the group as a whole, but also of each individual sonata'. The reviewer recommended that the edition should become the standard performing edition although he did not like the continuo realisations. He believed that some individual chords were wrong, but commented that the accompaniment did lie comfortably under the fingers. This was in contrast to the views expressed in a letter David Lasocki had received from Dr Angelo Zaniol of Venice University, who described Walter Bergmann's continuo realisations as 'exemplary'. Christopher Ball also wrote[6] to David Lasocki thanking him and Walter Bergmann for their 'admirable edition'.

The return of Grete to Carrick House to give both Walter Bergmann and Erica Bendix a break from

*London County Council/Inner London Education Authority

caring for her, gave him freedom to go out more. Michaela Petri was in London to make some Telemann recordings, and he met her mother for lunch and attended the recording studios. Michaela Petri was using Walter Bergmann's realisations, which the studio staff liked very much and they asked if they could meet him. He had devised several new parts because Schott were not happy about him using existing published editions. He was delighted that Michaela Petri came and played with him at home. Other visitors included Catherine Marwood, Richard Platt, his talented young pupil Patrick Welche and Edgar Hunt. The latter had come to see him on a somewhat awkward and delicate mission. Only two students had registered for Walter Bergmann's class at the Recorder Summer School, and Hunt suggested that he might like to just come for two days instead of the whole week. Walter Bergmann was extremely hurt and offended by the suggestion, convinced that numbers would go up in spite of the close proximity of the course. He could not see that it was time for him to retire gracefully, and that Hunt had given him a way out by which he would not be forgotten or ignored. He would not see the problems his deafness and frailty were causing and determined that he would attend for the whole week. He performed in the final concert, playing Arnold Matz's *Recorder Quartet* with Paul Clark, Edgar Hunt and Margaret Westlake, and accompanied Brian Bonsor, Edgar Hunt and Philip Thorby in a trio sonata. Before going to Doncaster, he visited Grete, and registered how much better life was at home for her than in the nursing home.

Seventy players attended the Baroque Chamber Week at Newland Park College, which followed on immediately from the Recorder Summer School on August 7th. Antony Hopkins was the guest lecturer, and was generous with his time, giving four lecture-recitals. The course was reviewed in the violin magazine The Strad, which described[7] the course as a week for 'caring accomplished enthusiasts' and not for 'purely academic specialists'. However it pointed out that 'all those who were there must have gone home with increased understanding and heightened sensitivity for music of the Baroque period'.

At the end of August Walter Bergmann wrote to Harold Newman (of Hargail) in America, summing up his present life.[8] 'Just a year ago Grete had a light stroke, which however reduced her activity to near nothing. She has slightly recovered from the stroke but the tempo of her activities is still very slow and her walking is very much affected. Our daughter, Erica, and I share in looking after Grete, one cannot leave her alone for any length of time. So I am much more at home than I used to be and it was very useful that the London County Council retired me twelve years later than they should have done. At the moment I am recovering from two very intensive recorder weeks.' Money was now coming in irregularly, and Walter Bergmann was hoping that Newman would be happy with another American publisher publishing works in which Hargail were not interested. There was some possibility of a gratuity from ILEA — a letter from the Assistant Education Officer, thanking him for his services for so many years, had mentioned this.

A meeting at Schott in October 1980 with the new Managing Director John Harper did nothing to raise his hopes of the firm promoting his compositions and editions more. Up to date they had published 237 works written or edited by him and he felt that the firm could provide more publicity for him. In November Walter Bergmann was frightened one evening by a reduction of vision in his good eye. It had righted itself by the following day, but he visited the optician, who assured him that all was well. If he could no longer drive, his activities would become even more restricted. However, his friends and family were becoming very concerned about his driving.

By the end of the year he was becoming very depressed. He attended a concert at St John's Smith Square to celebrate the 90th birthday of Hans Gal, but felt he could not attend the reception afterwards, which would finish too late when Grete was alone at home. His lack of hearing also frustrated him at events such as this, SRP committee meetings and at the Early Music Conference he attended. His unhappiness increased with the return of three works from the BBC, who had no interest in performing them. Visits from David Lasocki and Faith Whitely to discuss future publications cheered him a little, as did the broadcast of Michaela Petri playing his arrangement of Handel's *Concerto* for treble recorder. Michaela Petri and her mother Hanne came to visit him to discuss the possibility of more new editions for performance. By December he was extremely tired and found it difficult to prepare music for Christmas meeting of the London SRP. The meeting was nearly a complete disaster, as there were insufficient string players for his arrangement of Bach's Christmas *Pastorale*. At the last minute, a young player, Karen Winkelmann stepped in. Over Christmas, Grete was ill and weak and by the New Year she was restricted to a wheel chair, an enormous problem in the flat, which was on two floors. They had no feeling of celebration over the festive season.

At the beginning of 1981, Walter Bergmann was becoming worried as to whether he would be strong enough to continue to look after Grete and to earn sufficient money to care for her properly. It was proving difficult to get permanent help. Their initial helper, Betty Burke had been hit by tragedy; first her husband died, then her son died following an accident.

At a concert in January, given by Frans Brüggen in the Wigmore Hall, he was asked by Dr Stanley Sadie if he would write a review for *The Musical Times* of the forthcoming tercentenary Telemann celebrations to be held in Magdeburg, East Germany to which he had been invited. He was also busy writing an article for *Recorder and Music* entitled *Double Centenary*, which was about Telemann and Johann Mattheson, both born in the same year, 1681. Walter Bergmann believed[9] that they were both underrated for the contribution they had made to the development of German and 'may be even European music of the eighteenth century, though on different lines: Telemann as a composer with a mountain of publications; Mattheson as a theoretician with 31 books and 2 periodicals of the utmost musical importance to his credit'. In spite of his personal worries, he adjudicated at Eastbourne and lectured at Charney Manor.

Walter Bergmann enjoyed his visit to Magdeburg for the week of the Telemann celebrations, held from March 12th to 18th 1981. Preparations for the festival had taken two and a half years. It was organised by a group of musicologists, the Telemann Arbeitkreis, who had worked for over 20 years to encourage the recognition of Telemann. As well as concerts, there was an international conference on Telemann's role in eighteenth century European culture attended by 160 academics. The local Magdeburg newspaper included a small article on Walter Bergmann in its coverage of the event. Performers came from East Germany, Denmark, Poland and Russia. There were modern premières of several of Telemann's works. Not all the performances at the Festival were good, but he enjoyed some of them enormously, in particular Telemann's church cantatas, a magnificat and part of a Passion, the violin *Concerto Suite in F*, the *Concerto* for viola and the opera *Der geduldige Sokrates*. All of the concerts were sold out. On returning to London, he was depressed that an excellent performance of Telemann's *Der Tod Jesu* he attended in the Queen Elizabeth Hall was half-empty.

In April Walter Bergmann worked on more continuo parts for Michaela Petri, which she used in a concert. Together they persuaded Faber to agree to publish a Michaela Petri series. This came to nothing, as the Danish firm Hansen insisted that they should publish such a series. May was a busy month, with adjudicating in Hereford, the annual London SRP concert, which included a Telemann cantata, and the SRP Festival held in Edinburgh. Theo Wyatt drove Walter Bergmann to Edinburgh. It was a long journey, leaving at 7.15 a.m. and arriving at 5.45 p.m.. After dinner, he was taken to see Scottish Ballet, which he enjoyed, but he did not get to bed until after midnight. The following day he adjudicated all day; trio sonatas in the morning, and recorder consorts in the afternoon, with only a cup of tea for lunch. During the morning he was extremely tired. He felt[10] that he spoke badly and got muddled when making the winning announcements. The afternoon went more smoothly and he enjoyed the prizewinners' concert and the concluding playing session conducted by Brian Bonsor. He returned to London with Theo Wyatt the following day straight after lunch and the SRP annual conference. He noted in his diary how efficient Theo was in chairing the SRP conference, driving and with life in general.

At home life continued to be stressful. Grete Bergmann needed someone with her all the time, and it was a heavy load for Erica Bendix and Walter Bergmann. They had found an excellent daily help, Mrs Ryan, whom they hoped would stay. He wrote[11] miserably of himself, saying he had aged greatly over the last year. His sight and hearing were poor, his left knee weak and he had prostate problems; he could not do anything in a hurry. His head was full of musical ideas, but he could not do anything about them. He was anxious to get as much work as he could so that there was money coming in regularly, not really appreciating that if he was not there Erica had to be available for her mother. After the SRP Festival he was home for 2 nights before leaving to teach at Knuston Hall, from where he went to spend some time at Ursula Groke's home 'to recover from many stressing weeks'[12]

At the beginning of June Mrs Ryan left after approximately 8 weeks. The burden of Grete Bergmann's care fell on Erica Bendix again, with some support from the District Nurse and a home help. Peter Bendix felt that she had left because too much had been demanded of her while Walter Bergmann was away. The situation was becoming more and more stressful and causing grief and anguish to all involved. An advertisement for help brought 30 replies, of which only five were suitable. Walter Bergmann enjoyed Catherine Marwood's wedding in July, but at home problems were not resolved. The new help left after only two weeks. Erica and Peter Bendix had Grete to stay for two weeks to cover the period of the two summer schools. Both seemed to go well from Walter Bergmann's point of view, but he found the Baroque Ensemble Week, held at the South Thames Polytechnic in Dartford, a great strain. He conducted all the evening sessions and gave two lectures on baroque ornamentation and Mattheson. Norman Platt was the visiting guest and he directed and lectured on music by Monteverdi. Walter Bergmann initially decided that it would be the last course he did, but then was persuaded to change his mind.

Grete Bergmann celebrated her seventy-seventh birthday while staying with the Bendixes. Her two sisters Liselotte and Irene came to visit her. Walter Bergmann had arranged a month previously for a parcel to be delivered on her birthday, and was very upset to discover it had been delivered 3 days late. Back at home, life continued as before. Friends came frequently to cheer him up and visit Grete. One brought him a present of an electronic watch and calculator. He had great fun playing with it. Fritz Bergmann asked him to join him for two weeks holiday in the Alps, but it was not possible. He could not leave home and Fritz became ill with sciatica.

On September 15th Walter Bergmann took Grete out in her wheel chair. It was a beautiful sunny day and she was feeling cheerful. Suddenly she was sick and passed out. Within half an hour she was in hospital and unconscious for three hours. It was another stroke. He was fearful for the future. How could they cope if she was even more incapacitated? Would death not be better for her than an even more miserable existence? He went to Northampton to conduct the SRP and examine candidates for the Society's teaching certificate, staying overnight at Grove with Ursula Groke. On his return, he went straight to the hospital to be with Grete. She had pulled through the stroke and was transferred to New End Hospital for rehabilitation. Walter Bergmann was able to spend four days in October with Fritz Bergmann in Neckargemünd.

Grete came home on his return. Life went on. He prepared at Grove for the 1982 Baroque Chamber Week; he heard Michaela Petri play and discussed music for further concerts with her; he was interviewed by the BBC about the SRP. He worried about what appeared to be an endless succession of tax demands, and his health. He was well enough to play in a concert at the beginning of December given by the SRP London Branch Recorder Orchestra, which included a performance of his *Chaconietta*. He played continuo in Handel's *Concerto Grosso Op. 6 no.7*. It was to be one of the last concerts Walter Bergmann played in. Grete Bergmann was becoming steadily weaker, but at Christmas was well enough to enjoy a meal with the Bendixes and three more guests, including Margaret Murray.

He still went to the Knuston Hall course in January 1982, though thought unlikely he would be asked back. Soon after Grete Bergmann was taken into hospital, as she now required professional nursing care. It was both a great sadness and a relief. On her admission, Walter Bergmann sat with her until the doctor came to see her, but he could not understand any information he was given. On returning home, Erica Bendix was waiting, and she invited him to go with her, her husband and Erika Seelig, who had continued to be a staunch friend, for a Chinese meal. Erica drank two glasses of wine, broke down and rushed out of the restaurant. Peter Bendix could not find her, and Walter Bergmann and he spent an anxious night. She returned home the next day, having spent a night with a friend. She was apologetic; the strain of the preceding months, coupled with the knowledge that her mother would probably not return from hospital had been too much. On January 15th, they were summoned to the hospital, as she was very poorly. They were warned that she was unlikely to recover, but in the evening she rallied, and Walter Bergmann spent all of the next day at her bedside. Over the following days she slowly improved. He managed to teach his private pupils and do a little work for Michaela Petri, but he was in a turmoil as to what might happen next and whether Grete should be helped to recover or allowed to die. She was quite lucid and clear about what was happening to her. The medical diagnosis was that she had had a heart attack and not another stroke. Her progress continued to fluctuate. She was insistent that she should remain in hospital, as it would be too onerous for her to be looked after at home. The hospital and Walter Bergmann agreed with her; Erica believed she really wanted to die at home. Throughout February, they both visited Grete Bergmann daily.

Life reshaped itself round hospital visiting and returned to partially resemble how it had been before Grete Bergmann became ill. But Walter Bergmann's own health was placing constrictions upon him. He found driving difficult because his left leg was unreliable. Friends rallied round. The SRP central committee met at Belsize Square; Theo Wyatt brought the lunch with him. He enjoyed going to a Kent Opera Production of Handel's *Agrippina*, directed by his old friend Norman Platt at Sadler's Wells. He adjudicated and taught on courses as usual. Following the SRP Annual Festival at Hatfield in May, where he adjudicated the trio sonata competition, he taught on another weekend course at Knuston Hall, which raised his spirits, as it went well. 'I was on top of myself and feel a bit encouraged to go on with my life.'[13] In June, Walter Bergmann took the decision to take his three eighteenth century recorders to be auctioned at Sotheby's. Grete Bergmann came home for a night; Erica looked after her mother during the day and a nurse came for the night. It was a happy occasion, only marred by the fact she had to return to hospital. They hoped she could come home regularly once a month.

Walter Bergmann was busy over the summer with correcting work for Faber, who had commissioned more work from him. He had little time to write in his diary. He went to the Recorder Summer School, now in Leeds. It was to be his last; he finally made the decision to retire. Several of his works, including his two sonatas, were performed in his honour and he made a presentation to course participants of his newly published Telemann album on the day of publication. He noted that it was right to retire 'but painful. Everybody was very nice. It was my week.'[14] As well as his fee, Walter Bergmann received a farewell collection for him amounting to £150. He had a week's break before the sixth Baroque Ensemble Week at Dartford. This was tiring, but memorable for a performance of Telemann's *Concerto Grosso* in B flat for recorders, oboes, strings and continuo, which Walter Bergmann nicknamed 'The Seventh Brandenburg', because he felt it deserved that title.

The September edition of *Recorder and Music* celebrated Walter Bergmann's 80th birthday. His photograph appeared on the front cover, and Schott took the back cover, offering their congratulations. The page included a photograph of him playing the recorder and advertised a range of his compositions. Faber Music took a full-page advertisement, also offering their congratulations. The Editor, Edgar Hunt, paid fulsome tribute to him and to 'his work and influence where fields of art and education combine'. Dividing his output in four categories, these being arrangements of classics and folk tunes, compositions for educational use, editions of Baroque music and a few original works, Hunt commented that in most of his work, Walter Bergmann had 'with great skill, kept within the limitations of the players for whom he was writing. There were no such limitations in the case of his *Sonata* for descant recorder and piano and *Sonata* for treble recorder and piano.' In his tribute[15] to him Hunt wrote 'Recorder players owe a great deal to Walter Bergmann' not just for his music, but 'for keeping recorder playing alive during World War II through his classes at Morley, and for all he has done to integrate the recorder and its music in the

20th-century world of music. If someone asked: 'shall we play our recorders or shall we play music?' those would not be alternatives to him'. He could not have asked for more.

The London SRP gave him a birthday 'feast' on September 18th just before his actual birthday. Yet within himself he was sad and unhappy. On the eve of his birthday he wrote[16] briefly in his diary 'These have been sad weeks and there is no-one's shoulder on which I can lean.' By the middle of October he had received around 145 letters for his 80th birthday, all thanking or commending his work with recorders. Less happy were continuing arguments with Schott over his publications. He was overwhelmed by people's kindness but at times awkward, irritable and frustrated by deafness and continuing family arguments. He could still be incredibly thoughtful and kind. He was invited by a head teacher, Janivere Rowell to hear her school recorder group play from the new Telemann album. 'He came and was delightful and delighted. Not only did he give me an inscribed copy, but when one of our number (Debbie) wrote to thank him, he wrote back with a specially composed snatch of music on the notes D E B.'[17]

The October edition of *Early Music* contained a full-page advertisement for Sotheby's sale of Walter Bergmann's three recorders to be held on November 4th. He was delighted that they were advertised as 'highly important musical instruments'. One of the three instruments sold for £1292.

A special concert organised by the SRP was held in Walter Bergmann's honour on November 13th at Morley College. It was a gathering of a large number of his musical friends and the programme showed the width of his work. The concert was introduced by John Amis. Ilse Wolf sang Purcell songs; Ross Winters played Barsanti's *Sonata in G minor* for recorder and continuo with Alan Wilson; Janet Coles was the soloist yet again in the *Sinfonietta* with the London SRP Orchestra (director Nancy Winkelmann); Steven Rickards (countertenor) and Kathleen Stubbings (recorder) performed his *Pastorale*; 40 London school children took part in a performance of *The Drummer Boy* with members of the Orff Society and the Mid-Herts Branch of the SRP; the Danesholme Quartet, a group of four young players from Northampton played his arrangement of *Greensleeves*, and the concert concluded with a performance of the *Sonata* for treble and piano played by Philip Thorby and Brian Bonsor. It was a happy and special occasion, as the photographs in the 1983 March edition of *Recorder and Music* illustrated.

By November 1982 Grete Bergmann's condition had stabilised. She had begun to enjoy eating a little, and Walter Bergmann took food she especially liked into the hospital for her, for example bread, liver sausage and onion. For the rest of the year he had no inclination or time to write in his diary except to make a note of the many letters he wrote after his birthday mail. By the end of 1982, Walter Bergmann's eyesight was worrying and troubling him again. At the beginning of January 1983 he was examined by a specialist at Moorfield Eye Hospital who found that nothing significant had changed, except for a small correction required in his glasses. In spite of his growing infirmity, he was still accepting new recorder pupils, though he had ceased to advertise for them. The pupil was a young seven year-old boy, who he thought was probably very gifted. Working with young, gifted musicians still gave him immense pleasure.

Shortly afterwards, Walter Bergmann had a frightening experience, which heightened his awareness of his age and vulnerability. One evening he opened the front door to a man who said he knew him and was an acquaintance of Dick Coles. After he had invited him into the house he realised that the man was mentally disturbed. He said that he had come to ask about Schumann and then told Walter Bergmann that he was 80 and senile. He opened all the doors in the flat and took off his shoes. After a worrying few minutes Walter Bergmann managed to persuade the man to leave, saying that as he was 80 he was entitled to be senile! He then rang Dr Coles who did indeed know the man and confirmed that he was mentally ill. Walter Bergmann was extremely shaken by the incident, and realised how much more careful he ought to be. He was cheered the following day by the arrival from Faber of the second album of music for descant recorder and piano. 'Hurray' he wrote[18] in his diary, 'it is my best album'. In February he unexpectedly received some flowers from the frightening visitor — presumably an apology.

Walter Bergmann's pace of work was visibly beginning to slow down, although he was still playing in public occasionally. In March he accompanied the pupils of a close friend and ex-pupil, Sheila Kinsley, in a concert at the Blackheath Conservatoire of Music. Although unable to entertain at home, he desperately still wanted to offer hospitality to visitors. Finances were tight, but when La Noue Davenport and his wife visited, he took them both to a Chinese restaurant with John Thomson, Sheila Kinsley and Erika Seelig. A week later, he took Michaela Petri out to an Italian restaurant with Erika Seelig. Close friends knew that he really could not afford to entertain. Old friends such as Norman Platt came and spent time with him and then took him out for a meal. He adjudicated again at the SRP Festival and was invited as a guest to the 1983 Recorder Summer School. He stayed one night, and gave one lecture and conducted one evening session. It made him feel that he was not forgotten. The Baroque Ensemble Week was a much greater challenge. He was aware that he had less control of the course, and his failing sight and deafness were an enormous problem, but he still could not take the decision to retire.

Grete Bergmann's condition was difficult for all the family. Sometimes matters were quite clear to her; on other occasions she was very confused. She was able to talk a little, but Walter Bergmann found it very difficult to understand her, though he could sometimes guess what she said. In September no mention was made of his birthday, so that Grete was not upset. Their grandson, David Bendix, fetched Walter Bergmann from a morning visit to the hospital, and took him to a special lunch Erica Bendix had cooked, and they then played cards for two hours. Hilde Volhard, Erika Seelig and Ursula Groke then spent the afternoon and evening at home with Walter Bergmann.

Faber were still keen to receive new material for publication from him, and it was agreed that they would publish his arrangement of Handel's *Overture for St Cecilia's Day* (1739), which was dedicated to the SRP and to which the royalties would be given. At the end of September Walter Bergmann was already planning for the following year's Baroque week. He met to discuss it with Philip Thorby, who had agreed to teach on the 1984 course. In spite of his infirmities, he still travelled by train and went to Birmingham in November to conduct the SRP. Paul Clark, Musical Director of the Birmingham SRP, came to see him in December. They had a 'most enjoyable talk of 9 hours, 2 meals and 2 bottles of wine'.[19] He was extremely relieved to receive a significant royalty cheque from Schott, this being the final cheque for publications sold in 1982. Walter Bergmann was disheartened and disappointed when the music he had spent four weeks arranging for the London SRP Christmas meeting for choir and recorder quartet did not work. He really felt his age. The December edition of *Recorder and Music* included an article by him entitled 'Henry Purcell's Use of the Recorder'. But it had originally been written for a conference in 1959. It included a complete list of all the known works in which Purcell used the recorder.

By the middle of December 1983 Grete Bergmann was very weak. 'How we shall get through Christmas is not clear' wrote[20] Walter Bergmann in his diary. He declined an invitation to Christmas festivities at Faber; partly because he did not feel like celebrating, and partly because he found so difficult to hear what was said in a large group. He went to Erika Seelig's seventy-fifth birthday celebrations, but could not hear anything that was said to him because he had forgotten to put in his hearing aid.

Grete Bergmann died in hospital on the morning of December 31st. On January 14th 1984, Walter Bergmann wrote in his diary 'I think a great deal about Grete and her warmth. Why was she so punished?' Life continued much as before, but without hospital visits. He received many letters of condolence. He now had a secretary, Solveig McIntosh, who had been engaged the previous November to help with preparation for the Baroque week and any other work. He dictated an article on Telemann, which Edgar Hunt accepted for *Recorder and Music*. Walter Bergmann was dissatisfied with the article, but Hunt requested a second Telemann article. He was becoming dissatisfied with all his work, and his hearing was causing him much distress. He was amazed that he could still tune his harpsichord accurately. He still played occasionally in public, for example accompanying a pupil, Rebecca in a festival, where much to his delight she was awarded very high marks. Following her mother's death,

Erica Bendix left for a two-month trip to India. Walter Bergmann worried about her, but knew that she needed time to recover from the previous months. At the end of February the whole family were delighted when David Bendix was selected against stiff opposition for an excellent banking post in the City of London.

Walter Bergmann managed to hide his unhappiness on some occasions. At a weekend course at Charney Manor with Denis Bloodworth and Ursula Groke he was his usual humorous self and well enough to participate fully. After conducting a branch meeting of the Essex SRP in March he wrote[21] that it went well 'I was happy for half a day'.

The March edition of *Recorder and Music* celebrated 25 years of publication. It included articles by three members of the original editorial board, Walter Bergmann, Herbert Hersom and Anthony Rowland-Jones. Walter Bergmann's article was entitled 'Telemann on the Continuo'. He concluded it with his own philosophy of continuo realisation.;

'In our time in print there cannot be the perfect realisation of the continuo because of the widely different conditions of its use. How can we cope with this problem?

I will conclude with my own way of dealing with it. When writing down the realization of a continuo I presume that the technical abilities of the continuo player are equal to those of the (imagined) soloist(s). (In style and quality I follow the style and quality of the composition itself.) There cannot be a fixed 'best' realization of the continuo because of the changing conditions of its use which only the flexible continuo could master. There is no 'best', only 'better'.[22] The magazine also included a short obituary to Grete, remembering her as 'a gracious hostess'.

Erica Bendix returned from India at the beginning of April brown, fit and well. Later in the month she took Walter Bergmann, Hilde Volhard and Erika Seelig to a performance of Verdi's *Sicilian Vespers* at the Coliseum. Walter Bergmann found it a wonderful performance. The following day he tackled answering the letters of condolences for Grete with Erica Bendix and Erika Seelig. They sent out a printed acknowledgement, which Walter Bergmann hated doing, but it was the only practical way to answer so many letters. Grete's death had left him very thoughtful about both the past and future. He started reciting the Lord's Prayer each night before he went to sleep, seldom for himself, often for Grete and sometimes for strangers[23]. He wondered how long he had to live. Life continued. He still regularly conducted the London branch of the SRP, and close friends such as Erika Seelig and Sheila Kinsley regularly visited him and helped him entertain and organise musical evenings. His daughter Erica helped him with paperwork and typed letters for him. He was impressed with her efficiency and competence.

The 1984 SRP Festival was held in Guildford. Walter Bergmann wanted to be invited, which was a problem for the Festival Director, Evelyn Nallen, and the Guildford SRP. Nobody wanted to offend Walter Bergmann, but his increasing frailty and severe deafness made involving him no longer a practical possibility. Evelyn Nallen was also in a position to invite prominent professional musicians to participate in the festival. The adjudicators of the competitions were Paul Clark, Friedrich von Huene, Melvyn Tan and John Turner. Performers at the festival included Evelyn Nallen herself and Michael Copley and Timothy Roberts (the Cambridge Buskers). Conductors included Brian Bonsor, Antony Hopkins, Robert King and Philip Thorby. A solution to the problem was found by honouring Walter Bergmann through the consort competition; Faber donated a Walter Bergmann prize of £200. He was still sad, as it was the first SRP festival in which he had not taken an active part.

At the end of May 1984, Walter Bergmann flew to Frankfurt, where he was met by his nephew, Rolf, who drove him to Neckargemünd to spend a few days with Fritz and Anneliese Bergmann and to celebrate Fritz's 85th birthday. Walter Bergmann took two bottles of champagne with him. From Neckargemünd he went to stay for 11 days in a designated 'cure hotel', which catered for those recovering from illness and stress, or others requiring a rest, in the Odenwald, a forested area south of Frankfurt, renowned for its mountain air and health resorts. He spent time reading, sleeping and eating. He met with Rolf and his son Bernard every day. Walter Bergmann found himself dreaming about his childhood. Once when he woke up, he had in his head a melody he had sung as a member of the school choir in a festival in 1916. Rolf insisted on contributing towards the cost of his stay. The weather was not good, but Walter Bergmann enjoyed the rest and the opportunity to relax.

The Baroque Summer School took place as usual in August, this time held at Wycliffe College Oxford. Walter Bergmann was 'assisted' by Philip Thorby, who was not happy with the situation he found during the week. He felt that the time had come for Walter Bergmann to retire with dignity – others close to Walter Bergmann felt the same, and were concerned, like Philip Thorby, that he was being used and manipulated to make sure the course continued under the auspices of his name. There were occasions when Walter Bergmann's deafness meant that he had no idea what was going on around him. There was also unpleasantness between those friends who devoted a great deal of time to looking after him, and felt that they were not being treated fairly. In the Autumn Walter Bergmann decided to go to Hamburg to visit his old friend Dietrich Gerhardt, who was unhappy as his marriage was in difficulties. Two friends wanted to accompany him, and Erica Bendix offered to go as well. He did not know what to do without offending at least two people!

The September edition of *Recorder and Music* published Walter Bergmann's second article on Telemann entitled 'Dull like Telemann'. He took this quotation from an article about two twentieth century composers, in which the work of one was described as 'dull like Telemann'. It gave him the opportunity to write about a cause close to his heart – the under-estimation of Telemann as a composer, which still existed in 1985. In his article Walter Bergmann reminded his readers how long it had taken for Bach to be appreciated as a composer. It was the recorder movement in the 1930s that had rediscovered the music of Telemann and this, he believed was part of the problem. 'The recorder movement was then and remained for decades an amateur music movement and was as such shunned by the musical profession. It is silly but the reputation of amateurism sprung over to Telemann's music, which was not taken seriously after the war.'[24] He also pointed out that Telemann's music was not always well performed. 'Telemann's works are often under-rehearsed because conductors and agents under-rate their difficulties'. He believed that 'one day our musicians will be as familiar with Telemann's music as they are with Bach's *Brandenburg Concertos*'.

Friends like Sheila Kinsley continued to help him fulfil engagements. She drove him in October to Northampton for an SRP teacher's certificate examination. He was unhappy at his gradually deteriorating health. He wrote 'I am cracking up: 82 years old. Incontinent. Eyes (left) and Ears (right) bad. Right arm objects to writing'.[25] He felt that Ian Kemp had not referred to him sympathetically in his new biography of Michael Tippett, published just before Tippett's 80th birthday. He was still fortunate to be receiving a significant income from royalties and he had some income from private pupils. He also continued to receive a pension, but he had to remember that he had to pay tax on his earnings. He had to accept he was at the end of his working life and that old age had caught up with him. Yet another musical friend, Gustav Scheck died in 1984. Walter Bergmann wrote the obituary for *Recorder and Music*.

After 1984, Walter Bergmann did little arranging. His final arrangement and published edition was Telemann's 7 *Wedding Dances* arranged for recorder quartet. His *16 Duos for two treble recorders*, published at the end of 1983, were reviewed in the March 1985 edition of *Recorder and Music*. Paul Clark praised[26] the duets, saying that in spite of the amount of duet material available, it was 'typical of Walter Bergmann to have found something still to be done'. The volume concluded with a page of hints and suggestions. Of these, Clark wrote, 'Among the words of wisdom is this: Articulation is the soul of recorder playing. Dr Bergmann's insistence on good phrasing is very necessary – good phrasing seems to be a dying art – and his encouragement of the players to learn both parts is similarly good advice.' Clark regarded the duets as 'A publication of the highest standard, such as we have come to expect from Walter Bergmann'.

He was able to go again to the Charney Manor Course with Denis Bloodworth and Ursula Groke, and coped with conducting ensemble music from the 16th to 18th centuries. 'The last?' he noted[27] in his diary. In June Erika Seelig accompanied him to stay with Fritz again and to make a repeat visit to Odenwald. The Baroque Chamber week was held as usual in August. It was the last time he participated. In December he conducted the London SRP's Christmas meeting – again for the last time.

By 1986, old age and deafness had severely curtailed Walter Bergmann's musical life. His friends took him to concerts and appropriate musical occasions, where it always pleased him when people recognised and greeted him. He still continued to teach a small number of private pupils and he delighted in their success. His diary entries end in February 1986, with the recording of Anneliese Bergmann's death. His memory had begun to fail. Schott invited him to the opening of the Early Music Shop in the basement of Schott's London premises in Great Malborough Street. To those who had not seen him for a while, the change in him was noticeable; he appeared old and confused.

The Society of Recorder Players celebrated its 50th birthday in 1987. John Turner of Forsyth put together a compilation of music and letters entitled *A Birthday Album for the Society of Recorder Players*. The book included new compositions and arrangements for recorder by Arnold Cooke, Alan Ridout, Hans Gal, the Cambridge Buskers, Colin Hand and Alan Bullard. Walter Bergmann was unable to write anything new, but he asked that the canon from his descant recorder sonata should be included with a message from him. In his message as President of the SRP, Sir Michael Tippett mentioned how he came involved with recorders through working at Morley College with Walter Bergmann and putting on performances of Purcell. The Dutch recorder player Kees Otten paid tribute in a long letter to his musical friends in the society including Edgar Hunt, Carl Dolmetsch and Walter Bergmann. In particular he remembered 'the fine music-making' with Walter Bergmann and Brian Bonsor at the Recorder Summer School. Walter Bergmann attended a special reception held at the Artworker's Guild in London, which was the original meeting place of the SRP. Carl Dolmetsch and Edgar Hunt were present along with one other original member, Enid Hunt. Kees Otten was one of the guests. All those present were saddened by Walter Bergmann's isolation through deafness and obvious confusion. It was his last public appearance.

The final months of his life were difficult for all those concerned with advancing senility, confusion and ill health. The responsibility of caring for him fell on his daughter Erica, but old friends did what they could to help. He died on January 13th 1988. Edgar Hunt wrote of his death in the editorial column of the March 1988 edition of *Recorder and Music*. He wrote[28] that 'With the death of Walter Bergmann recorder players have a lost a great friend who was able to bridge the gap between the amateur and the professional'. There were 'many young musicians, singers and instrumentalists, whom he helped onto the ladder of professional success.' Hunt observed that those who worked with him remembered his 'impish sense of humour' and that Walter Bergmann had been one of the first to recognise the outstanding talent of Frans Brüggen. In his obituary[29], Edgar Hunt referred to the great contribution Walter Bergmann had made to British music in his collaboration with Michael Tippett and the revival of Purcell and the countertenor voice and in keeping interest in the recorder alive during the war, which provided a basis for the reforming of the SRP in 1946. Hunt also referred to the important role Walter Bergmann had played in the publication of a wide range of music for the recorder through his work at Schott and his own editions and compositions. Next to the obituary, Schott published a full-page advertisement of works by Walter Bergmann.

In the following edition of *Recorder and Music*, Herbert Hersom paid tribute to Walter Bergmann from the point of view of a teacher, writing[30] 'these pages cannot ignore the tremendous impact on music in schools by one who was never too busy to help children'. 'He loved youngsters: he loved music: and he loved every opportunity he had of putting the two together. He encouraged teachers in every way he could. We are greatly indebted to him for the copious supply of editions, arrangements and compositions he made with the needs of young people in mind.'

Walter Bergmann was mourned by many people. He was a unique character who cared passionately about music. He retained a sense of humour to the end of his life. He could be unreasonable and impractical, but always generous — and always short of money. He set high standards for himself and others, and at times could be harsh to those he believed had failed to reach those standards. Throughout his life he fought insecurity within himself. He championed those he felt were undervalued and needed support whether it was Telemann or a young player. His judgement failed him sometimes, particularly regarding himself, but rarely where young gifted musicians were concerned. Of course he had his critics; there is no denying he enjoyed female company, sometimes unwisely, but his personal judgement did not usually cloud his musical judgement, when he could be ruthless. Above all he needs to be remembered for the significant role he played in the revival of early music, particularly the music of Purcell and Telemann, and in the revival of the recorder and editing, arranging and composing of music for the recorder.

As scholarship has developed, and the professional early music scene has moved on, it is easy to look at editions of forty or fifty years ago with a critical eye. But it is important to remember the role of those such as Carl Dolmetsch, Edgar Hunt and Walter Bergmann, in discovering and performing so much music and bringing it to the attention of the musical world, and in raising the playing standards and profile of the recorder. The 1998 Schott Recorder Catalogue contained just under one hundred works or publications edited, arranged or composed by Walter Bergmann currently in publication ten years after his death. At time of publication, his *First Book of Descant Solos and of Treble Solos* still provided pieces for the Associated Board practical examinations at grades one, two and three. His name is affectionately remembered within the world of recorder music.

1 'Meine geistige Lähmung hat sich etwas verbessert.' Diary 28, 03.01.80
2 *Early Music Magazine*, January 1980, p.43
3 Letter from J.P. Adams to WB, 28.03.80
4 Diary 28, 03.06.80
5 *Early Music,* July 1980, p.398
6 Christopher Ball to David Lasocki, 19.01.80
7 *The Strad,* January 1981
8 WB to Harold Newman, 29.08.80
9 *Recorder and Music, Vol.7 no.1,* March 1981
10 Diary 28, 29.05.81
11 Diary 28, 29.05.81
12 Diary 28, 29.05.81
13 Diary 29, 10.06.82
14 Diary 29, 08.08.82
15 *Recorder and Music, Vol.7 no.7,* September 1982
16 Diary 29, 23.09.82
17 Letter from Janivere Rowell to Anne Martin
18 Diary 29, 28.01.83
19 Diary 29, 02.11.83
20 Diary 29, 21.12.83
21 Diary 29, 07.03.84
22 *Recorder and Music, Vol. 8. no.1,* March 1984
23 Diary 29, 22.04.84
24 *Recorder and Music, Vol. 8 no. 3,* September 1984
25 Diary 29, 30.10.84
26 *Recorder and Music, Vol. 8, no.5,* March 1985
27 Diary 29, 23.03.85
28 *Recorder and Music, Vol. 9, no. 5,* March 1988
29 Ditto
30 *Recorder and Music, Vol. 9, no. 6.* June 1988

Walter Bergmann; compositions

Published compositions
(all published by Schott unless stated; number given is WB's in his own catalogue of compositions and editions)
Septet (1945), dedicated to John Amis; originally written for pipes and recorders, or to be played by recorders; published in 1994 (2 descants and 5 trebles) by Forsyth
10 Canonic Studies for descant and treble recorder (1949) (22)
Pastorale for voice and treble recorder (1946) dedicated to Alfred Deller (23)
8 Canonic Studies for treble and alto pipes (1949) Cramer (55)
Prelude for flute and piano (1949) (75)
Prelude and Fugue for bassoon and piano (1950) (90)
Variations on Le Mois de Mai for descant, treble and tenor (1962) (334)
Sonata for descant recorder and piano (1965) dedicated to Frans Brüggen pub. 1966
Chaconietta for cello and 6 recorders (1969), published 1978 (431, 543))
Sonatella for tenor recorder (1971) published in *For the Tenor Recorder Player* Magnamusic (455)
The Passionate Shepherd to his love for 2 counter tenors, 2 treble recorders and harpsichord (1971 rev. 1979) (457)
Pastorella for soprano voice and sopranino (1971), dedicated to Carl Dolmetsch; (originally written for counter tenor and descant recorder, (445)); published in *For the Sopranino Recorder Player* in 1972 by Magnamusic (468)
American Indian Suite and *Peruvian Suite* (1972) for descant recorder and piano, published in 1973 by Hargail
Sonata for treble recorder and piano (1973) commissioned for Amico Dolci published 1974 (474)
7 Canonic Studies for bassoon (1976) (504)

Unpublished compositions include
2 Sonatas for oboe, written for Dietrich Gerhardt (1932 and 1934)
Sonatina for treble recorder and piano (1942)
Quintet for recorders (1943)
Sonata for flute, written for Delia Ruhm (1942) Incidental music for *The Tempest* (songs) (1951) (135 –139)
The First of April, 8 Variations for 9 recorders, string orchestra, harp and percussion (1957) (252)
The Rehearsal, a children's opera (1971 rev. 1976) (458)
4 songs for countertenor and lute (1973 rev. 1983) (398, 473, 608)
Variation and Themes for recorder orchestra (1974) (481)
Tooters' and Tutor's Limerick for voices in canon, descant and treble recorder and Piano (1977) (531)
Variations on a German Folksong for 5 recorders and piano (1977, rev. of 1968) (532, 420)
Music on the Death of Alfred Deller for vocal quintet (1980) (575)

Compositions and music publications for school use; recorder tutors and teaching materials include
For 3 descant recorders with percussion ad lib. published in the *SRP Junior Branch Magazine No 5* March 1951 (115)
Matthew, Mark for unison soprano voices and 2 descant recorders (1957)
The Common Cormorant, a canon for recorder and voice (1957) (273)
Limerick, published with above (1958) (274)
The Drummer Boy for unison voices, recorders, percussion and piano (1967) (387)

Matilda for children's voices, violin, cello, piano and percussion (1966 rev. 1967) (388)
Three to Seven Notes, first ensemble book for 2 descant recorders (1967), Faber (405) with Hilda Hunter, *Initial Duets Bk 1* and *2* for descant and treble recorders, (1968/9) Faber (415 and 442) (republished 1983 as one book)
Accent on Rhythm for descant, treble and tenor recorders Faber (1968)
Accent on Melody for 2 descant recorders and piano Faber (1969)
Casey Jones for unison voices and school orchestra (1971) Hargail (453)
Solo Book for Bass Recorder (1971) (451)
Solo Book for Tenor Recorder (1971) (455)
Solo Book for Sopranino Recorder (1972) (468) all Magnamusic
Solo Book for Soprano Recorder (1973) (469)
Solo Book for Alto Recorder (1973) (470)
Old Brass Wagon for unison voice and school orchestra (1971) (461)
Descant Recorder Lessons (1973) Faber, Schirmer and Zen On (450)
7 Canonic Studies for Brass (1976)
With Faith Whiteley, *First Violin Book* (1977) OUP
Yo-yake-Koyake, Variations on a Japanese children's song for recorders (1977) Zen On
First Book of Treble Recorder Solos (1978) Faber (562)
First Book of Descant Recorder Solos (1978) Faber (563)
with Lyndon Hilling, *First Book of Bassoon Solos* (1979) Faber (556)
Second Book of Bassoon Solos (1980) Faber (577)
Second Book of Descant Recorder Solos (1982) Faber (603)
Second Book of Treble Recorder Solos (1982) Faber

Edited music, composers include
Arne
J.C. Bach
J.S. Bach
Barsanti
Baston
Blow including *Ode On the death of Henry Purcell*
Boismortier
J. Clarke
    including ode written on the death of Henry Purcell
Corelli
Croft
Dieupart
Festing
Finger
J. Fischer
Flackton
Henry Hall including *Music on the death of Henry Purcell*
Handel
Haydn
Hook
Hotteterre
Pelham
Humphrey
Kuhnau
Locatelli
Loeillet
Mattheson
Pepusch
Pez
Henry Purcell, including songs with Michael Tippett
D. Purcell
Quantz
Schickhardt
Telemann, including *Sonatas* for recorder, *Ino* and

Pimpinone
Woodcock
Valentino
Publishers include Bärenreiter, Faber, Hargail,
Magnamusic, Nova, Peters, Schott and Zen On.

Translation work includes (English to German) Songs by
H. Purcell, including *Fairest Isle*
English folksongs, e.g. *Greensleeves*
A Child of Our Time and *King Priam* by Michael
Tippett
The Ledge by Richard Rodney Bennett

BIOGRAPHICAL NOTES

Amadeus Quartet; Internationally renowned string quartet, which made its formal debut in London in January 1948. Its members consisted of 3 refugees from Nazi Germany and Austria, Norbert Brainin, Sigmund Nissel and Peter Schidlof, who were all pupils of Max Rostal, and an English player, Martin Lovett. They remained together until Schidlof's death in 1987. Britten composed his third quartet for them.

Amis, John, (1922 – 2013); critic, writer, administrator and broadcaster; presenter of programmes on radio and TV; originally studied to be professional singer.

Arno, Michael (1936 – 1988); Gifted amateur recorder player, who became a professional player; GSM Silver Medallist. He formed the Lydian Consort and played with Collegium Saggitarri and Alan Bush.

Barthel, Rudolf (1908 – 1978); German violinist and recorder player; In the early 1950s he established the first recorder 'choir' or large ensemble group of around 50 players in the Neukölln Volkshochschule, Berlin, pioneering the idea of a recorder orchestra. Initially Barthel used descant, treble, tenor and bass recorders, and then he added sopranino (and higher recorders), great bass and contrabass; also used soloists and small groups; repertoire used included works specifically written for the orchestra and early music adapted to use the full range of the orchestra.

Bennett, William (1936 –); flautist, orchestral player and soloist; member of LSO, English Chamber Orchestra and Academy of St Martin's in the Fields.

Berkeley, Lennox (1903 – 1989); Composer, studied with Nadia Boulanger; Professor of Composition RAM 1946 – 1968; wrote *Recorder Sonatina* (1940) for treble recorder and piano.

Bixler, Martha (1927 -); American recorder player and teacher; studied with La Noue Davenport and played with New York Pro Musica Renaissance Band.

Black, Neil (1932 - 2015); oboist; orchestral player and soloist; member of English Chamber Orchestra, Academy of St Martin's in the Fields, London Mozart Players, Principal Oboist LPO 1958-60, Monteverdi Orchestra; Professor RAM 1960-70; specialist in Baroque and Classical Music.

Bonsor, Brian (1926 – 2011); Scottish teacher, composer, pianist, recorder player; Music Adviser in the Scottish Borders 1970 – 1983; author of recorder tutors *Enjoy the Recorder* and composer of recorder ensemble music, particularly for school use; Musical Adviser SRP.

Bowen, Kenneth (1932 –); Welsh operatic tenor, conductor and teacher; sang with Glyndebourne, Welsh National Opera and Kent Opera; Professor of Singing RAM from 1967 and Head of Vocal Studies 1987 – 91.

Brainin, Norbert (1923 – 2005); Austrian born violinist; see Amadeus Quartet;

Brannigan, Owen (1908 – 1973); much loved English operatic bass; created roles of Noye in *Noyes Fludde* and Bottom in *A Midsummer Night's Dream*, both of which Britten wrote specifically for him; also sang and recorded songs from his native Northumberland.

Britten, Benjamin (1913 – 1976); Composer, created life peer in 1976; composed wide range of music and established modern British opera; President of the SRP 1959 – 1976; wrote *Alpine Suite* (1955) and *Scherzo* (1955) for recorder quartet and used the recorder in *Noyes Fludde* and *A Midsummer Night's Dream*.

Brüggen, Franz (1934 – 2014); Dutch virtuoso recorder player, flautist and conductor; studied with Joannes Collette and Kees Otten; Professor of Recorder and 18th-century music at the Hague Royal Conservatory;

editor of recorder music and has commissioned new works for recorder including Berio's *Gesti*; Vice-President SRP.

Camden, Archie (1888 – 1979); Bassoonist, soloist and orchestral player and teacher; first native English bassoon soloist, who established bassoon as solo instrument; member of Halle orchestra and BBC Symphony Orchestra; Gordon Jacob composed Bassoon concerto for him; taught in Manchester and at RCM.

Cantelo, April (1928-); Soprano specialising in Baroque music, Mozart and songs by Richard Strauss; member of the Deller Consort; created the role of Helena in Britten's *A Midsummer Night's Dream*.

Carner, Mosco (1904 – 1985); Austrian musicologist, who settled in London in 1933; conductor, critic and author;

Clark, Paul (1927 – 2013); Recorder player, teacher, arranger and publisher based in Birmingham; Musical Adviser SRP.

Collette, Joannes (1918-1995); Dutch recorder player, also player of flute, viol and harpsichord; Professor at Utrecht and Maastricht conservatoires; taught Frans Brüggen.

Conrad, Ferdinand (1912 – 1992); German recorder player, flautist and teacher, pupil of Gustav Scheck; early music pioneer in 1930s; 1939 – 1953 member of specialist orchestra, Lübeckischen Kirchenorchester, which performed Renaissance and baroque music on original instruments; Professor at Hanover Conservatoire 1953 – 1969 teaching recorder; founded own performing group in 1955.

Dart, Thurston (1921 – 1971); English harpsichordist, musicologist, editor and teacher; Professor of Music at Cambridge and King's College, London; specialist in Renaissance and Baroque music, particularly Bach, Bull and keyboard and consort music of the 16th, 17th and 18th centuries.

Davenport, LaNoue (1922 – 2000); American recorder player and player of early instruments, teacher and editor; originally Jazz trumpeter who developed interest in early music; studied with Erich Katz, who was one of the most important figures in the early music movement in the USA from 1943; participated in first performance of New York Pro Musica (1953); later director of Pro Musica consort and assistant director of Renaissance band; also closely involved in the American Recorder Society; Vice-President SRP.

Dawes, Frank (1910 – 1977); piano teacher, writer and editor specialising in Elizabethan keyboard music, Maurice Greene and the music of Clementi.

Deller, Alfred (1912 – 1979) countertenor responsible, with Michael Tippett, for the revival of the countertenor voice; joined Canterbury Cathedral choir in 1940, where Tippett heard him in 1943; Deller made his London debut at a Morley College concert in October 1944, singing Purcell's *Music for a while*; made his first recording, of Purcell songs, with Walter Bergmann in 1949; revived English lute song with Desmond Dupré; founded Deller Consort and the Stour Festival (1963); Britten composed role of Oberon for him in *A Midsummer Night's Dream*.

Deller, Mark, (1938 –); Countertenor; son of Alfred Deller and followed Father as chorister at Canterbury Cathedral; lay vicar at Salisbury Cathedral; member of Deller consort and Director of the Stour Festival.

Dent, Edward, (1876 – 1957); Musicologist, teacher and author; Professor of Music Cambridge 1926 – 1941;broadened Cambridge music degree course; had particular interest in opera (Scarlatti and Mozart); first President of International Society for Contemporary

Music (ISCM); supported musicians escaping from Nazi Germany.

Dinn, Freda, (1910 – 1990); violinist and teacher of violin and recorder, educationalist; taught violin and ran the orchestra in the Junior Dept at RCM; succeeded Stanley Taylor as recorder professor at RCM 1967-1971; lecturer Froebel Institute of Education 1946-1961; taught recorder at Mary Ward Settlement from 1937 until Walter Bergman succeeded her in 1952; Musical Director of the Society of Recorder Players after the war; one of original tutors for the Recorder in Education Summer School.

Dolci, Amico, (1957 –); Italian recorder player; studied with Edwin Alton, Edgar Hunt, Ferdinand Conrad and Hans-Ulrich Staeps; his Father commissioned Walter Bergmann's Sonata for treble recorder and piano.

Dolmetsch, Carl, (1911 – 1997); solo recorder player and recorder maker, youngest child of Arnold Dolmetsch; played a number of other instruments including viols; first modern recorder was made by Arnold Dolmetsch as a result of the young Carl Dolmetsch leaving a bag of Bressan recorders on Waterloo station in 1919; from 1932 formed a partnership with the harpsichordist Joseph Saxby, which lasted into the 1980s; Director of the Haslemere Festival and the Dolmetsch Consort; co- founded the SRP with Edgar Hunt and Max and Stephanie Champion (Dolmetsch and Hunt first joint Musical Directors); promoted the recorder as a solo instrument and its music; commissioned works for recorder; Lennox Berkeley, Hans Gal, Gordon Jacob and Edmund Rubbra all composed for him; editor of recorder music; Vice-President SRP.

Dolmetsch, Natalie, (1905 – 1989); viol player, teacher and editor of viol music; founded the Viola da Gamba Society; Chairman of the Dolmetsch Historical Dance Society.

Downes, Ralph, (1904 – 1993); organist, studied RCM; 1928 appointed musical director and organist at Princeton USA; from 1936 organist Brompton Oratory, London; resident organist of the LPO; designed organ for the Festival Hall, London.

DuPré, Desmond, (1916 – 1974) lutenist and viol player, studied RCM (initially cellist); accompanied Alfred Deller and played with the Deller Consort; also played with Julian Bream, Musica Reservata and Thurston Dart; President of the Lute Society.

Edmunds, Christopher, (1899 – 1990); composer, lecturer; Principal Birmingham School of Music 1945 – 1956); composed *Sonatina* for descant recorder and keyboard, and established recorder teaching at Birmingham.

English, Gerald, (1925 –); tenor, educated RCM; sang in St Paul's Cathedral Choir and Deller Consort; operatic singer; performed wide range of music including Bach, Britten, Tippett and Henze; Professor RCM 1960 – 1977; Director Opera Studio, Victorian College for the Arts, Melbourne.

Esswood, Paul, (1942 -); countertenor, studied RCM; lay vicar Westminster Abbey; performed in oratorio and opera, particularly Monteverdi and Cavalli; international career; founder of Pro Cantione Antiqua; taught RCM 1973 – 1985.

Eulenburg, Kurt, (1879 – 1982); German publisher of miniature scores; moved firm to London in 1939; Eulenburg settled in London in 1945; eventually Eulenburg Miniature Scores became part of Schott..

Flagstad, Kirstin, (1895 – 1962); Norwegian soprano with international operatic career; made debut at Bayreuth in 1934 and became known for Wagnerian roles; gave first performance of Strauss' *Four Last Songs*; Director

Norwegian State Opera; made many recordings, including Wagner, Sibelius and Grieg; gave final stage performance in *Dido* and *Aeneas* at the Mermaid Theatre in London.

Fowler, Fred, (d. 1983) teacher; attended the first recorder course for teachers given in Bradford by Edgar Hunt in 1937; promoted the recorder in schools and taught teachers in Wakefield; joint author, with Edmund Priestley, of one of first school recorder tutors, *The School Recorder Book*.

Fricker, Peter Racine, (1920 – 1990); composer; studied RCM and at Morley College with Seiber; Director of Music Morley College 1956 – 1964; taught composition RCM 1955 – 1964; from 1964 Professor of Music University of California and composer in residence; works include orchestral, choral, vocal and chamber music, including *Suite* for recorder trio (1956).

Gal, Hans, (1890 – 1987), Austrian composer, musicologist, pianist and conductor; educated Vienna University and lecturer there 1919 – 1928; Director Mainz Conservatory 1929 – 1933, when had to return to Austria, becoming conductor of Vienna Concert Orchestra and Vienna Madrigal and Bach Society; his works were banned in Germany; left Austria for Britain in 1938 and settled in Scotland in 1945; lecturer Edinburgh University; became interested in the recorder in 1950s, when children in his family began to play the recorder; compositions include opera, orchestral, choral and chamber, including several works for recorder e.g. *Quartettino,* for recorder quartet (1960); Vice-President SRP.

Goehr, Walter, (1903 – 1960); German conductor and composer; studied with Schoenberg; conducted Berlin Radio Orchestra 1925 – 1931; left Germany for London, becoming musical director for Columbia recording company; joined circle of musicians associated with Tippett at Morley College, and conducted there from 1943; conducted first performances of Britten's *Serenade* and Tippett's *A Child of our Time*; conducted first modern performance of Monteverdi *Vespers 1610*; editor of Monteverdi.

Goodman, Roy, (1951 –); conductor, director, violinist and teacher; choral scholar Kings College, Cambridge; Co-director Parley of Instruments 1979 – 1986; Conductor Hanover Band 1986 - .

Goossens, Leon, (1897 – 1988); oboist; initially orchestral player in 1930, pursued career as soloist from 1945; did much to promote oboe as solo and chamber instrument; Bax, Britten, Elgar, Jacobs and Vaughan Williams composed music for him.

Hamburger, Paul, (1920 – 2004); Austrian-born pianist, accompanist and critic; studied Vienna and London; worked with English Opera Group and Glyndebourne; made recordings with artists such as April Cantelo and Heather Harper; taught GSM and RCM.

Hemsley, Thomas, (1927 – 2013); baritone; chorister St Paul's Cathedral 1950 – 51; debut in *Dido and Aeneas* at Mermaid Theatre in 1951; international career including Bayreuth , Zurich, Glyndebourne; sang with Kent Opera and English National Opera; created role of Magnus in first performance of Tippett's *The Knot Garden* (1970); visiting professor RCM and RNCM.

Hersom, Herbert, (1919 – 1998); teacher, lecturer and arranger; Musical Adviser SRP and Director and tutor of the Recorder in Education Summer School; founder member Kingsway Choral Society; Music Adviser for recorder; Chairman of London Schools Music Association; promoted and taught the recorder in school from the 1950s; member of the Oriel Consort.

Hess, Myra, (1890 – 1965); solo pianist; studied GSM

and RCM; international career; debut in 1907 playing Beethoven *Piano Concerto No 4* conducted by Beecham; particular interests included Bach, Scarlatti, Mozart and Beethoven; organised National Gallery concerts during World War Two.

Hindemith, Paul; (1895 – 1963); German composer, viola player, teacher and conductor; studied Musikhochschule Frankfurt; Professor of Composition Musikhochschule Berlin 1927 – 1937; compositions unacceptable to Nazis and left Germany in 1937, initially for Switzerland and then to USA in 1950; Professor at Yale University from 1940 – 1953 and at Zurich University 1951 – 1955; settled in Switzerland; compositions include opera, orchestral, choral and chamber works, including *Recorder Trio* (1932).

Hoffnung, Gerard, (1925 – 1959); German-born artist, cartoonist and tuba player; came to Britain as a child and refugee; drew series of acutely observed humorous musical cartoons; organised concerts.

Holst, Imogen, (1907 – 1984); conductor, lecturer and writer; daughter and biographer of Gustav Holst; Artistic Director Aldeburgh Festival from 1956; founder and conductor of the Purcell Singers 1953 – 1967.

Hopkins, Antony, (1921 – 2014); composer, conductor, pianist, broadcaster, lecturer and writer; studied RCM; associated with Morley College during War Years; composed music for film, stage and radio and works for children; broadcast successful radio series 'Talking about Music' for over 20 years; taught RCM and London City University; compositions include Suite (1953), dedicated to WB, for descant recorder and piano.

Huene, Friedrich von, (1929 – 2016); German-born recorder maker, flautist, recorder player and teacher; emigrated to USA in 1948; served in US Air Force Band; graduated in music in 1956 and joined workshop of Boston flute maker in 1956; set up own workshop making recorders in 1960; studied construction of Renaissance and Baroque recorders; designed Rottenburgh recorder for the German firm Moeck; Vice-President SRP.

Hunt, Edgar, (1909 – 2006); recorder player, flautist, teacher, editor, writer and lecturer; Head of Renaissance and Baroque Music Trinity College of Music, London; one of most important influences on the recorder movement in Britain; joint co-founder of SRP in 1937 (see Dolmetsch); co-founder and Chairman Recorder in Education Summer School; editor *The Recorder Magazine*; member Galpin Society; music editor Schott; designed first plastic recorders; author of *The Recorder and its Music*. Vice-President SRP.

Hunter, Hilda, (1919 –); oboist, lecturer and recorder teacher; lecturer Wolverhampton Polytechnic; teacher on summer schools; author of educational recorder music.

Jones, Philip; (1928 – 2000) trumpeter, teacher and editor of music; studied RCM; orchestral player (RPO, LPO and BBC Symphony) and soloist; founded Philip Jones Brass Ensemble; taught RNCM and GSM; Principal Trinity College of Music, London 1988 - 1994.

Kenworthy, C. (Ken) (1918 – 2000); attended WB's recorder classes at Morley College; founder member Oriel Consort; edited *Recorder News* 1948 – 1963; arranged music for recorders and encouraged Theo Wyatt to found 'Oriel Library' publications; his arrangements of Bach *Contrapunctus IV* and *IX* were the first Oriel publications.

Küng, Franz, (1906 – 1983); Swiss recorder-maker; began making recorders in 1938; made distinctive recorders, including great and contrabasses.

Lasocki, David, (1947 –); recorder player, lecturer,

musicologist, editor and writer; studied recorder with Edgar Hunt and Gustav Scheck; completed research into recorder players in England 1540 – 1740; specialises in history of woodwind instruments and editing 18th century music; editor *The Recorder Education Journal*; Music Librarian University of Indiana until 2011.

Lehane, Maureen (1932 – 2010); operatic and concert singer; studied GSM; debut Glyndebourne in 1967 as Melide in Cavalli's *Orminde*; international career; Handel specialist; edited Purcell songs with husband Peter Wishart.

Leigh, Walter, (1905 – 1942); composer and organist; studied Cambridge University and with Hindemith; killed in action at Tobruk; compositions mainly for the stage; chamber works include *Sonatina* for recorder and piano (1939).

Lidka, Maria, (1914 – 2013); German-born violinist, pupil of Max Rostal; came to Britain before World War Two; soloist and chamber music player; taught RCM.

Lovett, Martin, (1927 –), cellist; studied RCM; see Amadeus Quartet.

Luxon, Benjamin, (1937 –); baritone; studied GSM; operatic and lieder singer; performed with ENO, Netherlands Opera, at Glyndebourne and Covent Garden; created title role in Britten's television opera *Owen Wingrave*.

Marriner, Neville, ((1924 – 2016); conductor and violinist; studied RCM and Paris; taught RCM 1949 –1959; principal second violin LSO 1956 – 1968; founder (1959) and director Academy of St Martin's-in-the-Fields.

Matthews, Denis, (1919 – 1988); pianist, lecturer and writer; studied RAM; gave first performance of Rubbra's *Piano Concerto* 1956; noted for performances of Mozart; 1971 appointed first Professor of Music at University of Newcastle.

Matz, Arnold, (1904 – 1991); German violinist and viola player; close friend of WB from boyhood; member of the Leipzig Gewandhaus Orchestra; professor at Leipzig Musikhochschule; composed *Sonata Contrappuntistica* (1979), dedicated to WB, for treble recorder and piano.

Mellers, Wilfrid, (1914 – 2008); composer, critic, writer and lecturer; studied Cambridge University and with Rubbra; lectured Cambridge, Birmingham and Pittsburgh Universities; from 1964 Professor of Music at York University until retirement; compositions mainly choral and vocal, but some chamber including *Sonatina* (1956) for treble recorder and piano; published several books including *Man and his Music* with Alec Harman.

Meyer, Ernst, (1905 – 1988); German musicologist and composer; studied with Hindemith; in 1930 completed PhD on 17th century German ensemble music; began research in other northern European countries and in 1933 had to leave Germany because of left-wing activities; settled in Britain until 1948; worked for the WEA and helped establish Free German League of Culture; wrote film music; published *English Chamber Music from the Middle Ages to Purcell*; edited first modern edition of Schmelzer's *Sonata a 7*, which he discovered in manuscript in Uppsala University; from 1948 – 1970 Professor of Music Humboldt University, E. Berlin.

Müller-Hartmann, Robert, (1884 – 1950); German composer, teacher and critic; lectured Hamburg University 1923 – 1933; musical adviser N. Deutscher Rundfunk 1931 – 1933; settled in Britain in 1933; friend of R. Vaughan Williams; compositions include Suite for recorder trio (1951).

Munrow, David, (1942 – 1976); recorder player and early music specialist, teacher, arranger and broadcaster; founder of Early Music Consort; lecturer Leicester

University and from 1969, taught recorder at RAM; broadcast 'Pied Piper' series on BBC Radio, which brought early music to a wide audience; he contributed significantly to the early music revival, making performances of early music accessible and full of life.

Murray, Dom Gregory, (1905 – 1992); organist, composer, conductor and editor; in 1930s regular organ recitalist on BBC radio; composer of church music and authority on Gregorian chant; became interested in recorders, directed the Bath SRP and arranged a significant amount of recorder music.

Murray, Margaret, (1921 – 2015); pianist, cellist, recorder player and teacher; studied RCM; specialist of Orff- Schulwerk, translated and edited English edition.

Murrill, Herbert, (1909 – 1992); studied RCM and University of Oxford; composer, organist, teacher and manager; Head of Music BBC from 1950; taught composition RAM from 1933; compositions include opera, vocal music and instrumental; wrote *Sonata* (1950) for treble recorder and harpsichord.

Nallen, Evelyn, (1952 –); recorder player, and teacher; studied with the Dolmetsch family, Kees Boeke, Walter van Hauwe and Peter Holtslag; performed widely in Britain and abroad; interest in contemporary music; Musical Adviser SRP.

Nissel, Sigmund, (1922 – 2008); Austrian-born violinist; see
Amadeus Quartet.

Norrington, Roger, (1934 -); conductor and tenor; choral scholar Clare College Cambridge, studied conducting with Adrian Boult at RCM; 1962 –1973 founded and conducted Heinrich Schütz Choir; musical director Kent Opera 1966 – 1984; conductor Bournemouth Sinfonietta 1985 – 1989; worked with London Baroque Players, LPO, London Classical Players and many other international orchestras.

Oriel Consort; recorder consort founded in 1950 by four members of WB's Morley Evening Class; Theo Wyatt later took the name for his publications of recorder consort music.

Otten, Kees, (1924 – 2008); Dutch recorder player, clarinettist, jazz player, writer and teacher; educated Amsterdam Conservatoire; international career; in 1963 formed ensemble group Syntagma Musicum; Professor of Recorder in Amsterdam, The Hague, Rotterdam and Utrecht; pupils included Frans Brüggen; made significant numbers of recordings; Vice President SRP.

Parrott, Ian, (1916 – 2012); composer, musicologist and writer; educated RCM and Oxford University; Professor of Music University of Wales, Aberwystwth; interest in Welsh music; compositions varied including opera, orchestral and chamber music; wrote *Arabesque and Dance* (1972) for treble recorder and harpsichord.

Pears, Peter, (1910 – 1976); tenor; studied RCM and with Elena Gerhardt and Dawson Freer; close companion of Benjamin Britten and created many operatic tenor roles for Britten including Peter Grimes, Captain Vere in *Billy Budd*, Quint in *The Turn of the Screw* and Aschenbach in *Death in Venice*; gave first performances of works such as *The Holy Sonnets of John Donne* and *Serenade* for tenor, horn and strings; one of founders of the English Opera Group and the Aldeburgh Festival; also known for other repertoire such as Bach, Schütz and Elgar.

Peter, Hildemarie, (1921 -); German recorder teacher and writer in the 1950s; pupil of Gustav Scheck; published *The Recorder, its tradition and task* (1958).

Petri, Michaela, (1958 -); Danish virtuoso recorder player; studied with Ferdinand Conrad in Hanover; international solo career; numerous recordings.

Pitsch, Kurt, (? – 1982); Austrian amateur recorder player involved in the recorder revival in the 1950s; arranged recorder summer schools in Austria and Italy.

Platt, Norman, (1920 – 2004); baritone, actor, producer, broadcaster and translator; studied Cambridge University; Vicar Choral St Paul's Cathedral 1948 –1952; member of the Deller Consort 1950 – 1964; principal Sadler's Wells Opera; founder of Kent Opera; taught Morley College and Goldsmith's College.

Pritchard, John, (1921 – 1989); conductor; international career; conducted Glyndebourne Opera, RLPO, LPO, BBC Symphony, Cologne Opera; Huddersfield Choral Society etc; conducted first performances of Britten's Gloriana and Tippett's *Midsummer Marriage* and *King Priam*.

Purves, Alison, (d. 1991); soprano; wife of Antony Hopkins;

Reizenstein, Franz, (1911 - 1968); German-born composer and pianist; studied with Hindemith; settled in London in 1934; studied at RCM with R.Vaughan Williams, and with the pianist Solomon; taught piano RAM (1958 – 1968) and RMCO (1962 – 1968); also taught composition at University of Boston; composer of orchestral, vocal, chamber and piano music; wrote *Partita* for treble recorder and piano (1946).

Reynolds, Gordon, (1921 – 1995); organist, teacher, music educationalist, broadcaster and writer; lecturer in music Whitelands College; taught harmony at Royal Military School of Music; organist and choirmaster (from 1967) Chapel Royal; editor of *Music in Education*; broadcaster BBC Schools' Programmes.

Ring, Layton, (1922 -); New Zealand-born harpsichordist, recorder and viol player, lecturer and music editor; settled in Northumberland; member of the Dolmetsch Ensemble; harpsichordist to Northern Sinfonia; specialist on William Lawes.

Ritchie, Margaret, (1903 – 1969); soprano and teacher; studied RCM; member of Sadler's Wells and English Opera; sang Lucia in Britten's *Rape of Lucretia* at Glyndebourne; from 1960 ran summer school for singers in Oxford.

Rostal, Max, (1905 – 1991); Austrian-born violinist, teacher and writer; child prodigy; international career as soloist and chamber player; studied violin with Carl Flesch and composition with Matyas Seiber; appointed assistant to Flesch at Berlin Musikhochschule; professor Berlin 1930 – 1933; settled in London in 1934; taught GSM 1944 –1958; 1957 – 1982 Professor Cologne Musikschule and 1958 – 1986 at Berne Conservatoire, settling finally in Switzerland; founded European String Teachers' Association; several concertos written for him, including works by Alan Bush, Franz Reizenstein; also Fantasia by Seiber.

Rowland-Jones, Anthony, (1926 -); recorder player, lecturer, teacher and writer; books include *Recorder Technique* (1959) and *Playing Recorder Sonatas* (1992); studied recorder with WB at Morley College; involved in encouraging and establishing the recorder in the north of England; Musical Adviser SRP.

Rubbra, Edmund, (1901 – 1986); composer, pianist, writer and teacher; studied composition with Gustav Holst; lectured University of Oxford 1947 – 1968, GSM from 1961; reviewer for *Monthly Musical Record*; interest in 16th and 17th century English music; compositions wide and varied including several works for recorder e.g., *Meditazioni sopra 'Coeurs Desoles'* (1949), *Notturno* for recorder quartet (1962), *Passacaglia Sopra 'Plusieurs Regrets'* (1964) and *Sonatina* (1964) all for treble recorder and harpsichord.

Salaman, Esther, (1914 – 2005); mezzo-soprano and

teacher; wide-ranging singing career including oratorio and opera; taught singing GSM and at summer schools including Dartington; worked with English Opera Group; married Paul Hamburger.

Salkeld, Robert, (1920 – 2011); recorder player, teacher examiner and editor; taught recorder Morley College 1950 – 1969; Professor of Recorder LCM 1961 - 1969; edited music for school use.

Sarti, Laura, (1924 -) born Trieste; mezzo-soprano and teacher; operatic career; Professor of Singing GSM.

Saxby, Joseph. (1910 – 1997); American-born harpsichordist and pianist; studied piano RCM and harpsichord with Arnold Dolmetsch; accompanied tenor John McCormack on his final American tour; formed partnership with Carl Dolmetsch, with whom he played for 60 years;

Scheck, Gustav, (1901-1984); German flautist, recorder player, teacher and writer; studied with Gurlitt; early music pioneer; first flautist Hamburg Philharmonic Orchestra; in 1934 formed partnership with cello and gamba player August Wenzinger and harpsichordist Fritz Neumayer; Professor of flute Berlin Musikhochschule; in 1946 founded Musikhochschule in Freiburg in Breisgau, director until 1962; interest in contemporary flute music, as well as Baroque and Renaissance music; published *Die Flöte und Ihre Musik* in 1975; pupils include Hans-Martin Linde, Ferdinand Conrad and Hildemarie Peter.

Schidlof, Peter, (1922 – 1987); Austrian-born viola player; **see Amadeus Quartet.**

Scholes, Percy; (1877 – 1958); music critic, organist, teacher and broadcaster; founded *Music Student*, forerunner of the *Music Teacher*; music critic *The Observer* 1920 – 1925; music editor *Radio Times* 1926 – 1928; expert on Burney; edited *Oxford Companion to Music* (1938).

Seiber, Matyas, born Hungary (1905 – 1960); composer, cellist, writer and teacher; studied Budapest Academy of Music with Schiffer and Kodaly; Professor Frankfurt Musikhochschule 1928 – 1933 teaching theory and jazz; settled in England in 1935; taught at Morley College from 1942 – 1957; co-founded the Committee for the Promotion of New Music; founded and directed the Dorian Singers; much respected teacher of composition; wide range of compositions including choral, orchestral, film music and chamber music

Sidwell, Martindale, (1916 – 1998); organist and choirmaster; Director of Music Church of St Clement Danes in London; founded and conducted Martin Sidwell Choir; Professor of Organ Trinity College of Music and RSCM.

Spiegl, Fritz, (1926 – 2003); Austrian-born flautist, writer, editor, humorist and broadcaster; studied RAM; principal flautist RLPO 1948 – 1963; worked as music journalist for *Liverpool Daily Post*, *Classical Music* and *The Listener*.

Staeps, Hans Ulrich; (1909 – 1988); German-born recorder player and composer; studied Musikhochschule Cologne and at University of Münster; Professor of Music at Vienna Conservatoire from 1956; taught on summer schools in U.K. and U.S.A.; compositions include significant number for recorder, e.g. *Sonata in E flat* for recorder and piano (1951), *Sieben Flötentänze* for recorder quartet (1954), *Berliner Sonate* (1979) for 3-part ensemble in octaves;

Stevens, Denis; (1922 – 2004); musicologist, conductor, violinist and writer; studied University of Oxford; BBC music producer specialising in early music 1949 – 1954; taught RAM 1956 – 1961; visiting professor at various American universities including California, Cornell and Columbia; co-founder and director of the

Ambrosian Singers; edited Monteverdi Vespers 1961.
Strasser, Jani, (1900 – 1978); Hungarian- born bass, teacher of voice and composer; settled in England; taught Old Vic London 1946- 1951 and at Glyndebourne.
Teyte, Maggie (1888 – 1976); soprano; studied London and Paris; international operatic career; sang Melisande under the direction of Debussy in 1908; recitals and recordings of Debussy, Faure and other French composers; wide range of operatic roles; made final operatic performance in 1951 as Belinda in *Dido and Aeneas* at the Mermaid Theatre.
Thomson, John Mansfield, (1926 – 1999); New Zealander, writer, editor and recorder player; founding editor *Composer Magazine* until 1966; pupil of WB; music book editor for Faber; editor *Recorder and Music* Magazine 1966 – 1967 and 1971 –1974; founding editor Early Music 1973 – 1983; 1983 joined Stout Research Centre at University of Victoria, New Zealand; editor of *The Cambridge Companion to the Recorder* (1995)
Thorby, Philip, (1952 -); recorder, viol and early instrument player, teacher and conductor; succeeded Edgar Hunt as Head of Baroque and Renaissance Studies Trinity College of Music; Director of Musica Antiqua of London; interest in wide range of Renaissance and Baroque music including opera and choral music.
Tippett, Michael, (1905 – 1998); composer, broadcaster, administrator, conductor and teacher; studied RCM; Director of Music Morley College 1940 – 1951; President of the SRP 1976 – 1998; wide range of compositions including opera, symphonies and chamber work; used the recorder in a small number of works; *Four Inventions* for descant and treble recorder (1954), *Bonny at Morn,* unison folksong with recorder trio (1956), *Crown of the Year*; a cantata including recorders (1958).

Vyvyan, Jennifer, (1925 – 1974); soprano; studied RAM; debut in 1947 in English Opera Group production of *Beggar's Opera*; created roles in Britten operas – e.g. the Governess in *The Turn of the Screw*, Titania in *A Midsummer Night's Dream* and Miss Julian in *Owen Wingrave*; international operatic and concert career.
Wailes, Marylin, (1896 – 1990); recorder player, editor and writer; member of the New English Consort; specialist on Martin Peerson; taught at City Literary Institute.
Walmesley, Clare, (d. 1987); soprano; operatic and concert career; married Paul Hamburger.
Watts, Helen, (1927 – 2009); contralto; studied RAM; international operatic and concert career; numerous recordings including Handel and Bach.
Weir, Judith, (1954 –); composer; studied Cambridge University; wide range of compositions including opera and orchestral music.
Whitworth, John, (1921 – 2013); countertenor, organist and music adviser; choral scholar Kings College Cambridge; solo career; lay vicar Westminster Abbey 1949 – 1971; Music Adviser for Leicestershire; numerous recordings including Purcell.
Wingerden, Jeanette van, (1939 -); Dutch recorder player and teacher; studied with Kees Otten and Frans Brüggen; Professor at the Hague Royal Conservatoire.
Winters, Ross, (1951 -); recorder player and teacher; studied Oxford University and with Hans Linnartz and Walter van Hauwe; taught RCM 1978 – 1994 and RCM Junior Dept, and at LCM.
Wolf, Ilse, (1921 - 1999); German-born soprano and teacher; settled in UK; specialised in lieder and oratorio; recordings include Bach, Monteverdi and German Lieder.
Wolfes, Felix, (1892 – 1971); German-born conductor, composer, pianist and teacher; studied with Reger and

Pfitzner; worked as operatic assistant and coach in Halle and Elberfeld ; debut as conductor 1923 in Breslau; 1931 Director of Dortmund Opera; after 1933 worked as accompanist in Paris and conducted at Monte Carlo Opera; 1938 emigrated to U.S.A.; assistant conductor Metropolitan Opera and vocal coach Boston New England Conservatory; edited operas of Pfitzner and Strauss; composed songs.

Wyatt, Theo, (1920 – 2017); civil servant, musician and music publisher; Chairman SRP 1973 – 1985; organiser of summer schools, particularly consort playing; member of the Oriel Consort; founder publisher of Oriel Library publications for recorders and viols; Vice-President SRP.

Zorian, Olive, (1916 - 1959) violinist; founder-leader of the Zorian String Quartet; leader of the English Opera Group orchestra 1952 – 1957; wife of John Amis.

Abbreviations

ENO	-	English National Opera
GSM	-	Guildhall School of Music, London
ISCM	-	International Society for Contemporary Music
LCM	-	London College of Music
LPO	-	London Philharmonic Orchestra
LSO	-	London Symphony Orchestra
RAM	-	Royal Academy of Music, London
RCM	-	Royal College of Music, London
RLPO	-	Royal Liverpool Philharmonic Orchestra
RMCM	-	Royal Manchester College of Music
RNCM	-	Royal Northern College of Music, Manchester
RPO	-	Royal Philharmonic Orchestra
RSCM	-	Royal School of Church Music
SRP	-	Society of Recorder Players
WB	-	Walter Bergmann
WEA	-	Worker's Educational Association

188

BIBLIOGRAPHY

Bessel, R. (ed.). *Life in the Third Reich*. Oxford; OUP 1987

Campbell, Margaret. *Dolmetsch, the Man and his Work*. London; Hamish Hamilton, 1975

Foreman, Lewis. *From Parry to Britten*. London; Batsford 1987

Hardwick, Michael & Mollie. *Alfred Deller, A Singularity of Voice*. London, Cassell 1968

Haskell, Harry. *The Early Music Revival*. London; Thames & Hudson, 1988

Hunt Edgar. *The Recorder and its Music*. rev. ed. London, Eulenburg 1977 new edition Peacock Press 2002

Kemp, Ian (ed.). *Michael Tippett, A Symposium on his Sixtieth Birthday*. London, Faber 1965

Matthews, David. *Michael Tippett, An Introductory Study*. London, Faber 1980

O'Kelly, Eve. *The Recorder Today*. Cambridge University Press 1990

Recorder and Music Magazine. 1963 – 1993 published Schott; 1993 – Peacock Press

Rickards, Guy. *Hindemith, Hartmann and Henze*. London, Phaidon 1995

Rowland-Jones, Anthony. *Recorder Technique*, London, OUP 6th imp. 1971

Thomson, John Mansfield (ed.). *The Cambridge Companion to the Recorder*. Cambridge University Press 1995

Tippett, Michael. *Those Twentieth Century Blues, An Autobiography*. London, Hutchinson 1991

Turner, Barry. *And the Policeman Smiled*. Guild Publishing 1990

Index by Margaret Binns

Titles of compositions are listed following the subject headings under composers' names

Amadeus Quartet 46, 93, 177
amateur musicians, WB's attitude to 16, 57, 70–1, 85
American Recorder Society 123, 127–8, 136
Amis, John 47, 54, 148, 157, 158, 164, 177
Arno, Michael 111, 113, 122, 134, 177
Austria, International Summer School 65, 66–7, 72

Baghuis, Elly 108, 124
Baines, Francis 85, 90, 100
Bamforth, Dennis 108, 114, 123, 133, 136, 139
Baroque Chamber Music Week 147, 152, 154, 159, 161, 167–8
Barthel, Rudolf 72, 177
Bendix, David (WB's grandson) 88, 147, 152, 166
Bendix, Erica (née Bergmann) see Bergmann, Erica
Bendix, Peter (WB's son-in-law) 82, 85, 125
Bennett, William 96, 97, 177
Bergmann, Alice (née König) (WB's mother) 1–3, 6, 11
Bergmann, Anneliese (WB's sister-in-law) 67, 149, 169
Bergmann, Erica (WB's daughter)
  arrives in England 36–7, 40
  at Oxford Baroque course 147, 152
  birth of 17
  cares for Grete after her stroke 154–5, 158, 161
  during World War Two 39, 40, 42, 46
  engagement and marriage to Peter Bendix 82, 85
  helps with children's opera 126, 132
  musical ability 51, 53
  schooling 50, 64
  spends year in Israel 73
Bergmann, Fritz (WB's brother) 1, 3, 6, 11, 13, 27, 62, 65, 67, 78, 114, 143, 147, 149, 162, 167
Bergmann, Gabrielle (WB's niece) 82, 85
Bergmann, Grete (née Haase) (WB's second wife)
  arrives in England 36–7
  birth of Erica 17
  death of 166
  during World War Two 39, 40, 42, 44
  first sees WB 6
  ill health of 55, 78, 107–8, 150, 153, 154, 157, 161, 162–3, 164
  marriage to WB 38
  moves to London 49, 50
  pre-marital relationship with WB 15, 22
  runs a restaurant 68, 78
  suffers a stroke 154, 162
  tries to leave Germany 26–7, 33, 34
Bergmann, Hans (WB's brother) 1, 3, 6, 11, 27, 86, 101, 104, 138–9, 144, 145
Bergmann, Marthel (née Kolb) (WB's first wife) 12–15, 17, 19–20, 22, 25, 128
Bergmann, Oskar (WB's father) 1–3, 6, 20
Bergmann, Rolf (WB's nephew) 73, 149, 153, 158, 167
Bergmann, Vera (née König) (WB's stepmother) 1, 11, 26, 27, 58, 62
Bergmann, Walter
  adjudicating 65, 121–2
  children's Christmas opera 119, 122, 123, 124, 126, 128, 132
  collection of recorder pictures 22, 25–6, 33, 128
  contract with Faber 107, 109–10, 113, 115, 121, 122, 124, 158, 163, 165
  death of 169
  driving of 88, 92, 93, 160
  eightieth birthday 163–4
  engagement to Issi Matz 10, 11
  eyesight 73, 104, 111–12, 130, 131, 159–60, 164
  finds pupil dead 76

INDEX

frightened by intruder 164–5
Golden Rules for Ensemble Playing 77–8
hearing problems 123, 124, 150, 152, 166
ill health of 73, 74, 76, 78–9, 150
imprisonment 23–4
income 21, 40, 83, 115–16, 135, 142, 168
interest in photography 97, 116
internment 42–5
introduced to recorder and its music 16, 21–2
Jewish ancestry 1–2, 19–20, 22
leaves Germany for England 25–6
legal training and work 9, 10–11, 14, 18, 20–1, 22–3
marriage to Grete Haase 38
marriage to Marthel Kolb 12–15, 17, 19–20, 22, 25, 128
Morley College involvement 47–8, 49–58
musical strengths and weaknesses 29–30
pension problems 115
pleasure from teaching children 81, 83, 88, 116
poems published 128–30
pre-marital relationship with Grete Haase 15, 17, 20, 22
private pupils 119, 141, 150
pseudonym (T.S.Walker) 65
relationship with Hilde Volhard 34–5, 36, 37
resigns from Morley College 71
resigns from Schott 109–10
sells recorders 163, 164
seventieth birthday celebrations 133–4
Society of Recorder Players involvement 64, 65
trained as fitter 53, 54, 55, 58
work at Schott 48–9, 58, 63, 67–8, 78, 82–3, 96
Drummer Boy 106, 110, 114, 116, 123, 164
Matilda 105, 106, 114, 116
Pastorale 62, 69, 96–7, 115, 120, 142, 149
Pastorella 119, 120, 142
Septet 61, 63–4

Sonata for Descant Recorder and Piano 103, 104, 106, 113, 119, 125
Sonata for Treble Recorder and Piano 133, 134, 136, 137–8, 140
Berkeley, Lennox 52, 58, 177
Bevan, Maurice 74, 81, 94, 102, 106, 112
Bixler, Martha 135–6, 139, 177
Black, Neil 81, 94, 97, 100, 101, 177
Bloodworth, Denis 166, 168
Blow, Ode on the Death of Henry Purcell 65, 74, 75, 80, 81, 91, 112
Bonsor, Brian 73, 76, 95, 106, 123, 126, 128, 152, 164, 177
Bowen, Kenneth 81, 177
Boyde, Carl 16–17, 30
Brainin, Norbert 46, 93, 177
Brannigan, Owen 89, 177
British Broadcasting Corporation (BBC), WB's dealings with 69–70, 71, 75–6, 91, 133
Britten, Benjamin 72, 137, 146, 177
  Morley College involvement 51, 52, 53, 61
  Alpine Suite 75, 86
  Midsummer Night's Dream 86, 87
  Noyes Fludde 89, 94
Brown, Wilfred 74
Brüggen, Franz 177
  buys WB's Stanesby recorder 143
  jointly edits Schickhardt sonatas 101, 110, 138, 140, 142, 150, 151, 152–3
  WB as accompanist 103, 105, 113–14, 120–1, 123, 125–6, 130, 140

Camden, Archie 91, 178
Cantata Choir 82, 85, 87, 94
Cantelo, April 81, 86, 178
Carner, Mosco 64, 178

Carrell, Norman 70, 75
Cashmore, Donald 86, 95
Champion, Max 46, 52, 57
Champion, Stephanie 46, 52, 54
Charney Manor course 136, 141, 147, 151, 157, 166, 168
Clark, Paul 115, 119, 123, 130, 133, 165, 168, 178
Clarke, Jeremiah, *Music on Henry Purcell's Death* 82, 85, 94, 99, 102
Cleaver, Sylvia 80, 81, 85, 87, 94, 96, 105, 107, 144
Cobb, Eileen 142
Coles, Janet 115, 120, 130, 147, 151, 164
Coles, Richard (Dick) 111, 120, 124, 142, 165
Collette, Joannes 73, 77, 111, 178
Conrad, Ferdinand 73, 103, 111, 114, 121, 133, 139, 152, 178
Corcoran, Ronald 97
Craig, Douglas 99, 115, 125

Dart, Thurston 61, 62, 64, 65, 66, 70–1, 178
Dartington Summer School 93, 125, 127, 131, 145
Davenport, LaNoue 86, 165, 178
Dawes, Frank 146, 147, 178
Deller, Alfred 178
  argues with WB 95
  BBC broadcasts 69–70, 91, 96
  death of 153–4
  debut at Morley College 55–6
  Provence summer school 127
  Purcell recordings 81, 112
  replaced in A Midsummer Night's Dream 87
  Stour Music Festival 100, 103, 122
  WB as accompanist 62, 63, 64–5, 75, 79, 92, 96, 100
  WB's Pastorale written for 62, 149
  WB's tribute to 154, 157, 158
Deller Consort 79, 100, 102
Deller, Mark 100, 112, 128, 178

Dent, Edward 25, 35, 65, 178
Dinn, Freda 49, 51, 52, 65, 72, 76, 94, 135, 178
Dolci, Amico 133, 145, 147–8, 179
Dolmetsch, Arnold 70
Dolmetsch, Carl 179
  at Roehampton/Keyworth summer school 64, 73–4, 76, 115, 131, 135
  Bressan recorders owned by 98
  compositions by 52–3
  performances by 37, 39–40, 77, 90, 94
  recorder teaching 52
  SRP involvement 72, 169
Dolmetsch, Marie 76, 88, 126
Dolmetsch, Natalie 76, 179
Dolmetsch, Richard 105
Dolmetsch, Rudolph 37
Downer, Eileen 83, 93, 101
Downes, Ralph 66, 137, 179
Dupré, Desmond 75, 92, 96, 133, 179

early music, WB first introduced to 16, 19
Early Music movement 70–1, 148
Edmunds, Chris 50, 76, 179
Edwards, John 33, 35, 36, 39, 47
Ehrlich, Robert 150
English, Gerald 71, 75, 76, 80, 81, 94, 95, 179
Esswood, Paul 119, 120, 179
Eulenburg Company 98, 102, 109
Eulenburg, Kurt 98, 179

Faber publishers, WB's contract with 107, 109–10, 113, 115, 121, 122, 124, 158, 163, 165
Fawcett, Norman 62, 64
Flagstad, Kirstin 66, 179
Flatz, Prunella 78, 106, 129–30, 139

Fowler, Fred 179
Frankl family 12, 15
Frankl, Susi 123, 128
Free German League of Culture 50, 55
Fricker, Peter Racine 75, 180

Gal, Hans 43, 44, 130, 136, 180
Gerhardt, Christoph 113, 116, 129
Gerhardt, Dietrich 15–17, 18, 25, 27, 29, 30, 72, 79, 130, 148–9, 168
Gerhardt, Suzanne 148–9, 151
Godman, Stanley 105–6
Goehr, Walter 47, 53, 54, 67, 180
Goodman, Roy 122, 180
Goossens, Leon 61, 180
Gosling, Susan 119, 122, 128, 133
Grainger, Percy 64
Groke, Ursula 141, 147, 149, 150, 153

Haase, Grete see Bergmann, Grete
Handel, G.F., editions by WB 36, 39, 40, 45, 152, 153, 158
Handel Verein, Halle 19
Harper, John 157, 159
Harradine, Archie 88, 89, 90
Hartog, Howard 67, 82–3
Haslemere Festival 37, 70, 92
Hemsley, Thomas 66, 180
Henckel, Herr 4–5, 6–7
Hensel, Fritz 13, 25, 30
Hersom, Herbert 76, 86, 113, 170, 180
Hess, Myra 39, 49, 180
Heyden, Rheinhold 16, 17
Hilling, Lyndon 150, 151, 153
Hindemith, Paul 10, 29, 64, 180
  Trio for recorders 52, 57, 61, 71, 149

Hoffnung, Gerald 77, 181
Holst, Imogen 71, 79, 86, 96, 181
Hopkins, Antony 50, 55, 57, 61, 122, 159, 181
Huene, Friedrich von 127, 142, 181
Hunt, Edgar 181
  at Schott 37, 48, 63, 109
  performances by 39, 77, 94
  recorder teaching 46, 94
  review of Schickhardt sonatas 152–3
  Roehampton/Keyworth summer school 64, 76, 115, 135, 159
  SRP involvement 72, 130, 169
  tributes to WB 163–4, 169
Hunt, Enid 77, 169
Hunter, Hilda 73, 74, 81, 86, 106, 126, 133, 135, 149, 181

ISM (Incorporated Society of Musicians) 85, 88, 101, 108, 119

Jeans, Katharine 111, 114, 122, 154
Jennings, Gloria 112, 115
Jones, Philip 64, 97, 181

Kaye, Elaine 98, 100
Kemp, Ian 80, 98, 102, 125, 141, 168
Kenworthy, C. (Ken) 50, 53, 71, 72, 97, 181
Keyworth Summer School (new venue for Roehampton course) 131, 135, 139, 145
Kingsley, Victoria 55, 57, 58
Kinsley, Sheila 165, 167, 168
Kolb, Marthel see Bergmann, Marthel
König family 1–2
Küng, Franz 94, 181

Lasocki, David 142, 151, 152–3, 158, 181
Lefkovitch, Leonard 79, 85
Lehane, Maureen 112, 182

Leigh, Walter 55, 67, 182
Leipzig Conservatoire 9
Leppard, Raymond 70
Leslie, Felicity 122
Lidka, Maria 47, 49, 56, 182
Linde, Hans-Martin 103, 108, 111
London College of Music, recorder group 87, 91
London Philharmonic Arts Club 54, 55, 56, 57, 61
London Recorder Consort 51, 52
Lovett, Martin 61, 182
Luxon, Benjamin 112–13, 182

McLaughlin, Eileen 81
McMullen, Elli 75, 79, 87
Makings, Peter 87, 96, 104, 106, 109, 115, 125, 138, 157
Marriner, Neville 57, 61, 113, 182
Martin, Colin 108, 114, 123, 133, 136, 139
Marwood, Caroline 150–1
Marwood, Catherine 125, 130, 141, 144, 146, 148, 149, 151, 159
   performs WM's treble sonata 133–5, 137–8, 150
Mary Ward Settlement, WB's classes at 71–2, 75, 91, 98
Marylebone Institute, WB's classes 91, 93, 114
Matlock Summer School 81, 86, 93, 104, 106
Matthews, Denis 77, 182
Matz, Arnold 5, 6–7, 9–10, 27, 81, 86, 105, 106, 131, 145, 149, 182
Matz family 7
Matz, Issi (von Arps-Aubert) 7, 9, 10, 11, 106, 127, 147
Matz, Rudi 7, 106, 144
Mellers, Wilfrid 72, 182
Mermaid Theatre 66
Meyer, Ernst 67, 182
Miles, Bernard, 66
Monteverdi, C. *Vespers of 1610* 62, 65–6
Morley College
   Festival of Britain events 65–6

recorder playing days 54, 57–8
recorder weekends 52–3, 61
WB first visits 41
WB involved with 47–8, 51–2, 62
   WB's recorder classes 49–50, 52, 55
Morley College Choir 51, 52, 61, 62, 66
Morley College Recorder Ensemble 57, 58, 61, 65–6
Müller Hartmann, Robert 36, 45, 182
Munrow, David 119, 136, 144, 182
Murray, Dom Gregory 114, 136, 183
Murray, Margaret 95, 96, 132, 183
   at Orff summer schools 104
   performances by 98, 99, 100, 103
Murrill, Herbert 69, 183
'Musical Pills to Purge Melancholy' (Purcell cabaret) 88, 89–90, 92, 95, 99, 100, 101, 115, 125, 131
Muthesius, Miete 39, 40, 41, 46

Nallen, Evelyn 93, 96, 101, 138, 149, 167, 183
Neumann, Otto 12, 17, 19, 81, 109
Nissel, Sigmund 45, 46, 93, 183
Norrington, Roger 107, 112–13, 115, 136, 183
Northern Recorder Course 108, 110, 114, 121, 133, 136
Novak, Helene 106, 127, 131, 135
Novak, Hermann 11, 127

Orff, Carl 95, 104
Orff Institute summer courses, Salzburg 94, 104, 122–3, 131, 135, 139, 145
Oriel Consort 71, 74, 183
Otten, Kees 154, 169, 183

Parrott, Ian 74, 183
Pears, Peter 51, 52, 56, 102, 119, 130, 183
Peter, Hildemarie 73, 77, 105, 111, 183

Petri, Michaela 143, 144, 152, 159, 160, 161, 162, 165, 183
Pipers' Guild 58
Pitsch, Kurt 65, 73, 183
Platt, Norman 136, 148, 161, 163, 165, 183
    children's opera 119, 122
    'Musical Pills' 88, 89, 92, 95, 115, 125
    performances by 65, 75, 76, 79, 80, 85, 87, 94
    Regional Opera 106–7, 112–13
Plowman, Ron 71, 74
Pritchard, John 77, 184
Purcell, Henry 61–2, 81, 82
    Dido and *Aeneas* 66, 80, 106–7, 112
    Music for a While 55–6, 57, 58, 64–5, 114
    Ode for St Cecilia 47, 48, 51, 56, 63, 64, 76, 94, 141
Purves, Alison 47, 52, 54, 55, 56, 62, 64, 184

Rahlwes, Professor 4, 7, 19
Recorder and Music Magazine 97, 163, 166
Recorder News 72, 82, 97
recorders
    first plastic recorders 48
    pictures collected by WB 22, 25–6, 33, 128
    unfavourable views of 64
Regional Opera Company 106–7, 112–13
Reizenstein, Franz 43–4, 73, 184
Reynolds, Gordon 76, 184
Richter, Karl 70
Ring, Christine 74, 76
Ring, Layton 74, 75, 76, 184
Ritchie, Margaret 56, 57, 61, 63, 66, 92, 184
Roehampton summer school (Recorder in Education) 64, 67, 72, 73–4, 76, 86, 92–3, 95, 104, 106, 115, 124
    moves to Keyworth 131
Rostal, Max 34, 39, 42, 47, 49, 184
Rowland-Jones, Anthony 90, 97, 166, 184

Rubbra, Edmund 73, 100, 184
Ruhm, Delia 61, 62
Ryan, Jane 113, 121
Ryan, Jennifer 75, 80, 85, 97, 105

St Pancras Festival concerts 85, 89, 94, 97, 99
Salaman, Esther 48, 49, 51, 61, 184
Salkeld, Robert 71, 91, 184
Sarti, Laura 85, 87, 94, 103, 122, 185
    in 'Musical Pills' 89, 92, 95, 99, 125
    in Regional Opera Company 107
Saxby, Joseph 52, 64, 71, 74, 76, 92, 185
Scheck, Gustav 110–11, 168, 185
Schickhardt sonatas
    edited by WB and Frans Brüggen 101, 110, 138, 140, 141, 142, 146, 150, 151–2, 152–3, 157
    Schott edition of 152–3
Schidlof, Peter 46, 185
Schmelzer, Johann 67
Scholes, Percy 72, 185
Schott & Co
    changes at 87, 109, 157
    plastic recorders 48, 63
    publication of WB's works 40, 46, 78, 159, 170
    recorder music publications 72, 78
    WB first visits 37–8
    WB resigns 109–10
    WB works for 48–9, 58, 63, 67–8, 82–3, 96, 104
    WB's pension 115
Schumann, WB's love of 4, 7, 10, 141, 145
Schwedler, Maximillian 9
Seattle Summer School 123, 127–8, 135, 139–40
Seelig, Erika 34, 35, 61, 74, 106, 127, 131, 141, 154, 166, 167
Seeliger, Martha 13
Seiber, Matyas 47, 185

Sidwell, Martindale 81, 185
Silbiger, Dr 74, 76
Society of Recorder Players (SRP)
   annual festival 130, 138, 144, 149, 161, 167
   fiftieth anniversary 169
   founding of 46–7
   Junior Section 65
   structure of 72
   teacher's examination 142
   WB's involvement 64, 65, 83
Spiegl, Fritz 77, 154, 185
Spinks, Charles 91
Staeps, Hans Ulrich 66–7, 73, 185
Standen, Richard 86
Steffens, Max 37, 47, 49, 63, 68, 74, 87, 105, 115
Stegmann, Herr 20, 24–5, 36, 81
Stevens, Denis 69, 70, 80, 185
Stour Music Festival 98, 100, 103, 106, 122, 138, 149, 158
Strasser, Jani 56, 61, 185
Strecker, Hugh 37, 38, 40, 41, 45, 48, 58, 63

Tadman, Joyce 72, 76
Taylor, Christopher 81
Taylor, Richard 81
Taylor, Sam 142
Taylor Recorder Trio 71
Telemann, G.P.
   WB's promotion of 46, 75, 76, 99, 160, 166, 168
   Ino 99–100
   Pimpinone 99, 106–7, 112
Telemann Orchestra 65–6, 71, 99
Teyte, Maggie 66, 185
Thomson, John 107, 109, 110, 113, 121, 151, 154, 186
Thorby, Philip 152, 164, 165, 167, 186
Tippett, Michael 186
   and Alfred Deller 55–6
   imprisonment 51–2
   Morley College involvement 41, 46, 47–8, 51
   resigns from Morley College 67
   sixtieth birthday 102
   and WB 48, 53, 67–8, 101, 102, 130, 141, 146, 157
   A Child of our Time 53–4, 56, 101
   Crown of the Year 102–3
   King Priam 87, 91, 92, 93, 95, 97
Todhunter, Joan 51, 57
Twiggy 96, 128
Twittenhof, Wilhelm 16, 17, 104

Versteeg, Jan 12, 17, 19, 29, 30, 36, 93, 106, 122, 128
Viol, Friedrich 12, 15, 17
Volhard, Hilde 23, 34–5, 36, 37, 39, 41, 46, 49, 132, 154
Vyvyan, Jennifer 66, 86, 93, 186

Wailes, Marylin 49, 51, 75, 186
Walmesley, Clare 86, 87, 93, 94, 103, 122, 186
   in 'Musical Pills' 89, 92, 95, 99, 115, 125
   in Regional Opera Company 107, 112
Walter, Rose 37
Walton, Michael, 67
Watts, Helen 86, 186
Weir, Judith 136, 186
Welch, Patrick 150, 159
Westlake, Margaret (Thorby) 152, 159
Whiteley, Faith 145, 146, 151, 154
Whitworth, John 75, 80, 81, 91, 186
Wilson, Helen 51
Wilson, Josephine, 66
Wingerden, Jeanette van 103, 145, 186
Winkelmann, Karen 150, 160
Winters, Don 123, 135, 139

Winters, Ross 111, 120, 130, 136, 139, 141, 149, 164, 186
Wolf, Ilse 73, 75, 76, 78, 80, 94, 99–100, 164, 186
  in 'Musical Pills' 89, 92, 95
Wolfes, Felix 4, 7, 13, 24, 25, 126, 186
Wolff, Hellmuth 18, 150
Wyatt, Kitty 80, 85
Wyatt, Theo 71, 80, 86, 98, 100, 103, 133, 161, 187

Zen On, publish WB's work 140, 146, 149, 152–3
Zilling, Eva 78, 145
Zimmermann, Charlotte 18–19, 20–1, 23–4, 26–7, 81
Zorian String Quartet 61, 187

www.ingramcontent.com/pod-product-compliance
Lightning Source LLC
Chambersburg PA
CBHW080245170426
43192CB00014BA/2572